Imagined Empires

The publisher gratefully acknowledges the generous support of the Ahmanson Foundation Humanities Endowment Fund of the University of California Press Foundation.

Imagined Empires

A HISTORY OF REVOLT IN EGYPT

Zeinab Abul-Magd

UNIVERSITY OF CALIFORNIA PRESS
BERKELEY LOS ANGELES LONDON

University of California Press, one of the most distinguished university presses in the United States, enriches lives around the world by advancing scholarship in the humanities, social sciences, and natural sciences. Its activities are supported by the UC Press Foundation and by philanthropic contributions from individuals and institutions. For more information, visit www.ucpress.edu.

University of California Press
Berkeley and Los Angeles, California

University of California Press, Ltd.
London, England

©2013 by The Regents of the University of California

Library of Congress Cataloging-in-Publication Data

Abul-Magd, Zeinab, 1976
  Imagined empires : a history of revolt in Egypt / Zeinab Abul-Magd.
    pages   cm
  Includes bibliographical references and index.
  ISBN 978-0-520-27552-2 (cloth : acid-free paper) —
  ISBN 978-0-520-27553-9 (paper : acid-free paper)
  1. Egypt—Politics and government.   2. Peasants—Political activity—Egypt—History.   3. Working class—Political activity—Egypt—History.   4. Government, Resistance to—Egypt—History.   5. Revolutions—Egypt—History.   6. Imperialism—History.   7. Egypt—Colonial influence.   8. Elite (Social sciences)—Egypt—History.   I. Title.
  DT82.A675 2013
  962'.3—dc23   2013003749

Manufactured in the United States of America

22 21 20 19 18 17 16 15 14 13
10 9 8 7 6 5 4 3 2 1

In keeping with a commitment to support environmentally responsible and sustainable printing practices, UC Press has printed this book on Rolland Enviro100, a 100% post-consumer fiber paper that is FSC certified, deinked, processed chlorine-free, and manufactured with renewable biogas energy. It is acid-free and EcoLogo certified.

CONTENTS

Acknowledgments   vii

Introduction: Imagined Empires, Real Rebels   1
1 · Ottomans, Plague, and Rebellion (1500–1800)   17
2 · The French, Plague Encore, and Jihad (1798–1801)   43
3 · The Pasha's Settlers, Bulls, and Bandits (1805–1848)   70
4 · A "Communist" Revolution (1848–1882)   95
5 · Rebellion in the Time of Cholera (1882–1950)   122
Epilogue: America—The Last Imagined Empire?   147

Notes   157
Bibliography   187
Art Credits   198
Index   199

ACKNOWLEDGMENTS

This book was supported by my graduate work in Georgetown University's History Department and by grants from Georgetown's Graduate School and Oberlin College. Its production would not have been possible without the invaluable and precious support of many colleagues and friends in the United States and Egypt. First of all, the greatest thanks are due to Judith Tucker, my former advisor at Georgetown University. Late Faruk Tabak of Georgetown thoughtfully helped with earlier stages of writing the manuscript. Many thanks are due to Timothy Mitchell, Khaled Fahmy, and Peter Gran, who were very generous with their time and ideas in discussing earlier versions of the book. Many graduate colleagues have been of indispensable help throughout the years of researching and writing, especially Dina Khalifa, Dina Shehata, Nadya Sabiti, Sara Scalenghe, Mohamed Said Ezz El-Din, Aurelie Perrier, and many others at Georgetown's Center for Contemporary Arab Studies.

I would also like to thank all the great historians and researchers at the National Archives of Egypt whom I met and had fruitful discussions with, especially Emad Hilal, Magdi Guirguis, Nelly Hanna, Gennifer Derr, Shana Minkin, Alan Mikhail, Lisa Pollard, and Will Hanley. At Oberlin College, I have found much support from many colleagues, including Frances Hasso and Sam White. Furthermore, I have to advance many thanks to Max Strasser and Avi Asher-Schapiro, my wonderful students who copyedited the manuscript. Finally, in Upper Egypt, the dear region about which this book was written, I would like to thank all the revolutionary youth of the south and my parents.

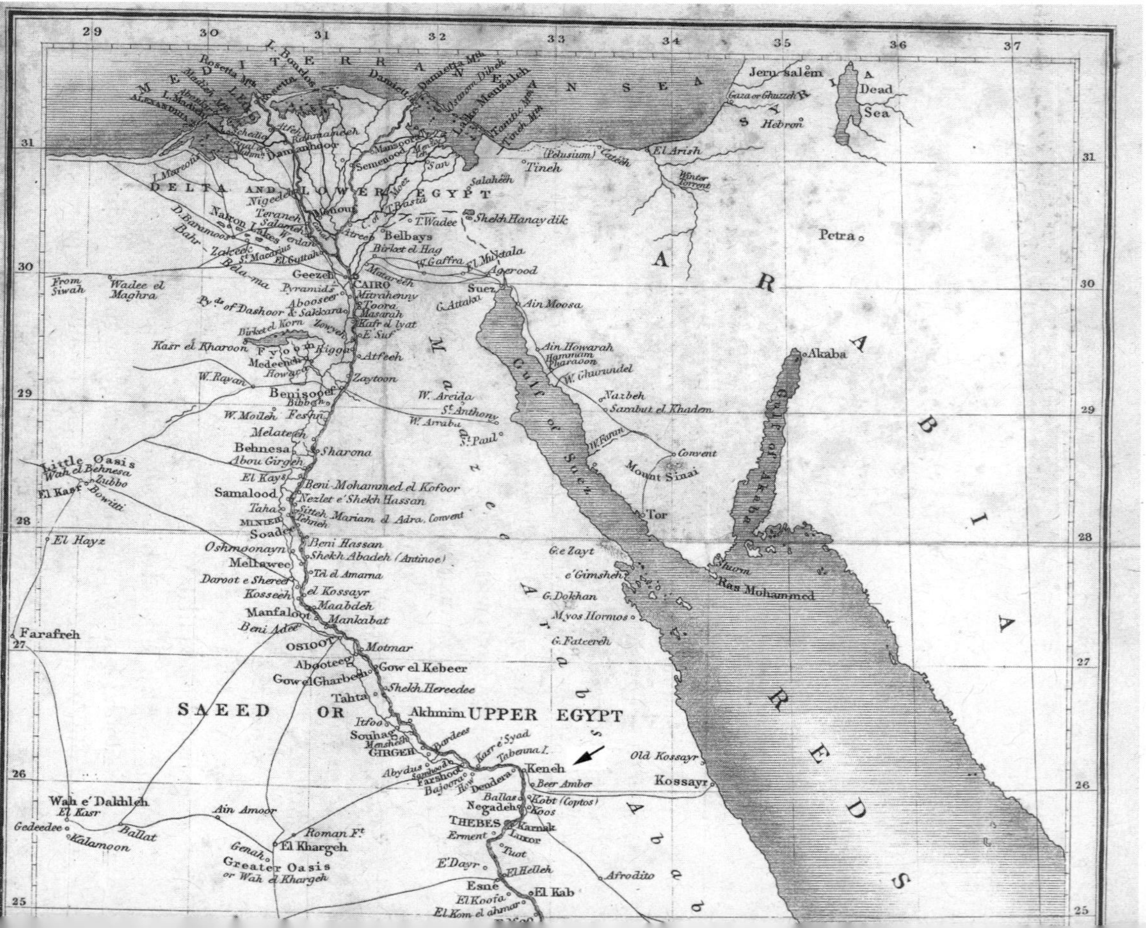

MEDITERRANEAN SEA
DELTA AND LOWER EGYPT
ALEXANDRIA
Rosetta
Damanhoor
Damietta
Lake Menzaleh
Mansoora
Semenood
Belbays
Tineh
(Pelusium)
Catieh
El Arish
Winter Torrent
Jerusalem
Gaza or Ghuzzeh
Hebron
Dead Sea
SYRIA
Petra
Natron Lakes
Geezeh
CAIRO
Pyramids
Suez
Agerood
Ain Moosa
Birket el Korn
Fyoom
Kasr el Kharoon
Medeeneh
Benisooef
Wadee el Maghra
From Siwah
Little Oasis
Wah el Behnesa
El Kasr
Bowitti
Behnesa
Samalood
MINIEH
Soadee
Beni Hassan
Shekh Abadeh (Antinoe)
Tel el Amarna
Mellawee
Manfaloot
OSIOOT
Motmar
Abooteeg
Gow el Kebeer
Tahta
Akhmim
Souhag
GIRGEH
Abydus
Farshoot
Dendera
Keneh
Kobt (Coptos)
Koos
Negadeh
THEBES
Karnak
Luxor
Erment
Esne
El Kab
Farafreh
El Hayz
SAEED OR UPPER EGYPT
Wah e' Dakhleh
Gedeedee
Kalamoon
Ballat
Ain Amoor
Roman Ft.
El Khargeh
Greater Oasis or Wah el Khargeh
Arabah
St. Anthony
St. Paul
Gulf of Suez
Tor
Mount Sinai
Convent
Gulf of Akaba
Akaba
Ras Mohammed
Myos Hormos
Old Kossayr
Kossayr
Afrodito
ARABIA
RED SEA

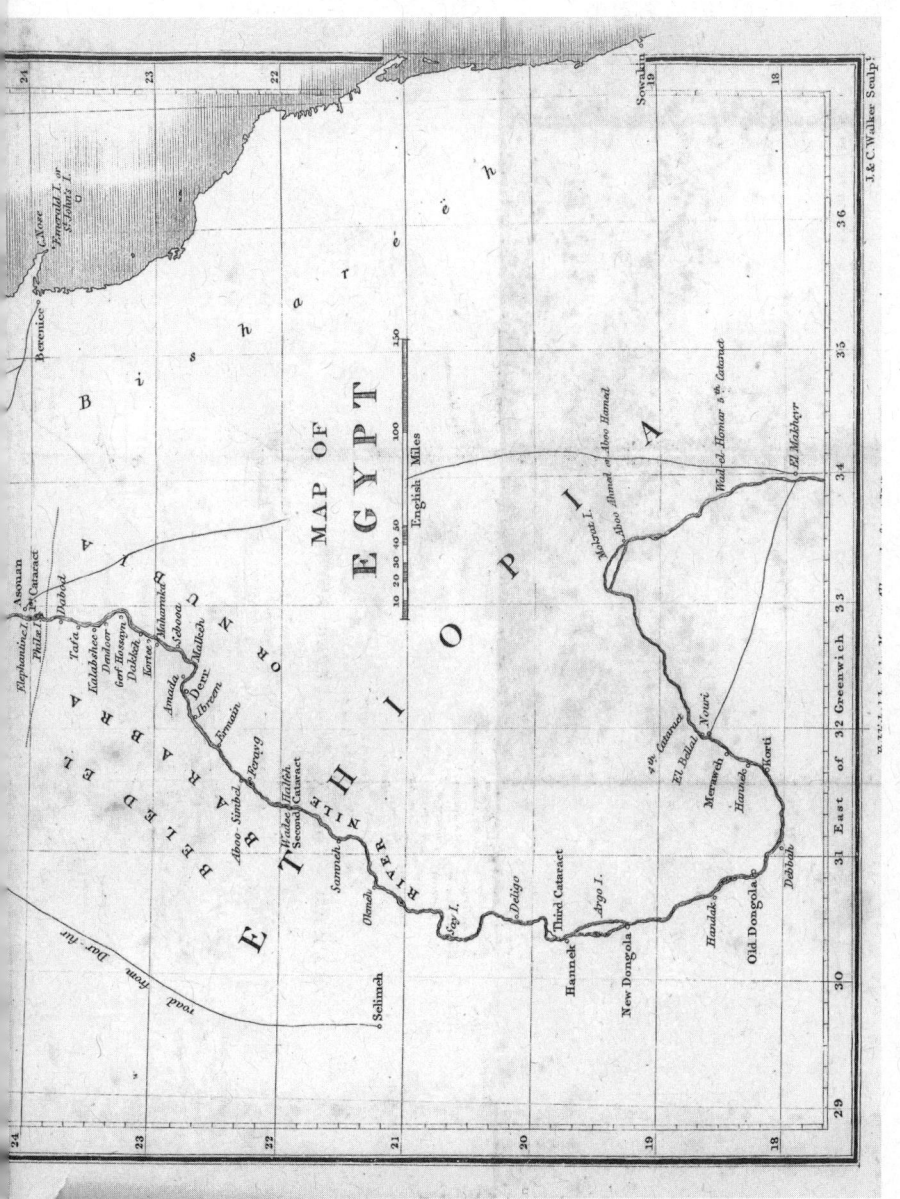

FIGURE 1. Nineteenth-century map of Egypt that shows Qina Province (Keneh) located in the south/Upper Egypt (see arrow).

INTRODUCTION

Imagined Empires, Real Rebels

Empire is almighty. It is an all-encompassing political entity capable of penetrating places big and small, near and far, and establishing full hegemony. The semidivine omnipotence of empire is made manifest not only in its ability to control the high politics of the metropolis but also in its penetration of the daily life of peoples in the remotest places—in the periphery of the periphery of the empire. Wherever it appears, empire is competent, fast, and successful in achieving its goals and altering people's lives. But that is a myth. Omnipotent empire was imagined. Although empire managed to extend into the farthest places on earth, it failed in that which it thought itself to be most competent, instead leaving behind environmental devastation and revolt. The history of Qina Province, a small place deep in the south of Egypt, over the last five hundred years proves this case.

On the eve of the Egyptian Revolution of 2011, I visited the southern half of the country, Upper Egypt, in order to conduct field research for this book. In the farmlands bordering a small town in Qina Province, I noticed an enormous cylindrical, silver building that looked alien to its surroundings. When I inquired about its contents, I learned that this was a silo for the wheat from the US Agency for International Development (USAID). The controversial American food aid to Egypt, which many analysts believe to be a tool of imperial hegemony through the establishment of grain dependency, had made its way to the farthest reaches of Upper Egypt. I also learned that the "informal empire" made an appearance in the province in many other ways.[1] For almost twenty years before the 2011 revolution, deposed President Hosni Mubarak's economic reform program—which followed the neoliberal "Washington Consensus"—deeply hurt the large number of sugarcane cultivators in Qina. The former legal codes of landholding, promulgated by the

Arab socialist regime of the 1960s, were reversed by a new code of private property, Law 96 of 1992. Peasants were evicted from land that the state had returned to the elite families of the pre-1952 colonial era.[2]

Under Mubarak's overthrown regime, the US presence in Upper Egypt was conspicuously strong, yet failing. Its failure throughout Egypt was a major reason for the eruption of the 2011 revolution. American market reforms, confidently advocated as the most efficient way toward economic development, did not yield results in Upper Egypt, even two decades after their application. The southern provinces, including Qina, were and still are known, to be the most underdeveloped regions throughout the country's modern history. The UN Development Programme's annual reports on Arab human development place Upper Egypt at the bottom of the ladder of human development, and several World Bank reports allude to the same fact.[3] On the eve of the 2011 revolution, protests against the failed empire spread across the south, especially in Qina Province. The southern provinces were the most rebellious among Egypt's regions against the central government in Cairo, which applied the dysfunctional US policies of market reform.

Gangs of bandits known as *matarid al-jabal,* who take refuge in the mountains surrounding the Nile in the south, have grown to symbolize ruthless crime as well as audacious resistance against the state and its failed free market policies. Many popular TV series and movies present a criminal, yet romantic, image of these bandits. They even make their appearance on Facebook: an opposition group of youth, resenting the authoritarian regime that subjugated itself to American domination, named itself after a memorable proclamation by a legendary southern bandit, 'Izzat 'Ali Hanafi. The story of 'Izzat, whose execution filled the newspapers while I was conducting my archival research in 2006, was made into the most popular Egyptian movie two years later. In a key scene in the film, the angry, outlawed protagonist, or 'Izzat, says, "From today, there is no government. I am the government." (*Min el naharda mafish hakuma. Ana el hakuma.*) This fierce political statement immediately grew popular among youth across Egypt and was quickly adopted as the name of the Facebook opposition group.[4] Eventually, the south, the north, and Cairo all rose to overthrow the US-friendly, neoliberal regime on 25 January 2011.

Over the last five centuries, many other informal and formal empires have made disturbing appearances in Qina Province and have similarly failed. They were all "imagined empires" that confidently went south and stumbled in applying imperial policies in which they claimed to be, or were under the illusion of being, the most efficient. The failure of these empires generated environmental destruction while altering established systems of land and river management and leaving behind sweeping epidemic diseases. More importantly, they provoked massive subaltern revolts championed by peasants, women, laborers, and ever-ruthless bandits. This book looks at five world empires that showed up in Qina Province: the Ottoman (1500–1800), the French (1798–1801), Muhammad 'Ali's (1805–48), the "informal" British (1848–82), and finally the formal British (1882–1950) empires. This book relates a microhistory of the villages and small towns of the province that goes beyond this little-known place to investigate the global history of imperialism and nonelite, nonnationalist rebellion against empire.[5]

This book goes south to Qina Province in order to explore the ignored history of Upper Egypt and to deconstruct established myths about early modern and modern world empires.[6] The book's five chapters, each about one empire that manifested in Qina, investigate the modes of imperial hegemony, the discursive images that empires advocate about themselves, and the empires' failure to fulfill such images because of their inability to control local resources and subjugate Qina's peoples. Many of these empires claimed to introduce "modernity" to the colonized peoples of Qina, particularly through market forces, but their form of modernity only dispossessed peasants, repressed laborers, and further subjugated women. With the indispensable assistance of co-opted local elites of the south, imperial modernity and its market economy disrupted existing systems of landownership, irrigation, trade, and more and left behind immense waves of the plague and cholera. Qina's lower classes, who were harmed—sometimes killed—by imperial incompetence, devised their own modes of both daily-life resistance and massive uprisings against the empire, in which audacious bandits assumed leadership roles. At the end of this book, the epilogue raises questions about an imagined US Empire and its failed market economy in the south, which partially resulted in Qina's participation in the 2011 revolution.

WHY QINA PROVINCE?

During the Egyptian Revolution in 2011, the small towns and villages of Qina were engaged in many actions of protest, including sit-ins, marches, and strikes. The province's inhabitants were building on a long tradition of expressing discontent and rebelling. For many centuries, Qina Province was the vibrant capital of an autonomous state in Upper Egypt, and it witnessed many great revolts. Its numerous villages, Nile cities, and Red Sea ports were thriving centers of commercial agriculture, long-distance trade, and manufacturing activities. Egypt's passage to modernity under consecutive empires terminated the independent state in Upper Egypt, peripheralized the south within the Egyptian centralized government and economy, and relegated its seat, Qina, to utter marginalization.

The historiography of imperialism in Egypt has long focused only on Cairo and the Delta in the north, ignoring Upper Egypt and its revolutions. Narratives of imperial hegemony and local resistance have been written from the point of view of the north, and the voice of the south has gone unheard. The domination of nationalistic, elite, and Cairo-centered approaches in Egyptian history has rendered the narratives of subalterns in a place like Qina Province irrelevant in the larger tale of the country. Upper Egypt does have a different story to tell about its relation with empire—imagined empires. Qina, a seemingly remote and insignificant province, stands out as an alternative case to study, and its uprisings reveal many myths of imperialism.

In 1819, a French traveler by the name of Edouard de Montulé, observed that "after Alexandria, Damietta, Rosetta and Cairo, [the city of Qina] is probably the most important city in Egypt."[7] De Montulé was so impressed by the luxurious life in the city—graceful white buildings, bazaars, restaurants, and bakeries—that he declared it comparable to Paris.[8] About two decades before this date, Vivant Denon, a French Egyptologist who accompanied Napoléon Bonaparte's troops to Upper Egypt, described a vivid scene of Qina's regional market, with goods from Arabia, East Africa, North Africa, and the entirety of the Indian Ocean. In 1799, Denon stated,

> We left Kous [Qus], and arrived at Keneh [Qina], where we found a number of merchants of all nations. By encountering the natives of very foreign countries, remote distances seem closer. When we begin to reckon the days required for the journey, and the necessary means of affecting it, the space to be passed over ceases to be immense. The Red Sea, Gidda, Mecca, seemed like neighboring places to the town where we were; and India itself was but a short way beyond them. In the opposite direction the oases were actually no more than three days' journey off us, and ceased to appear to our imagination as an undiscovered country.... The journey to Darfur may be accomplished in forty days, a hundred more are required to reach Tombuctoo. A merchant whom I found in Keneh ... had often been in Darfur, where the caravans arrive from Tombuctoo.... Here we also found many Turkish, Meccan and Moorish merchants, come to exchange coffee and Indian cottons for corn.[9]

Qina Province had maintained this prosperity for hundreds of years before these two accounts were written. Between the twelfth and the fourteenth centuries, historians from the Ayyubid (1171–1250) and Mamluk (1250–1517) periods described scenes of busy trade and pilgrimage routes, advanced educational institutions, and flourishing sugarcane cultivation and sugar industry in and around Qina. Ibn Jubayr (d. 1217) described Qina Province's city of Qus as "full of markets, with extensive facilities and services, full of peoples because of the abundance of the imported and exported commodities brought by Yemeni, Indian, and Abyssinian merchants and pilgrims because it was the stopping place of all, the forum of friends, and the meeting point of the pilgrims of North Africa, Egypt and Alexandria."[10] A recent historian, W. J. Fischel asserts that "Qus, next to Cairo, was the most important commercial center of Egypt at this period."[11] According to Abu al-Fadl al-'Umari (1301–49), this city had large commercial complexes and numerous inns for the accommodation of international merchants, in addition to luxurious houses, schools of higher education, public baths, gardens, vast farms, and more. Qina Province was home to various kinds of craftsmen, merchants, large landowners, shari'a scholars, and wealthy Muslims and Christian Copts.[12]

Qina Province owed its rise to prominence to being an integral part of what many world historians call the Indian Ocean world economy. Before the advent of a modern European "world system," the Indian Ocean world economy incorporated the Red Sea, the Arabian Sea, and the entirety of the Indian Ocean and served as the engine for Afro-Asian trade. European trade was on the periphery of this global system and was mainly a recipient of its commodities.[13] Upper Egypt, especially Qina and its Red Sea ports, was a central meeting point in a regional market that incorporated places such as Hijaz, Yemen, India, Sudan, Abyssinia, and Morocco, and the Upper Egyptian market was an essential trade circle in the vast Indian Ocean market. The economic prosperity of Upper Egypt allowed the formation of an autonomous state in the south, whose capital was always a Nile port city within Qina Province. During the Mamluk period, an Arab tribe, the Hawwara, controlled landownership, long-distance trade, and the sugar industries in Upper Egypt, and it founded a powerful dynasty in the south.[14]

When the Ottoman Empire invaded Egypt in 1517, it did not conquer the south. Rather, it made peace treaties with the region's ruling elite, leaving the native dynasty in power in return for an annual tribute. During the three centuries of Ottoman imperial rule in Egypt, the country was divided between a military Mamluk regime in the north, whose capital was Cairo, and a civil tribal regime in the south, whose capital was Qina. The southern regime reported directly to the Ottoman sultan in Istanbul and maintained administrative autonomy. Later attempts by the Ottomans to annex the south to the northern regime only brought about rebellion and plague. On the eve of the nineteenth century, the French mounted a campaign to "liberate" Egypt from the Mamluk despots of the Ottoman Empire, but they only did so in Cairo and the north. The French failed to control the south and faced a fierce war of Jihad led by native Arab tribes and Hijazi volunteers. This conflict led to a new wave of the plague, and eventually the French had to install the same Mamluk tyrants—the ancien régime—to rule over the autonomous state of Upper Egypt.

When Muhammad 'Ali Pasha (r. 1805–48) came to power in Egypt, he attempted to subjugate Upper Egypt and unify the north and south under a centralized government, ruled from his seat in Cairo. After six long years of vicious wars to conquer the south, Upper Egypt became the "first colony" in Muhammad 'Ali's expanding empire. He used the resources of Qina and the other provinces of Upper Egypt to support his military expansion and conquest of new territories outside Egypt. Shortly afterward, between 1820 and 1824, a series of unprecedented massive revolts erupted in Qina Province to overthrow the pasha's government. Muhammad 'Ali crushed these revolts and subsequently marginalized the south within his unified state and empire.[15]

The pasha's empire did not survive long. It collapsed in the face of "informal" British imperialism in the mid-nineteenth century. A European-led, capitalist world system emerged to undo and replace the old Indian Ocean one, cutting off Qina Province from its regional trade connections. Cairo's incumbents—who were the grandsons of Muhammad 'Ali and inherited his unified state—shifted Egypt's economic center to the cotton-producing north, the Delta, in order to meet the demands of the British industrialists. Moreover, the informal British Empire pressured Cairo to introduce market measures, such as free trade, to the south. Once more, in 1864, the increasingly impoverished inhabitants of Qina Province embarked on a massive revolt against Cairo's regime.[16] When the British Empire formally colonized Egypt in 1882, it was time again to fully subjugate and incorporate the ever-rebellious south. The colonial regime worked with Cairo's ruling elite to forge a nation-state, unifying the north with the south in one capitalist market. But the introduction of colonial capitalism in the south failed, generating a cholera epidemic and provoking novel forms of subaltern unrest—against both the empire and the nation-state—in Qina Province.

Thus, Upper Egypt, and particularly Qina Province, had a fundamentally different relation with world empires than the north did. Nonetheless, the prevailing nationalistic historiography of Egypt ignores this and positions the perspectives of Cairo and the Delta as the one narrative of a presumed "nation." The integration of the south into a northern regime, followed by the south's peripheralization within the centralized state from the nineteenth century onward, also facilitated the region's marginalization in historical accounts. Both Arabic and English histories of Egypt are overwhelmingly Cairo- or north-centered. Moreover, they celebrate bourgeois struggles against colonialism in which elite Cairene female and male heroes champion nationalistic resistance against the empire, and they intentionally miss subaltern struggles in the south.[17]

Only a few historians have attempted to recount the history of Upper Egypt. Peter Gran sheds light on the ignored narrative of the impoverished south, especially under British colonialism. From a Marxian stance, Gran applies Antonio Gramsci's concept of the "Southern Question" to Upper Egypt. "In ... a certain kind of capitalist nation-state hegemony, ... the Northern ruling class exploits the Southern peasantry with the collusion and assistance of the Southern ruling elite by playing the Northern worker against this Southern peasant," Gran explains.[18] He argues that British colonialism generated such a phenomenon in Egypt when it expanded capitalist cotton cultivation and helped create a modern industrial sector in the Delta, turning Upper Egyptians into a mere peasantry. In another treatment of southern Egypt's history, Martina Rieker applies a subaltern studies approach to the question of Upper Egypt under British rule, also within the nation-state confinements. She argues that under the British administration the successful process of building a modernized state made the populations of Cairo and the Delta into citizens and reduced the southern population to cheap labor.[19] This book attempts to add nuanced analysis to the invaluable contributions of Gran and Rieker by expanding the time period of Upper Egyptian history under study from the Ottoman to the contemporary era and by inviting the empire as a unit of analysis.

The dominant unit of analysis in Middle Eastern history has long been the nation-state, which renders local stories of the margin or low-class resentment unimportant within the larger heroic tale of bourgeois national independence and elite nation building. As this book shifts the unit of analysis from the nation-state to the empire, it recovers the history of Upper Egypt from the universalized nationalist narratives and restores the silenced voices of the subalterns of the south. This book retrieves the history of Upper Egypt from within alternative histories of failed empires. It frees the south from the nationalistic narrative and then investigates particular ramifications of colonialism and unique modes of resistance in its remote capital province, Qina.

THEORIZING THE EMPIRE

While narrating the story of Qina Province and the empire, this book relies on variant theoretical approaches to analyze the relation between the local southern communities and their external hegemons. Marxist, dependency, world-system, postcolonial, and subaltern studies approaches have previously deconstructed major myths about early modern and modern empires in global history at large and Middle Eastern history in particular. They have attempted to reveal the destructive faces and present an undermining critique of colonialism. This book brings many insights of these theories into the study of Upper Egypt and through their lenses attempts to show novel intricacies in the case of Qina.

In *Empire,* Michael Hardt and Antonio Negri affirm that empire is still alive and well. With a Marxian stance and postmodern rhetoric, Hardt and Negri indicate that today's empire is different from traditional imperialism. Whereas imperialism in the past was based on a European nation-state's territorial expansion outside its borders of sovereignty, the new existing empire "is a *decentered* and *deterritorializing* apparatus of rule that progressively incorporates the entire global realm within its open expanding frontiers.... The rule of Empire operates on all registers of the social order extending down to the depth of the social world.... The object of its rule is social life in its entirety.... [It is] the paradigmatic form of biopower."[20] Thus, contrary to what many think, empire concerns not just the United States; rather, it is a global system governed by NGOs, multinational corporations, the United Nations, the International Monetary Fund, the European Union, and, to a significant degree, the United States. In Hardt and Negri's argument, there is a tone of fascination, albeit with criticism, for empire as a legendary entity whose "rule has no limits." It is "a regime that effectively encompasses the spatial totality."[21] The global exploited subjects, or the "multitude" as the authors call them, could try and resist the empire, but they would have to invent new tools of mobilization through interconnectedness to take the empire down—perhaps in the distant future.

About a century before the birth of Hardt and Negri's postmodern empire, Marxist theory asserted that modern imperialism was, in the words of Lenin "the highest stage of capitalism." A prominent Marxist critic of Western imperialism, Giovanni Arrighi defines empire as the main capitalist hegemon that dominates the world in one historical moment or another. Arrighi extended Gramsci's concept of hegemony—which he coined to analyze noncoercive, persuasive nation-state authority—to understand how empire has exercised power over subjugated states and economies. "The power of the hegemon is something more and different than 'dominance' pure and simple. It is the power associated with dominance expanded by the exercise of 'intellectual and moral leadership,'" Arrighi asserts.[22] He suggests that in early modern and modern global history, there were three successive capitalist hegemons: the Italians, the Dutch, and the British. He adds that the United States inherited the British Empire in becoming a global capitalist hegemon today. Despite recognizing the fallacies of Western capitalism, Arrighi assigns it a triumphant role in creating the modern world system that assimilated economies in and outside Europe into one interstate system.[23] He shows that the British Empire, for instance, was successful in establishing world hegemony through imposing free-trade agreements, and native resistance could not end this exploitive situation. "Under British hegemony," says Arrighi, "non-Western people did not qualify as national communities in the eyes of the hegemonic power and of its allies, clients, and followers.... Non-Western people ... had from the start resisted those aspects of Free-Trade Imperialism that more directly impinged upon their customary rights to self determination and to livelihood. By and large, however, this resistance had been ineffectual."[24]

The dependency and world-system theories, offshoots of Marxism, reach similar conclusions. They assert that modern European empires were successful in dividing the world into industrial, capitalist cores and economically dependent peripheries. The two theories perceive Western empires as able to reduce vast territories of the world into mere subjugated margins. Canonical texts within these theories, such as Immanuel Wallerstein's *Modern World-System,* Andre Gunder Frank's *Dependent Accumulation and Underdevelopment,* and Samir Amin's *Imperialism and Unequal Development,* have for decades provided the social sciences with profound insights into understanding Western empires and their presence in the Third

World, whether in Africa, Latin America, or the Middle East. The two theories trace the dynamics through which the European core came to dominate and peripheralize the economy of the controlled territories. They assert that the capitalist, industrial West expanded externally in pursuit of raw material and open markets in the colonies. Limiting the economic activities of the colonized lands to the primitive production of raw material kept them in a peripheral, undeveloped status in the modern world economy controlled by European cores located in Britain and France. Dependency and world-system theories assert that colonized societies in the Third World went through almost identical experiences in this regard.[25]

Postcolonial theory, a more recent approach, attempts to deconstruct Eurocentric discursive practices concerning imperialism. It positions the colonized as an object of close surveillance, with the purpose of close control, of the metropolis. The colonizer observes the natives, monopolizes the process of "representation" of them, allows them to move only within the confines of the images the imperialist forges, finally trapping them in certain social constructs—especially regarding race. Prominent postcolonial theorists such as Edward Said, Gayatri Spivak, and Homi Bhabha are heavily informed by Michel Foucault's concept of knowledge and power, meaning that Western ownership of knowledge has served as an indispensable tool of imperial domination. "The most formidable ally of economic and political control had long been the business of 'knowing' other peoples because this 'knowing' underpinned imperial dominance and became the mode by which they were increasingly persuaded to know themselves: that is, as subordinate to Europe," Bill Ashcroft, Gareth Griffiths, and Helen Tiffin affirm in *The Post-colonial Studies Reader*.[26]

Postcolonial theory is primarily informed by Foucauldian insights into how the European modern state developed new discourses and institutions of intensive, yet noncoercive, control of the citizen. Foucault uncovers the genealogy of how the birth of modern political economy accompanied the birth of the nation-state that further disciplines the bodies and lives of its subjects—rather than setting them free from early modern monarchical and church repression. Nineteenth-century centralized governments, primarily Victorian England, created certain institutions, such as schools, hospitals, and prisons, that put their subjects under close supervision and gave the state an elusive control over their bodies. Postcolonial analysts demonstrate that nineteenth-century empire imported these tactics of power to the colony and, thus, maximized its penetration of the natives' daily life.[27] For example, Ann Laura Stoler writes that "many students of colonialism have been quick to note that another crucial 'Victorian' project—ruling colonies—entailed colonizing both bodies and minds. A number of studies... have turned on a similar premise that the discursive management of sexual practices of colonizer and colonized was fundamental to the colonial order of things. We have been able to show how discourses of sexuality at once classified colonial subjects onto distinct human kinds, while policing the domestic recesses of imperial rule."[28]

Since the late 1970s, historiography of the Middle East has applied the above theoretical approaches to explore the region's colonized societies in the nineteenth and twentieth centuries. During the 1980s, many books were published detailing how the Ottoman Empire and its Arab provinces, such as Egypt, Syria, Lebanon, and Iraq, were incorporated into the modern world system or integrated into a European-led world economy. For instance, eminent historians almost unanimously affirm that Egypt under British colonialism (1882–1952) was turned into a mere producer of raw material, namely cotton, for English textile industrialists. This process destroyed traditional, native industries and transformed the country into a peripheral economy with agrarian "retarded capitalism."[29] This caused Egypt to remain in an underdeveloped condition even after liberation from British rule. Egypt and other Arab countries experienced a state of economic "dependency" comparable to those of many other countries in Latin America, Africa, and Asia.[30]

The postcolonial approach to Middle Eastern history has added complex insights to the economic reduction and peripheralization narrative. Many historians in the field adopt Foucauldian concepts to argue that empire is penetrative beyond one's imagination—reaching under the native's skin. Its semidivine omnipresence is invisibly manifest through "biopower," that is, through the control of the bodies of its subjects by modern discourses and institutions such as the hospital, prison, and school. In other words, the postcolonial approach presumes that the colonizer does not control the colonized through coercion but rather through surveillance and discipline of her or his body. In this regard, recent literature on the Middle East uses Foucault's notions to study issues such as governmentality, biopolitics, medicine, marginalization, education, and sexuality within colonial contexts. Such studies imply that empire is an invincible, yet subtle, construct that can penetrate the native's own body through the softest practices of power without even being noticed.[31]

Timothy Mitchell applies existing theories, especially the postcolonial framework, in order to point out the inefficiency rather than the almightiness of empire. Mitchell is a leading critic of "modernity" as introduced by British imperialism to Egypt in the nineteenth and early twentieth centuries, and his *Rule of Experts* particularly deconstructs one facet of failed colonial modernity: the empire's market economy. Mitchell asserts that the economy is just another social construct produced by the modern social sciences—similar to class, nation, gender, race, and so on—yet it is neglected in postcolonial critique because of the general perception that statistics and figures constitute "universal" and "neutral" truth. Mitchell deploys Karl Polanyi's criticism of the free economy, which insists that the idea of a "self-regulating market" is a myth: such a market existed in European history only for a very short period and was never the norm. Mitchell argues that although the colonizer introduced the market economy—the conventional wisdom in today's liberal and neoliberal theories—to the colonized as an imagined universal model for reaching economic progress, this market never functioned in the ideal way that the empire claimed. The European colonizer brought this myth of a proficient laissez-faire economy to colonies like Egypt, only for it to fail and bring about environmental destruction. Instead of delivering the allegedly long-awaited modernity, European free market experts left the natives with diseases and biological catastrophes.[32] This book is heavily informed by Mitchell's critique of modernity and its market economy.

Using the insights of the above theoretical approaches, each chapter in this book closely deconstructs a historical myth that an early modern or a modern empire invented about itself. It attempts to undermine these myths through new Arabic archival evidence from Qina Province. As the book investigates issues of colonial modernity, market transformation, and environmental destruction in the province, it particularly adopts Mitchell's work to analyze these matters.

A word is due here about this book's adoption of the theoretical term *subaltern* to analyze low-class rebellion against the empire in Upper Egypt. Like the above theories, subaltern studies—an offshoot of the postcolonial theory—attempts to restore the voices of marginalized groups, such as peasants and women, and grants them greater and effective agency vis-à-vis the imperialist.[33] This theory takes Gramsci's concept of the subaltern, which he coined in *Prison Notebooks,* from its original Italian context to the study of colonial India. Subaltern studies also looks beyond conventional Marxist theory—beyond factory workers in uniforms—to forge a new notion of lower classes engaged in resistance against power structures, such as silenced peasants. Ranajit Guha insists that the historiography of anticolonial struggles has been a subject of a "bourgeois-nationalist elitism," one that celebrates only upper-class, urban, nationalist activism, led by the wealthy and Western-educated groups in the city, and almost ignores the narratives of the countryside and the underprivileged. This bourgeois monopoly is mainly a product of the British mind-set that granted respect and consideration only to the clean, rich elite—whether on the side of the colonizer or colonized.[34] Guha adds that "during the colonial period in India subaltern politics constituted an 'autonomous domain' which 'neither originated from elite politics nor did its existence depend upon the latter.'" He attributes the roots of these resistance politics to precolonial practices that reemerged under imperial rule, taking forms such as riots and popular movements.[35]

This book invites subaltern studies to investigate nonelite, nonnationalist rebellion against the empire and its co-opted ruling elites in Qina Province and southern Egypt. Furthermore, it places a significant emphasis on the social bandits of Qina and their rebellious operations against elite figures and properties, considering them an integral part of subaltern resistance.[36]

ON ARCHIVAL SOURCES

In order to tell a five-hundred-year story of incompetent imperialism, environmental destruction, and revolt in Qina Province, this book taps into a wide range of newly discovered archival and primary sources. It relies on sources that were not produced in the imperial center or even in Cairo: sources written in an unnoticed place and revealing unexpected truths. The book utilizes, for the first time, Arabic archival collections concerning Qina Province from the National Archives of Egypt (Dar al-Watha'iq al-Qawmiyya) that were only made available to researchers in the last few years.[37] This study complements this archival material with Arabic manuscripts and published books, documents from the British National Archives (formerly Public Record Office), military records, and various French travelers' accounts. Arabic documents about the province include collections from Islamic court records, official correspondence between the central government in Cairo and provincial bureaucrats, thousands of individual and collective petitions submitted by the lower classes to provincial and central authorities, minutes of the Supreme Court, parliamentary minutes, and much more.

For the period before and during the Ottoman Empire, the records of the shari'a court of the city of Isna and its rural vicinities in Qina illuminate political and socioeconomic developments in the province. These records uncover facts about the independent southern government and its relation to Istanbul and to subaltern and elite subjects; the archives also illuminate regional commerce, the landownership system, gender relations, Christian Copts, and more.[38] Classical works of history used here include al-Maqrizi's *Al-Khitat,* al-Damurdashi's *Al-Durra al-Musana,* al-Idfawi's biographical dictionary of Upper Egyptian scholars titled *Al-Tali' al-Sa'id,* al-Jabarti's *'Aja'ib al-'Athar,* and an unpublished manuscript about the Turkish governors of Upper Egypt with the title of "Risala fi man Tawalla al-Sa'id." Furthermore, Layla 'Abd al-Latif's study on the most famous autonomous ruler of Upper Egypt, *Al-Sa'id fi 'Ahd Shaykh al-'Arab Hammam,* is essential in understanding the period.

For the short-lived French Empire, this book uses accounts of French travelers, Egyptologists, military officers, and soldiers who landed in Qina Province. For the natives of Qina, the book relies on Isna Court records during the period of the Napoleonic campaign (1798–1801) to investigate the situation in villages and small towns. The same court records are also used to locate the Ottoman sultan's decrees, or *fermans,* which were disseminated in the province during the campaign. This book uses Arabic books that analyze the French presence in Upper Egypt, particularly Nasir Ahmad Ibrahim's *Al-Faransiyyun fi Sa'id Misr,* in addition to French and Arabic translations of correspondence between the campaign's generals in Upper Egypt and its headquarters of operations in Cairo.

As for Muhammad 'Ali Pasha's empire, several sources furnish vivid stories, making the voices of women and men from subaltern groups accessible and heard. Although shari'a court records remain an important source for this period, they are surpassed by the enormous and rich collections of the daily official correspondence between the central government in Cairo and every district and subdistrict in Qina Province, such as Sadir and Warid Mudiriyyat, Qina and Isna, which provide details about the viceroy's modern imperial institutions of hegemony, the provincial ruling elite, and how the subalterns of the province reacted to them. The people of Qina submitted thousands of petitions, or *'ardhala*s, either individually or collectively, directly to Muhammad 'Ali's court, to the general inspector of Upper Egypt, or to other high-ranking officials in order to complain about the ramifications of modern imperial hegemony. In addition, the minutes of the modern representative body that the viceroy created, the Council of Consultation, or Majlis al-Mashura, serve as an important source for understanding the pasha's modern institutions of internal colonialism. Legal codes promulgated by this council, such as *La'ihat al-Fallah* for agricultural organization and the Syasatname for the bureaucracy, are analyzed here as discourses of hegemony.

Concerning the middle period of the informal British Empire, the same previous sources—shari'a court records, official correspondence, and petitions—continue to provide the backbone of the narrative, but another source makes the story even richer and more vivid: the minutes of the Council of Rules, or Madabit Majlis al-Ahkam, an institution that served as both a supreme court and a legislature in Cairo. Cases that failed to reach a final verdict in local courts and civil councils in the province were referred to Cairo to be heard in the Council of Rules, which kept extensive minutes, sometimes tens of pages for each case. The lively details in these minutes show a province subject to the modernity of the market economy and uncover forgotten stories of rebellious bandits and other forms of subaltern resistance. Because there is a special focus on the legal codes in this part of the study, the minutes of the newly established Parliament, or Majlis Shura al-Nuwwab, show how both central and local ruling elites peripheralized the province through the promulgation of modern laws. Filib Jallad's encyclopedia of modern Egyptian laws, *Qamus al-'Idara wa-l-Qada'*, is another essential primary source in this regard. Furthermore, 'Ali Mubarak's geographical and biographical encyclopedia, *Al-Khitat al-Tawfiqiyya,* makes it easier for this book to follow modern transformations in the economic and social life in the provinces' villages under the informal empire. Luckily, an Englishwoman, Lady Lucie Duff-Gordon, happened to live in Qina when the massive 1864 revolt erupted there, and she provided an interesting account of the revolt in detailed letters to her relatives back home.

Finally, for the British colonial period, in addition to all previous sources in the Cairo archives, records from the British National Archives in London illustrate the failures of colonial capitalism. The annual administrative and financial reports of British high commissioners, consuls, and consular agents in Egypt are crucial for understanding British liberalism as a discourse of hegemony and how it functioned through allegedly democratic and capitalist institutions. Some confidential memoranda in the records of the British Foreign Office also reveal hidden facts about how foreign capital worked. The National Archives of Egypt also provide this part of the study with a new variety of sources, including the minutes of the Cabinet of Ministers, or *Maljis al-Wuzara'*; the minutes of the two bodies of the reformed Parliament, or

Majlis Shura al-Nuwwab and *al-Jam'iyya al-'Umumiyya*; and a collection of a new kind of petitions sent to the viceroy's court, called *iltimasat*. Furthermore, the annual provincial reports, *Majmu'at Taqarir al-Mudiriyyat,* and published collections of decrees and orders, *Al-Qararat wa-l-Manshurat,* show new faces of mythical imperialism and rebellion.[39]

ONE

Ottomans, Plague, and Rebellion

1500–1800

In the 1760s, the Ottoman sultan received a report on the state of affairs in Egypt that revealed unpleasant news. Egypt, one of the shiniest jewels in the empire's crown, was not one intact province under the sultan's full hegemony. The eminent officer who compiled the report described the existence of an autonomous state in the south. Seemingly enjoying no access to this state, the Ottoman officer gave brief and incomplete information about its government. According to the report, the autonomous regime in Upper Egypt was ruled by its own Arab tribal regime that did pay an annual tax to the sultan, but Cairo's Ottoman governor exercised no authority over it. About one of its legendary leaders, the report stated,

> The Arab named Shaykh Hammam is resident in . . . the province of Upper Egypt. He always has in his side four thousand Arab troops, and he controls by right of inheritance most of the villages of Upper Egypt. They [Hammam and his sons] never come to Cairo. . . . They always pay in full all the money and grains required for the treasury from their village, and they never oppose the tax collection. They themselves appoint and send twenty governors annually to the towns and provinces under their authority, and they collect approximately several thousand purses every year.[1]

Stories about this mysterious independent state recorded by other Ottoman officers reveal more surprises. Interestingly, the peasants who inhabited southern Egypt exercised a degree of leverage over their government to the extent that, on occasions of discontent, they could demand that the ruling elite pack up and leave. Highly impressed with this state, contemporary French observers and, later, Egyptian intellectuals of the nineteenth century called it a republic.[2] In one incident, in 1695, the ruling Hawwara tribe formed an alliance with separatist military factions in Cairo and went to war against the Ottoman governor. Amid the conflict, plague broke out and was exacerbated due to severe food shortages throughout Egypt. The discontented peasants of Qina, the capital of the southern state, asked their Hawwara leaders to take their belongings and families and leave. "We are people of plowing and harvesting, and more than half of us died. We will no longer fight and disobey the sultanate," said the farmers. The leaders of the tribe departed for the eastern mountains bordering the Nile, but they came back shortly afterward—despite local resentment—with the support of the Ottoman sultan and restored their regime.[3]

The existence of this state without a doubt comes as surprising news to many historians of the Ottoman Empire. Ottomanists traditionally have viewed Egypt as a unified province, controlled centrally by Cairo's military elite and the efficient imperial bureaucracy in Istanbul. Recent theoretical trends add that the imperial "core" in Istanbul made Egypt, along with other provinces in eastern Europe and the Arab lands, into a dependent "periphery." The entire new province was thus incorporated into a hegemonic Ottoman "world economy" that prevailed in the Mediterranean.[4] For Upper Egypt—a whole half of Egypt, in fact the richer half then—this is a mere myth. For three continuous centuries, ever since Sultan Selim's conquest of Cairo in 1517, an autonomous regime formed in the south under a local dynasty. Moreover, the south was a key part of what many world historians call the Indian Ocean world economy, the global hegemonic system of that period, of which the Ottoman Empire itself was a known dependent.[5]

This chapter argues that the Ottoman was an imagined empire in Upper Egypt. In the south of the country the core/periphery relationship was reversed: the consumerist imperial core was dependent on a capitalist periphery. Furthermore, when the empire attempted to make an actual appearance in the south, its presence only brought about environmental crises, including the onset of the plague, and eventually triggered subaltern rebellion. This chapter follows the formation of government and economic systems that existed under the independent tribal regime of the south. This state reached its maturity in the eighteenth century, under the government of the legendary Hammam that almost amounted to an early "republic"—as contemporary French observers asserted. Whenever the Ottoman Empire attempted to manifest itself in the south, the chapter demonstrates, its appearance only disturbed the political stability and disrupted an existing social contract between this state and its subjects, which generated subaltern rebellion that the empire then helped to crush. More importantly, the empire's appearance in the south killed people, as it carried with it an "imperial plague" all the way from Istanbul.

ONE SULTAN, TWO STATES: WILAYAT AL-SAʿID

Shortly after Sultan Selim I conquered Egypt, a "two-state" system was born in the new province. The official rulers of Egypt were the Mamluk officers of Turco-Circassian origin who took over Cairo's citadel after the Crusades in the thirteenth century. Nonetheless, one fierce Arab tribe, the Hawwara, established de facto control over Upper Egypt beginning in 1380, when, after prolonged wars against the Mamluks, the tribe dominated agricultural properties, trade, and industries in the south. The sultan subscribed to the existing status quo as he concluded peace treaties with the Hawwara and was content to receive the tributes and generous gifts that the tribe sent to Istanbul annually. Meanwhile, the sultan kept the loyal officers of the former Mamluk elite in power in the north but under the authority of an appointed governor pasha sent from Istanbul.[6] Thus, two separate states immediately took shape out of this postconquest arrangement: a settler, military regime in the north; and a native, tribal regime in the south.

Soon afterward, this two-state system was written into law. In 1525, when Sultan Suleiman the Magnificent issued the first book of imperial decrees to organize Egypt, *Qanunname-i Misir,* he regulated the administrative independence of Upper Egypt from Cairo. Wilayat al-Saʿid, or the province of Upper Egypt, was the official name the sultan used to refer to the southern state. According to the new imperial law, the appointed Ottoman pasha, Egypt's governor, in Cairo enjoyed no authority over the southern state's tribal rulers beyond tax collection, and he was not even authorized to punish them if they did not pay. The sultan reserved this right only for himself, and the Hawwara were to report directly to Istanbul. The imperial decree also laid out the Hawwaras' main administrative duties as rulers, including land reclamation, organizing irrigation, collecting taxes, sending annual gifts to the sultan, and crushing rebels from other Arab tribes.[7]

Another imperial law would consolidate the autonomous power of the Hawwara: the landownership code. After conquering Egypt, Istanbul introduced tax farms, or *iltizam*s, as a system of both landholding and tax collection. Each tax farmer won his piece of land, which could amount to several

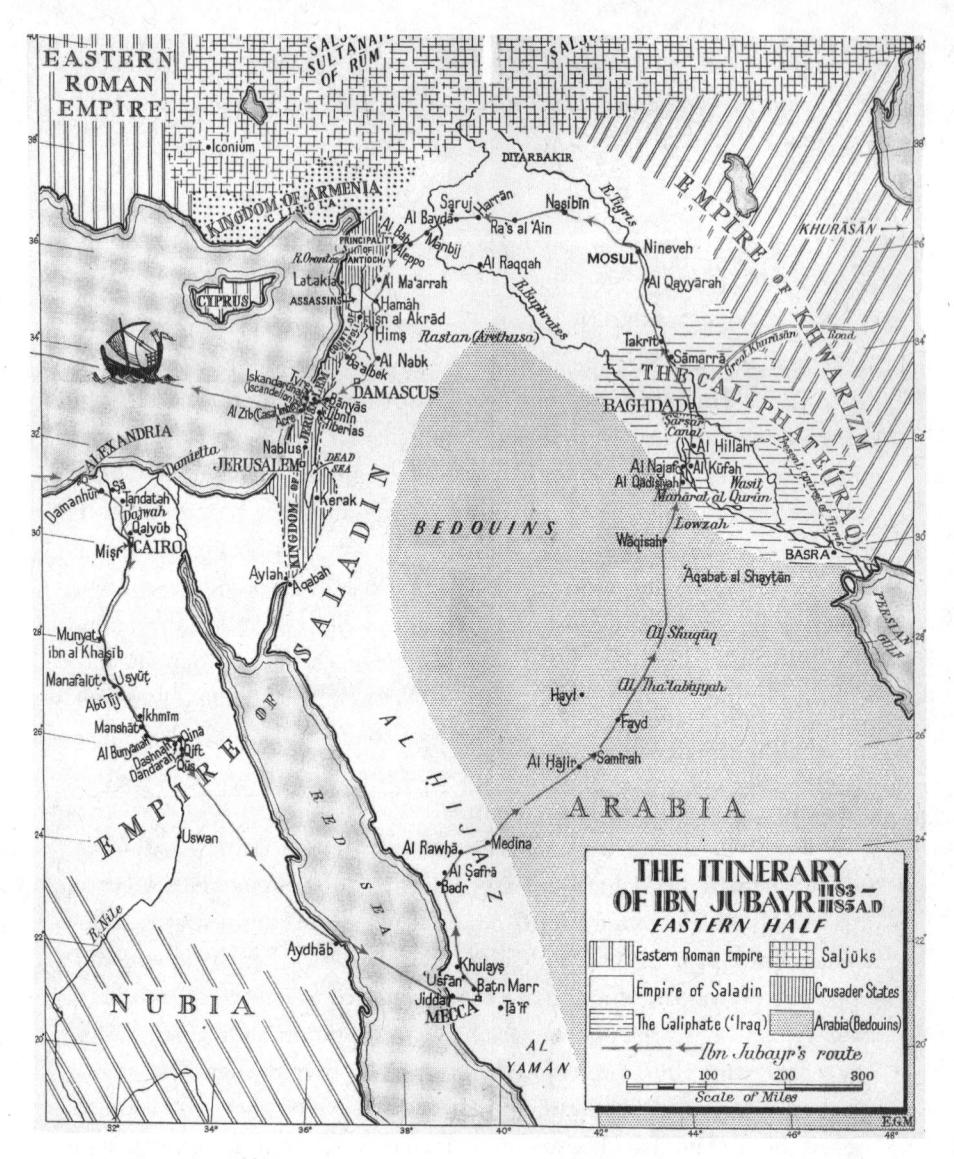

FIGURE 2. A twelfth-century trade route between Qina Province and its Red Sea port of 'Aydhab.

villages, through public auctions. The farmer would keep the land for a period of only three years, during which he maintained its cultivation through local tenants. At the end of each year, the tax farmer collected the land's fixed annual tax, sent it to the Ottoman governor in Cairo, and kept the remainder of the revenue for himself. In the northern military regime, Mamluk officers were the tax farmers of the Delta villages.[8] Hawwara tribal leaders were by far the largest, and at times the sole, tax farmers of the south. More importantly, as a sign of their independence, they maintained lifetime, hereditary rights to their landholdings. On the eve of the seventeenth century, they controlled about 65 percent of the land in Upper Egypt, and the Ottoman governor in Cairo collected revenue from the rest.[9] From the second half of the seventeenth century and through the eighteenth, Stanford Shaw recounts, the Hawwaras' "rule was formalized by their appointments as hereditary *multazims*."[10] In the mid-1700s, one Hawwara ruler, Shaykh Hammam, was the sole tax farmer in the entirety of Upper Egypt, from Asyut, through Qina, to Aswan.[11]

Aspiring to limit Hawwara power, the Ottoman pasha in Cairo appointed a governor—a Mamluk officer—in northern Upper Egypt. The city of Girga, closer to Cairo, was made into the seat for this new governor. Official records often referred to Upper Egypt as the province of Girga, or Wilayat Girga, in hope that the city's governor would impose control over the south. Nonetheless, the Hawwara not only established hegemony over incoming governors, they also controlled the very process of appointment in Cairo. When the Hawwara did not approve of a candidate, they blocked the grain tax intended for Istanbul. The Ottoman pasha and the Mamluk elite in Cairo were always forced to concede to the Hawwara. In one incident, in 1696, the Hawwara vetoed the candidacy of Mustafa Bey by threatening to forgo sending grain to the holy cities of Mecca and Medina in Hijaz, which would damage the sultan's image as the caliph of Muslims. Cairo's council thereafter excluded this candidate. Furthermore, when the Hawwara did not approve of a governor already in office, they simply terminated his tenure by ending his life. In general, the Mamluk governor of Girga stayed in power for an average of only one to three years. Around 1659, one governor, known for his despotic policies, managed to stay for five and a half years; however, his tenure ended abruptly with his murder. His successor faced a similar fate.[12]

The secret behind the rise of the Hawwaras' regime, from the Mamluk through Ottoman times, was the geographic importance of their seat of power: Qina Province, deep in the south of Upper Egypt. The capitalist commercial, agricultural, and industrial wealth of this province constituted the necessary material foundations for an independent state, as it allowed the Hawwara to rise first as an entrepreneurial and then as a political elite. Qina Province was an integral part of the Indian Ocean world economy, the old global system that encompassed the Red Sea, the Arabian Sea, East Africa, and the entirety of the Indian Ocean. As Andre Gunder Frank, Janet Abu Lughod, and many theorists of world economy assert, this was the hegemonic economic system from the rise of Islam until the nineteenth century, after which it was disrupted and replaced by a modern European-led system.[13] Through the Red Sea ports of 'Aydhab and Qusayr, the towns of the province (including Qus, Isna, Qina, and Farshut) were connected to Arabian and Yemeni ports and received important global commodities such as spices and coffee. The same towns also received East African trade, either via Nile sailboats or overland caravans, including luxury goods such as gold and slaves. These towns then served as Nile ports that reexported oriental and African commodities north to Cairo and on to the Mediterranean.[14]

Within the Indian Ocean world system, Qina Province was itself a major center of commercial agriculture. As a sugarcane, grain, and cotton producer, the province exported its own refined sugar and abundant grain to the north and sold its textiles to the regional market in East Africa.[15] The Hawwara tribe had monopolized agriculture production in the province since the Mamluk period, and the capital the tribe accumulated allowed them to grow into a dynasty. In fact, the Hawwara initially rose to power as the owners of sugarcane plantations and sugar refineries, when sugarcane was the most important cash crop in Qina Province, especially in the area of Farshut. The Mamluk sultans granted Hawwara notables large lands in Upper Egypt as fiefs, or *iqta's,* and the Hawwara soon transformed them into lucrative sugar plantations.[16] Upper Egyptian sugar was consumed domestically and exported to Middle Eastern and European countries, including, Italy, southern France, Catalonia, Flanders, England, and Germany.[17]

Evidently, there was a reversed core/periphery relationship between Istanbul and Qina, where the imperial core was actually dependant on the capitalist periphery to provide both sustenance and luxury consumption. After the conquest, the imperial granaries in Istanbul relied primarily on the Upper Egyptian grain tax, especially on wheat, to sustain its immense annual needs. As Shaw asserts, "most of the *muqata'at* [districts] of Upper Egypt were obliged to deliver their land taxes entirely in grain, and it was these grain payments which provided the entire supply used by the Imperial

Treasury to maintain those depending on it for sustenance."[18] In addition, it was the grain of Upper Egypt that the sultan—the caliph of Muslims—relied on to feed the inhabitants and pilgrims of the holy cities of Mecca and Medina each year. Grain from the south was shipped from Qina to the Red Sea port of Qusayr, unloaded at the port of Jeddah in Arabia, and shipped from there to Mecca and Medina.[19]

Furthermore, the sugar of Upper Egypt, especially from Farshut in Qina Province, arrived in Istanbul and Anatolia by land and sea in ever-increasing quantities in order to sustain the needs of the major Ottoman cities, as Shaw also points out. Istanbul annually requested and received hundreds of qantars of Upper Egyptian sugar. The empire also received its essential provisions of Yemeni coffee and African commodities, including gold and slaves, from the Upper Egyptian Red Sea and Nile trade routes. Yemeni coffee came from the port of Mocha to Qusayr and Qina and from there was shipped north. A large portion of the gold and African slaves imported by Istanbul arrived via Upper Egyptian trade routes from the Sudan and Abyssinia.[20]

The stability of the southern regime was based on a social contract between the ruling tribe and different subaltern groups in Upper Egypt. Peasants were the most important social group to which the Hawwara granted political agency; it was upon their grain and sugarcane that the dynasty built its capitalist fortune and subsequent hegemony. The peasants of Upper Egypt were largely either from Arab tribal descent or were Coptic Christians.[21] Arab peasants enjoyed considerable leverage based on tribal networks, making it difficult for rulers to control them. Arab peasants did not deal with the ruling elite in individual terms; rather, the entire clan of a village dealt collectively with their respective tax farmers. This tribal arrangement provided those peasants with considerable power vis-à-vis the Hawwara. Collective bargaining often forced the Hawwara to acquiesce to peasant demands.

This virtual social contract stipulated that Arab peasants would cultivate the land and pay dues to Hawwara tax farmers. In return, the Hawwara were obliged to provide security by protecting the villages against raids from unsettled Arab tribes. The Hawwara generally managed these tribal attacks more successfully than Mamluk tax farmers in the Delta.[22] Shaw affirms, "Their [Upper Egyptian peasants] lot was never as hard as that of the cultivators in Lower Egypt, for their masters were much better able to protect them from raids of other Arab tribes than was the central government."[23] Security was without question the main concern of peasants. When the Hawwara failed to deliver security, the legitimacy of the ruling dynasty was threatened.[24] Whereas the relationship between Mamluk tax farmers and the peasants of Lower Egypt was notoriously oppressive, Upper Egyptian peasants enjoyed a more dignified experience. Shaw writes that "the administration of this tribe [Hawwara] was equitable and beneficent; cultivation was maintained and the welfare of the peasants promoted far better than in Lower Egypt."[25]

The second group with which the Hawwara established a social contract were the Copts, the native Orthodox Christians of Egypt, especially the educated accountants among them. Replicating the model followed by Cairo-based Islamic empires ever since the Islamic conquest of Egypt in the seventh century, the Hawwaras' administration relied on Coptic expertise to run the financial system in Upper Egypt. The Hawwara hired Coptic *muʿallims* to manage the registers of their tax farms and private commercial businesses as well.[26] Nevertheless, the Coptic financial clerks were sometimes subject to persecution when their influence and fortune grew beyond the limits that the Hawwara permitted.[27]

Finally, unsettled Arab tribes, or the ʿUrban, were another important social group with whom a political pact was necessary in order to ensure the stability of the Hawwara regime. The ʿAbabida were the main tribe roaming Qina Province. They attacked villages and towns during daylight, robbed people in market places, and freed prisoners from jail.[28] Despite their criminal actions, the ʿAbabida and their shaykhs, as many European observers who were acquainted with them witnessed, were not naturally immoral people. They committed these crimes mostly as rebellious responses to state injustice. The tribe's shaykhs were fine men known for their generosity and hospitality; they kept their word and fulfilled their promises, as contemporary European visitors noted. The Hawwara co-opted the ʿAbabida through peace agreements and placed the ʿAbabida in charge of security matters. The ʿAbabida were tasked with protecting certain villages and defending the Qusayr port's trade routes against the raids of other Arab tribes.[29]

Hawwara tax farmers organized their relationship with peasants within the rules of Islamic law. They leased land to peasants through sharecropping contracts, according to which the tenant was obliged to pay the land's tax and hand in a share of the crops to the tax farmer. In addition, Qina's peasants held usufruct rights (*furugh wa nuzul*) to the land and could pass them down to their heirs. They exercised the rights to buy and sell agricultural land, which took the form of obtaining or relinquishing usufruct rights. They also enjoyed the right to mortgage their landholdings. In addition, peasants rented plots from Hawwara notables who held usufruct rights to large farms. The lease periods in these cases were as short as one year and as long as nine years. Justice was carried out in shari'a courts in order to minimize the exploitation of peasants.[30] Like their fellow Muslims, the Coptic peasants of Upper Egypt enjoyed usufruct rights, in accordance with Islamic law, and rented land from the tax farmers. Transactions in landholding occurred without discrimination between Copts and Muslims.[31]

The shari'a courts of Upper Egypt, the primary place of adjudication in the Hawwara legal system, reflected the south's autonomy. The provincial courts of Grand Cairo and the Delta were part of the state apparatus, and their judges often acted as part of the state bureaucracy. They adopted the Hanafi school of jurisprudence as the official legal framework, published the sultan's decrees (*fermans*) and other important administrative laws, and recorded grand military victories and political events in the empire. Among the duties of the provincial judge in the Delta was solving disputes among Mamluk tax farmers and investigating cases of negligence in land cultivation.[32] In contrast, the courts of Qina Province were entirely independent of Cairo. The registers of the city of Isna's court, for instance, had no first page (preamble, or *dibaja*) referring to an official affiliation of this court with the Ottoman regime in the north. They did not publish any Ottoman decrees, as they were not obliged to apply them, and did not record any Ottoman or Mamluk events, since these were irrelevant to political matters in the province.[33]

Four main schools of Islamic law dominated courts of the Muslim world at this time, and the Hawwara adopted one that differed from both Istanbul and Cairo. Whereas Istanbul adopted the Hanafi school as its official legal framework, and the Shafi'i school was dominant in northern Egypt, the Hawwara adopted the Maliki school because it was already used in southern courts and prevalent among Upper Egyptian scholars when the tribe came to power. Opinions from the Shafi'i school were still used in Qina's courts, for instance, but to a minor degree. Besides Islamic law, the Hawwara applied *'urf,* or the code of local traditions. *'Urf* in Upper Egypt referred to the Arab tribal code of ethics and collective government and was practiced in the Arab public councils, or *majalis al-'arab*. *'Urf* was also officially considered in local shari'a courts.[34]

The Hawwara built their own system of regional relations around Qina's trade routes. The traditional method of forming external alliances took place through intermarriage between dynasties, an act in which Hawwara family members participated with other ruling families in their Arab trade network. Hawwara family members married the daughters of the sharif of Mecca and became in-laws of the Hijaz ruling elite. The Meccan wives owned properties in Hijaz that their Hawwara husbands managed on their behalves. Interestingly enough, Hawwara influence in North Africa was so extensive that for a period the tribe ruled Cyrenaica, the western Libyan province. In the eighteenth century, the Hawwara ruler carried the title of the commander of Upper Egypt and Cyrenaica, or *amir al-Sa'id wa-Barqa*.[35]

The Hawwara built political alliances with specific Mamluk factions in the northern regime as well. Throughout the seventeenth and eighteenth centuries, Cairo had two primary Mamluk factions: the Faqqariyya and the Qasimiyya, who sought power and competed to form a strategic alliance with the Hawwara. Obtaining the governorship of Girga, in northern Upper Egypt, was crucial in the Faqqariyya-Qasimiyya rivalry because of both the economic resources of the south and the potential political benefits of an alliance with the Hawwara. Mamluk rebels opposing the imperial Ottoman regime traditionally escaped to Upper Egypt, where they received logistic support from the Hawwara and launched wars against their incumbent rivals in Cairo.[36]

FROM PLAGUE TO REBELLION

On the eve of the eighteenth century, the two-state system in Egypt faced a severe crisis. As war erupted across Egypt, both regimes almost collapsed. While Cairo's Mamluk factions fought each other in a dispute over power, the Hawwara sought further independence by withholding their taxes from Cairo. The empire desperately attempted to contain the collapse using its best military strategies. The political turmoil invited massive environmental devastation: the poor throughout Egypt suffered food shortages and high prices, and the plague broke out immediately afterward, both in Cairo and in the north. The empire's failure to restore political stability in the two regimes only contributed to the spread of the epidemic. Moreover, the empire's attempt to make its presence felt in Upper Egypt took place at the expense of the subalterns: it sabotaged their first considerable uprising against the Hawwara.

In 1695, an Ottoman chronicler reported that the two incumbent Mamluk factions of the military regime in Cairo—the Qasimiyya and the

Faqqariyya—intensified their competition over revenue and control of the Girga office. Their conflict was not new. It had erupted during several other major incidents through the previous decades when dissident factions revolted against the Ottoman governor pasha.[37] Capitalizing on political turmoil in the north to further their autonomy, the Hawwara stopped sending their grain tax to the pasha in Cairo. Ahmad al-Damurdashi, an eighteenth-century officer and chronicler, relayed that the "Hawwara had sized the villages producing the *kushufiya* [lands assigned to the Ottoman governor in Cairo] revenues by obtaining *taqasit* [title deeds] and turning them into *iltizam*s [tax farms] . . . and . . . were not concerned about the governor Pasha because they had agents among the notables of Cairo who purchased the *jiraya* [allowances in-kind] for 30 *nisf feddan* an *ardabb*. . . . The imperial granaries do not receive a single *ardabb* from the Hawwara."[38] Consequently, an economic crisis broke out not just in the north but across all Egypt. Commodity prices increased fourfold and some food staples, such as wheat, barely, and beans, disappeared from the markets. The crisis intensified in the next year, with low Nile inundation and a subsequently dire harvest.[39]

Amid the conflict, the plague broke out in Cairo. The Egyptian chronicler 'Abd al-Rahman al-Jabarti recounts that bodies of the impoverished dead were collected from the streets, washed in state public baths, and buried en masse.[40] It was an "imperial" plague, resulting from the empire's incompetence in maintaining the stability of the two-state system. According to the basic sultanic law regulating Egypt's administration, the Qanunname, a main duty of each state was agricultural organization, or ensuring the control of irrigation and drainage during the annual floods. Some contemporary European observers argued that the reason behind the sudden appearance of the plague was mismanagement of the Nile water after the flood, neglect of stagnant swamps, and low Nile inundation. This wave of the epidemic erupted during military conflict and a time of low Nile flood, when the two regimes neglected water control. Although this outbreak of the plague did not make it to Upper Egypt—as the region's dry air and hot weather mostly made it immune[41]—the impoverished population of the south was migrating to Cairo and sweeping its hungry streets, only to die there in the epidemic.[42]

Two years after this tragedy, in order to subjugate the southern regime of the Hawwara, Sultan Mustafa Khan issued a decree to send a Mamluk army equipped with the latest military technology from Cairo to Upper Egypt. The Supreme Council, or al-Diwan al-'Ali, of the governor pasha assembled to read the sultan's letter that commanded thus: "To Husayn Pasha. As soon as this noble receipt reaches you, you are to announce a general call for arms ... proceed to Girga and destroy the Hawwara tax farmers of Upper Egypt who sized the *kushufiya* villages [the tax farms of the pasha]. Take note and do not disobey."[43] The Mamluk officers obeyed. 'Abd al-Rahman Bey promised to recover the villages seized by the Hawwara, in return for which he would be appointed the governor of Girga for three years. He made sure to have an official deed registering this promise. He equipped his army with two cannons, ammunition, an artilleryman, and a *ferman* granting amnesty. More importantly, he formed an alliance with a dissident faction from the northern Hawwara against the tax farmers of the southern Hawwara who controlled the tribal regime.

In response, the southern Hawwara were ready with an army of peasants and Nubians. After a long fight, they lost the battle. The Mamluks occupied their capital town in Qina Province, Farshut, and the Mamluk soldiers plundered their properties and took their women. They looted the Hawwaras' oil mills' machinery, flour mills' grounding stones, slaves, horses, and camels in Farshut and sent the spoils north by boat. Many of the peasants of Upper Egypt died in the battle, but the ruling Hawwara tax farmers were unharmed.

It was time for the southern peasants, who resented the destruction that the Hawwara regime had inflicted on them, to rebel. The peasant leadership, of Arab tribal origin, visited the defeated leaders of the Hawwara in Farshut, saying, "We are people of farming. More than half of us died [because of the war]. We no longer want to fight and disobey the sultanate."[44] In response, the tribal ruling elite took their families and precious belongings and escaped through the western mountains with the goal of departing farther west. The next morning, peasant leaders walked from Farshut to meet with 'Abd al-Rahman Bey in his camp in order to serve him breakfast and show submission to his new order. They relayed to him what happened between them and the Hawwara and assured him again that they were the subjects, or *ra'iyya*, of the sultan. Then they pledged allegiance to Cairo and Istanbul. The bey appointed Mamluk tax farmers to replace the Hawwara in all of their former villages. News of the bey's victory and the Hawwaras' escape was relayed immediately to the sultan in Istanbul.[45]

However, after supporting the subalterns in the beginning, the Ottoman imperial center sabotaged their rebellion. It did not take the Hawwara long to return and restore their full control over Upper Egypt. "In every place, money... buys men prestige and glory.... It is the tongue for he who wants to be eloquent... and the weapon for he who wants to fight," read a poem recited by an Ottoman official during negotiations to reinstall the tribe.[46] The Hawwara purchased their regime back from the sultan and his proxy administration in Cairo. After the Hawwaras' departure to the mountains, they had taken refuge with an Arab tribal leader, al-'Ayd, who gave his home to their families and saved their remaining properties. They asked the Arab leader to find them a merchant going Cairo to carry a message to their allies among the incumbent Mamluk officers there. He found a suitable merchant and they rented a boat to carry him—and their important message—north. Upon receiving the message, the officers—the sultan's appointed bureaucrats—inquired about the amount of money that Hawwara leaders might have to assist in buying back their landholdings and restoring authority over the southern villages.[47]

As soon as the Hawwara received the response, they left for Cairo, bearing shipments of wheat to the Mamluk minister of mint. They arrived secretly at night and after dining spent the night at the minister's palace. An allied officer said, "Ask them if they have enough money to arrange to things." The Hawwara leaders responded, "Whatever you request is available. Just get us back our villages." The officer was so pleased by this response that he recited the abovementioned poem stating that money could buy everything. In a long session over a heavy meal and coffee, they agreed to plot against 'Abd al-Rahman Bey, have the pasha remove him from his position as the governor of Girga, and give the Hawwara back their tax farms. The plot succeeded and the newly appointed governor of Girga became a close ally of the Hawwara.[48]

AFTER REBELLION: A SOUTHERN "REPUBLIC"

Two decades after the onset of this environmental crisis and peasants' rebellion against the tribal regime, a republic was born in Upper Egypt. Upper Egypt was still an autonomous state governed by the returning Hawwara, but it was now based on a new social contract between the Hawwara and the subaltern classes of the south, to appease the latter. This republic emerged because of internal social conflicts and dynamics, in which the distant empire played no role aside from receiving annual tribute. Furthermore, the republic had its own political and social institutions, divorced from the imperial system. It was the state of Shaykh al-'Arab Hammam Ibn Yusuf.

Hammam was a legendary leader who founded a state that lasted for forty years, from the 1720s until 1769. He was born in Farshut around 1709 to a Hawwara ruler and was raised to inherit his father's position. Hammam unified Upper Egypt under one tax farmer, himself. Between the 1720s and 1730s he added extensive lands to his already vast inheritance and became practically the sole tax farmer in the entirety of Upper Egypt from Asyut to Aswan. His lands were officially lifetime tax farms that he could pass to his heirs or, in legal terms, were akin to private property purchased from the sultan.[49] With his independent position, he bypassed Cairo and established direct relations with Istanbul. James Bruce, a contemporary British traveler who had the pleasure to attend Hammam's court, observed, "This Shekh was a man of immense riches, and, little by little, had united in his own person, all the separate districts of Upper Egypt, each of which formerly had its particular prince [from the Hawwara leaders]. But his interest was great at Constantinople, where he applied directly for what he wanted, insomuch as to give a jealousy to the Beys of Cairo. He had in farm from the Grand Signior [the sultan] almost the whole country, between Siout and Syene [Asyut and Aswan]."[50]

For the officers of the French expedition, who occupied Egypt by the end of 1790s, Hammam's state was a model to follow in creating a "national" and "just" government in Egypt comparable to the French Republic.[51] For Rifa'a al-Tahtawi, the nineteenth-century Egyptian intellectual and translator of French civil law, Hammam's state was no less modern than the republican system that he studied in France. He called it *jumhuriyya iltizamiyya,* or a tax farming republic.[52] Al-Jabarti, the eighteenth century Cairene chronicler, attributed similarly legendary characteristics to the Hammam: "The honorable Excellency; the magnificent refuge; the noble and royal in origin; the shelter of the poor and princes; the station and comforter of travelers and caravans; the commander; the most affluent and generous whose generosity covered the near and the far; the honor of the state; and the grand ruler of Upper Egypt.... He encompassed in his mind the knowledge of all the matters of Upper Egypt."[53]

Bruce visited the town of Farshut and met with Hammam in the late 1760s. The Scottish man was impressed by the refined manners of this ruler: "We waited upon Shekh Hamam; who was a big, tall handsome man, I apprehended not far from sixty. He was dressed in a large fox-skin pelisse over the rest of his cloaths, and had a yellow India shawl wrapped about his head, like a turban. He received me with great politeness and condescension, made me sit down by him, and asked me more about Cairo than about Europe."[54] Richard Pococke, another British voyager, was similarly impressed by Hammam's manners upon meeting him. Pococke was accompanied by an Armenian interpreter and an Aleppine merchant doing business in Upper Egypt. When they arrived in Farshut, Hammam's secretary escorted them to Hammam's court. "The Sheikh was sitting in the corner of his room by a pan of coals," noted Pococke. "He rose both when I came and when I left him; his dress was after the Arab manner." Hammam asked the traveler many questions "with a good-natured smile."[55]

Hammam's state was a continuation of the reversed core/periphery case in the empire. He established monopolies over most Upper Egyptian trade and commercial agriculture and increased the dependency of the consumerist imperial core in Istanbul on its capitalist periphery. Hammam's monopolies emerged when Qina's market in the Indian Ocean system reached its highest point of maturity in the eighteenth century. In fact, it is not a historical accident that the "republic" of Hammam arose in this century when its economic foundations existed outside of the alleged Ottoman world economy. The city of Qina and the other towns of the province, including Qus, Farshut, and Nagada, gradually became some of the most important centers in Egypt for international trade. As historian Fred Lawson illustrates,

> Several Upper Egyptian cities served as bases for this trading network at the turn of the century. Arguably the most significant of these was Qina, a major transshipment point on the Nile river.... The older merchant center at Qus was also active in the Red Sea grain and cloth trade during the 1790s, while Farshut and Nagada maintained trading relations with the Hijaz.... Any mention of the Sudan requires consideration of the second major commercial network of which Qina province was a part during the late eighteenth and early nineteenth century—the trade between Sinnar, Dar Fur, and Abyssinia to the south with Cairo and Europe to the north. This network extended over a vast expanse of territory and handled a variety of commodities.[56]

Trade in coffee, which was often destined for Istanbul, expanded tremendously in Qina's Red Sea port of Qusayr, especially as the volume of trade in the Suez port shrank because of less favorable navigation conditions. Ten to twenty ships visited Qusayr every month, while Suez received no more than sixty ships during the whole year.[57] Hammam established a monopoly over Qusayr, where he seized an old castle and used it as a lodge for his guests. His own businesses carried wheat from Qina through Qusayr to the port of Jeddah in Arabia. He secured and protected the trade route between the Red

Sea and Qina by winning the loyalties of particular Arab tribes, the Bedouin highway raiders, who were roaming the road. He assigned the duty of securing the Qusayr route to the ʿUlayqat tribe.[58]

In addition, East African trade expanded in Farshut. Farshut was the final destination of *darb al-jallaba* (road of the importers) caravans coming from the Sinnar kingdom of the Sudan that carried slaves, ivory, and more. Again, one of the primary destinations of this precious cargo was Istanbul. Hammam made Farshut—his hometown—the seat of his state in Qina Province, and he monopolized much of the East African trade that passed through the city.[59] Farshut also played a major role in establishing Qina's position as a famous sugarcane and sugar producer.[60] Its sugar was an effective competitor with colonial American sugar in Istanbul, the Levant, and elsewhere in the East. Henry Light, a captain of the British royal artillery, noted that Farshut was the area "where the greatest quantity of sugar is made" and added that "the Levant chiefly derives its sugar from it [Farshut]. In no part of the East, which I visited, was colonial sugar to be found; that for the use of the seraglio at Constantinople comes from Fairshoot [Farshut], and is refined with extraordinary care."[61] Hammam monopolized both the sugar industry in Farshut and the entire agricultural production of Upper Egypt. He owned twelve thousand bulls solely for purposes of sugarcane cultivation. In order to sustain this commercial power, he employed numerous plowing machines, waterwheels, flour mills, cows, and oxen and built countless storehouses filled with commercial crops.[62]

Hammam gained a respected image in both Egyptian and European records because of the just government he founded in Upper Egypt. He established a power-sharing structure built on a new social contract with many of the region's subaltern and elite groups. The ultimate goal of this order was to sustain agricultural production, secure the movement of trade, and ensure political stability. In a continuation of the Hawwara government system, Hammam's contract incorporated peasants producing the commercial crops, educated Copts managing the finances of the state, and Bedouins protecting southern trade routes and carrying goods on their camels. Each of these groups played a vital role in maintaining the stability of Hammam's regime.

Hammam held a public council (called *hukuma*, or government) for villagers, town dwellers, and Bedouins to discuss socioeconomic occurrences and solve disputes through collective consultation. The council, organized at Hammam's immense ranch in Farshut, held daily, well-attended sessions.

Attendees casually came and left the council as they pleased and were served breakfast and lunch from the kitchen of their affluent ruler's residence.[63] In this council, peasants saw Hammam as a respected authority to whom they could appeal regarding disputes over usufruct rights, either between individual peasants or whole villages. The verdicts he issued in his council had the power of legal documents and were taken to the shari'a court to be notarized and applied by the judge.[64]

The second group with which Hammam founded a social contract was elite Copts, especially educated accountants. Hammam's government was composed of many departments, each of which had its own Coptic auditors working day and night. After spending the day and two-thirds of the night meeting with the people who frequented his public council, Hammam spent the third part of the night with his Coptic bureaucrats dealing with state finances and attending to administrative affairs.[65] Hammam's Coptic secretaries acted as his deputies in villages, collecting the grain tax from peasants and shipping it to Cairo.[66] For example, he tasked the brothers Bulus and Jirjis, sons of Manqaryus, with collecting the grain taxes and sending them north. The same brothers also managed, as his agents, his financial transactions.[67]

Coptic peasants in particular experienced a golden age under the rule of Hammam, as both eighteenth-century Arabic and foreign sources affirm. During the time of the Napoleonic campaign in Egypt (1798–1801), French scientists and officers asserted that they encountered pleasant memories of Hammam among wealthy and poor Copts of Qina Province three decades after his death. Copts told the French that they missed the days of security and justice under Hammam.[68] A Coptic notable who accompanied the returning French forces to France compiled a treatise on freeing Egypt from the Ottomans and founding an independent republic. The new government that he and his French supporters envisioned was to be "just . . . and national, like that of Sheikh Hammam in Upper Egypt."[69]

Finally, the nomadic Arab tribes were another important social group whose consent was indispensable for the political stability of Hammam's regime. Hammam requested that the 'Ababida—the most important tribal group in Qina Province—settle in villages and towns in order to put a halt to highway robbery. After a quarter of a century spent plundering, Shaykh Nimr, the tribal chief of the 'Ababida, finally settled in the city of Daraw and became a friend and trading partner of Hammam. Bruce narrates, "For the first twenty seven-years of his life, he [Nimr] never had seen the Nile, unless upon some plundering party; that he had been constantly at war with the people of the cultivated part of Egypt, and reduced them often to the state of starving; but now... he was old, a friend to Shekh Hamam, and was resident near the Nile." The two leaders formed a company for Red Sea trade. Hammam and Nimr's caravans carried cargos of wheat from Qina through Qusayr to Jeddah, and, of course, their caravans were the safest of all that passed through the desert between Qina and Qusayr.[70]

Hammam respected the shari'a court and abided by its rules in political and economic life. He used the court to register administrative matters, such as notarizing and collecting grain taxes from villages, as well as to register his private businesses. Hammam sometimes attended the court himself, but in most cases he sent legal agents with signed letters to the judge.[71] His deputies in large towns attended, on his behalf, cases regarding different types of tax registration, business transactions, and social matters. The local administrators of Hammam's government functioned through the court, as village and town notable shaykhs always attended court sessions that dealt with the economic and social life of the inhabitants of the province, which included buying and selling houses, shops, mills, and land; marriage and divorce; mortgage; and charitable endowment.[72] Under Hammam, the shari'a court in Qina was a place of adjudication for Copts and Muslims alike. Copts registered their transactions in the court and sometimes had Muslim village shaykhs as witnesses.[73] Hammam treated elite Copts with whom he had business as his legal equals in the court, since he exchanged properties with them and registered these transactions in order to maintain contractual rights for his minority citizens.[74]

Hammam also relied on an Arab tribal code of ethics to resolve communal and individual disputes in his public council.[75] In 1757, the people of two villages, Nimsa and Misariyya, violently assaulted each other and subsequently appealed to Hammam's council to resolve the dispute. Hammam concluded a peace accord between the two parties and mandated that the people of the two villages should first pay their dues to the treasury. If one side killed someone from the other side, the latter would be entitled to revenge and allowed to kill four persons and receive ten bags of blood money. Hammam forbade villagers from crossing the water canal that separated the two villages and decreed that transgressors would be mercilessly punished. On Sunday, which was the local market day, the two parties should mind their own affairs in the market and commit no transgressions against each other; otherwise, severe punishment would be inflicted on transgressors. The

Hawwara deputy tax farmers in the two villages were in charge with executing punishments. The notable shaykhs of each village accepted the accord and consented to its stipulations, and the document was registered in the shari'a court.[76]

Copts also frequented Hammam's council to resolve their disputes. In 1759, two Coptic brothers, Manqaryus and Sidarus, sons of Shunuda the goldsmith, quarreled with another Copt by the name of Habash Mikha'il over their shares in a house that the brothers had inherited from their mother, Ghazal, daughter of Jirjis the priest. Ghazal had inherited a share of the house of her father, who had bought it almost seventy years earlier and registered as his property in the shari'a court. The disputing parties presented the case before Hammam, who ruled that Manqaryus and Sidarus should retain their property rights to the house, a ruling that the two brothers brought to the shari'a judge to notarize.[77]

Hammam co-opted into his regime one elite Upper Egyptian group in particular: the Ashraf notables, who were Arabs claiming a Prophetic lineage. In his administration, some Ashraf families monopolized the judgeships of the shari'a courts of Qina Province. The shari'a scholars from the Habatir family were the only holders of this position in Isna Court throughout the eighteenth century and eventually transformed the position into a hereditary office maintained within the family. They continued to monopolize this post for part of the nineteenth century under Muhammad 'Ali. In 1692, Qadi Ahmad 'Ali Habatir was the official judge *(khalifat al-shar')* in Isna Court, and the position remained in his family, passing eventually to his great-grandson in 1839. Because of their elite status, the Habatir family enjoyed immense wealth and owned many different types of businesses and assets, including many houses and tracts of land.[78]

Hammam exerted considerable authority over Cairo's regime. The Ottoman governor pasha was forced to submit to Hammam's demands, even at the expense of the Mamluk elite. In one incident, Hammam mortgaged the lands of a village to a Mamluk officer, stipulating that he (Hammam) would relinquish his property rights to this village after a certain deadline. Hammam did not pay back the loan in time and yet refused to give up the village. He sent an emissary to the Ottoman governor in Cairo demanding that the governor not issue any decrees acknowledging the officer's right to the mortgaged lands. Hammam threatened that, should the governor issue such a decree, no more grain or cash provisions would be sent to Cairo. The Mamluk officer never managed to seize the village.[79]

Meanwhile, Hammam also built political alliances with rebellious Mamluk factions in Cairo and collaborated with them to overthrow the Ottoman governor. Oppositional Mamluk officers and their soldiers who took refuge in Hammam's court were Arabized—that is, adopted Arabic language and customs—and became part of Hammam's army.[80] Hammam chose an alliance with the Qasimiyya Mamluk faction. A prominent member of this faction, Salih Bey al-Qasimi, the head of the Pilgrimage Department, was a close friend of Hammam and acted as his business proxy in Cairo. Salih Bey was a large tax farmer in northern Upper Egypt, outside of Hammam's territory, and his soldiers stayed for prolonged periods with the Hawwaras' army and learned the clan's high code of ethics. During the annual pilgrimage season, Hammam sent his friend in Cairo a gift of three hundred camels and various other provisions for the caravan going to Arabia via the port of Suez. Salih Bey later fled Cairo in the wake of political tension and took refuge in Hammam's realm, where the pair planned a successful military coup against Cairo's Ottoman governor.[81]

The coup went as follows: In the mid-1760s, Hammam supported the most radical action against the sultan when he backed the insurgency of 'Ali Bey al-Kabir, the governor of Cairo. This coup was the product of an alliance between 'Ali Bey, the Qasimiyya faction, and Hammam. 'Ali Bey fled Cairo to the south, where Hammam gave him both refuge and logistical support for his separatist plans. Hammam at this time was also sheltering Qasimiyya rebels, including his friend Salih Bey, and integrated them in his own army. He then blocked grain and cash provisions from reaching Cairo and Istanbul. Upon receiving 'Ali Bey, Hammam mediated between the two groups of rebels to create a unified front. Hammam's military and financial support was crucial for 'Ali Bey's success in eventually deposing the pasha and taking full control over Cairo and the entire northern regime in 1768.[82]

ONE STATE, PLAGUE, AND REBELLION ENCORE

By supporting the coup of Mamluk officer 'Ali Bey al-Kabir, the legendary Hammam committed a fatal mistake. The coup soon resulted in his tragic death and the downfall of the Hawwara regime. The two-state system consequently collapsed as well, but the Ottoman Empire immediately intervened and installed a Cairo-based unified regime that ruled over all of Egypt. Thus, the empire made a second appearance in the south, but it would not be much time before plague and rebellion followed once again.

No sooner had ʿAli Bey established an independent state in the north than he perceived Hammam's power as an overt threat. He accused Hammam of sheltering other Mamluk dissidents and supporting them against Cairo. In 1769, ʿAli Bey sent forces to Upper Egypt to exterminate the Mamluk rebels and undermine Hammam's authority. ʿAli Bey's army formed a secret alliance with an ambitious cousin of Hammam, Ismaʿil ʿAbd Allah, who fought with the Mamluk troops. In the wake of the betrayal and with his unexpected defeat, Hammam withdrew from Farshut and fled southward to the village of Qammula. Later in that year and in this very village, Hammam died in his bed, at the age of sixty, out of deep grief. His sons were carried to Cairo and publicly displayed in the streets. The Hawwara were further humiliated when ʿAli Bey seized most of their tax farms. Some Hawwara leaders maintained large tax farms, but the tribal dynasty was overthrown and the clan never returned to power.[83]

The independent state of ʿAli Bey lasted only a few years before the Ottoman army restored full control over Egypt in 1773. The sultan then placed the whole country, including Upper Egypt, under a new Mamluk regime in Cairo. Istanbul abolished the two-state arrangement, after three centuries of existence, and allowed the Mamluk military elite in Cairo to establish authority over the tax farms, trade, and administrative system of the south. Thus, a new one-state system was born in Egypt, ending the six-century autonomy of Upper Egypt that survived from the Mamluk through Ottoman period.[84]

Replacing the Hawwara regime shattered the social contract that existed between the tribe and the subalterns of Upper Egypt. The south experienced political chaos and repression under the new Mamluk government, and discontented groups undertook various forms of resistance. Only four years after Hammam passed away, groups of Arab peasants challenged the authority of the state and the remaining Hawwara tax farmers by refusing to pay the land tax. The peasants of the Busayla village ceased paying both cash and grain tax. Shaykhs of other villages intermediated between Busayla and the tax farmer and threatened that the state would punish them by destroying their houses.[85] At the same time, Mamluk officers decreased the payments that the ʿAbabida Bedouins received for protecting villages and trade routes. The tribe immediately reacted by attacking travelers and plundering villages and later launched a war against the Mamluk government. It was almost impossible for the Mamluk officers to subdue the 'Ababida dissidents, who were highly skilled warriors. After every defeat the rebels managed to quickly reassemble themselves in a few days and return to fight the new imperial regime even more fiercely.[86]

Between 1784 and 1792, the plague struck Egypt again. This time the disease made it to the south—for the first time in five centuries. Before, as a contemporary French physician asserted, the plague had been an environmental phenomena "almost unknown" in Upper Egypt.[87] Ever since the great plague of the 1300s that had swept all of Egypt, the endemic had not returned to Upper Egypt, thanks to the efficient government of the independent Hawwara. As noted earlier, European observers of the period reported that the healthier and hotter air of Upper Egypt made it difficult for the plague to travel south, whereas Cairo and the Mediterranean coast remained more susceptible.[88] However, a British report from 1800 showed that the late-1700s plague had actually originated in Upper Egypt, killing thousands in one season. According to Colonel Wilson, "The Plague has long been supposed to have been brought from Turkey in the ships charged with old clothes, which constantly came to Alexandria from a market. But the plague has generated annually in Egypt during the last four years (although no such communication has been possible), and even chiefly commenced in Upper Egypt.... In Upper Egypt [last year], sixty thousand of the inhabitants perished.... There whole villages were swept away."[89] Thus, for Upper Egypt, the epidemic was without a doubt an "imperial" plague. It broke out precisely because of the new political order.

Among European physicians and travelers of this period, two theories arose to explain why the plague infiltrated the south. Both implicate the empire. First, Colonel Wilson insisted that this latest wave of the epidemic originated in Upper Egypt because of internal causes and local conditions.[90] Other European experts generally linked the outbreak to the overflow of the Nile and mismanagement of water. They asserted that a good system of irrigation, drainage, digging canals and sluices, and building dams would make it possible to prevent the plague.[91] In fact, Arabic and European sources alike show that the new Mamluk regime neglected water management and agricultural organization in Upper Egypt, as they were busy disputing over who would be in power. The Ottoman pasha in Cairo was too weak to eradicate internal Mamluk military contests. During this period, Mamluks feuded over Upper Egyptian grain and carried out military campaigns on southern soil, causing food shortages and price hikes. In Qina the new regime left canals to dry, and the once thriving capital and center of commercial agriculture was reduced to an unimportant provincial town.[92]

The second medical theory of the plague's origins attributed the epidemic to external causes emanating from the larger imperial system. This approach suggests that the "globalization" of the Ottoman Empire, which incorporated Upper Egypt only in the last few years of the eighteenth century, coupled with the new one-state system the empire installed caused the plague that reached the south. Clot Bey, a French physician who practiced in Egypt in the early nineteenth century, suggested that the plague had no connection to the overflow of the Nile or to poverty. He argued that these two internal conditions had existed in Upper Egypt in the past, and yet the plague had not visited the south.[93] Many other European physicians and observers affirmed that the plague was carried by ships coming from Istanbul and other parts of the Ottoman Empire to Alexandria and from there spread to the rest of Egypt. Guillaume Antoine Olivier, a contemporary French traveler, recounted,

> The plague visits the different countries of the Ottoman Empire, as the smallpox visits the different countries of Europe: Like the latter, it neither owes its origin to putrid exhalations nor to causes derived from the soil or the climate.... The plague visits Turkey and makes its appearance more or less often in a town, according as commerce or communications are most or less frequent.... Egypt carries on a somewhat considerable trade with Constantinople; and indeed, it commonly happens that the Turkish ships or caravels belonging to the Grand Signior bring the plague to Alexandria, where it spreads to Rosetta, Damietta, and Cairo, and thence into all the villages.[94]

The plague was pandemic throughout the empire from the beginning of the sixteenth to the mid-nineteenth century, causing a mortality rate of up to 70 percent in the affected places. The eighteenth century witnessed many waves of this epidemic in the Mediterranean basin of the empire;[95] and in a sense, Istanbul "traded" the epidemic with Cairo.[96] As Upper Egypt was now an integrated part of the empire's political and commercial system, Mamluk ships gained access to the south—facilitated by their wars on Upper Egyptian soil—and they carried imperial diseases with them. In the 1780s, the ships of two Mamluk factions of the new regime, led by Ibrahim Bey and Murad Bey, fought each other in Upper Egypt in what was also a time of low Nile inundation and food shortage. Furthermore, other dissident factions continued to take refuge in Upper Egypt. These troops without a doubt transmitted the epidemic to the south, especially since numerous Mamluk warlords of this period died from the plague while in Upper Egypt or after their return to Cairo.[97]

With the plague and Mamluk oppression in Upper Egypt, subaltern rebellion became a daily practice of the inhabitants of the towns, villages, and mountains in the desert. Nomadic Arab tribes and Coptic peasants in particular faced increasing oppression during this period. They rebelled in various ways against the empire and its Mamluk government. Their discontent was more distinctly expressed when the Napoleonic campaign arrived in Egypt, between 1798 and 1801, as many members of these two groups supported the French soldiers against the Mamluk army.

As for the unsettled Arab tribes, their rebellion was incited by both racial and economic factors. In the past, these roaming tribes had submitted themselves to the Hawwara primarily because they shared Arab tribal blood with them but also because of the economic advantages that the Hawwara provided. Arab tribes were, as an eighteenth-century European traveler put it, "looking down with contempt on Turks," and they believed that their lineage could be traced to Ishmael and was therefore superior to that of the Turks.[98] They detested the new domination of the northern Mamluk elite, who were a foreign oligarchy of Turco-Circassian origin. In addition, the Mamluk elite discontinued the Hawwara practice of offering economic privileges to the Arab tribes in exchange for safe passage on highways. As a result, the tribes returned to plunder, highway robbery, and raiding villages to both disturb the foreign state and make a living.[99]

For instance, al-Jazzar Pasha, the Ottoman governor of Syria, indicated in his 1785 report to the sultan that when the Mamluk officers suspended the salaries of the 'Ababida tribe in Qina Province, the frustrated members of the tribe exacted revenge by attacking travelers, pillaging villages, and destroying crops. A battle erupted between the two sides in which the strong, proficient warriors of the 'Ababida emerged triumphant. The conflict was settled only when the 'Ababida fully received their payment in addition to blood money for those who were killed in the battles. The two sides then wrote a deed registered in one of Qina's shari'a courts to confirm the settlement and record the terms of the ceasefire. Thousands of similar battles erupted between the Mamluks and Arab tribes. Al-Jazzar did, however, note that friendship between the Arabs and the Mamluks was not impossible.[100]

The 'Ababida tribe embarked on another more radical rebellion when they supported the French troops in Upper Egypt against the soldiers of the sultan. As soon as the French arrived in Egypt, their troops headed to Upper Egypt in order to occupy the rich region and control its agriculture and trade routes. The 'Ababida befriended the French officers and provided them with logistical support during the battles. Vivant Denon, an Egyptologist who accompanied the campaign, reported that during a battle in the Qusayr port on the Red Sea, "we entirely gained their [the 'Ababida] friendship by exercising with them in mock charges and showing so much confidence in them."[101] Similarly, peasant Copts, who suffered tremendously under Mamluk oppression after the collapse of Hammam's nearly ideal state, supported the troops of the French occupation. Like the 'Ababida tribe, Coptic peasants of Qina sided with the Christian invaders during the battles in their province. Denon asserted that commoner Copts sympathized with the French army because of their extreme animosity for the Mamluk troops who had plundered Coptic villages, such as Nagada, during the war. Denon said that "[the Copts'] zeal induced them to come and give us all the intelligence that they had been able to collect."[102]

After the campaign's defeat and the French departure from Egypt, the Ottoman sultan needed to propagate a new imperial discourse of hegemony in order to address the resentment in Upper Egypt. Sultan Selim III restored the one-state system and, once more, installed Mamluk military elite as rulers of Upper Egypt. Nevertheless, he sent a series of decrees (*fermans*) to Qina and the other provinces in Upper Egypt to appease and co-opt different discontented groups. The Ottomans incorporated the south's local shari'a law into the more centralized state apparatus and used the court system to disseminate these decrees. The sultan deployed a religious rhetoric, emphasizing his position as the "caliph" of Muslims who had defeated infidel invaders. One of the *fermans* arrived immediately after the French departure and expounded the sultan's policy of reconciliation with the peasants and Arab tribes of Qina, especially after the massive destruction that the Mamluk armies had inflicted on these two groups while fighting the French for the Ottomans. The same decree also aimed at incorporating all power groups in Upper Egypt into a new imperial order.[103]

This elaborate decree, as received by Isna Court, addressed elite and subaltern groups alike, including shari'a law scholars, judges, Arab tribal leaders, village shaykhs, and peasants. After declaring victory over the French, the sultan affirmed that it was his duty to protect and guard the poor inhabitants of the country—a mission entrusted to him by God as the caliph of Muslims. The decree added that some Mamluk soldiers had arbitrarily accused groups of peasants, Arab tribal leaders, and Bedouins of collusion with the French and consequently had confiscated their grain, animals, and wealth. The affected groups expected the sultan to apply a firm punishment to the transgressive soldiers. Instead, the sultan stated his plan to relocate the offending Mamluks outside of Egypt and bestow upon them lands and houses in other provinces in the empire, as a reward for defeating the French. The sultan implied that Upper Egyptian peoples whom they had hurt would never have to see them again, and a new Mamluk government hopefully would be more just.[104]

Another decree from Istanbul dealt with the Copts as a religious minority. Upper Egyptian Copts who had supported the French were clearly in trouble with both the Mamluks, who now had reasserted their authority, as well as the local Muslim population. The new regime forced these Copts from their homes and confiscated their properties. The Copts raised a petition to the Ottoman sultan, requesting protection and the retention of their properties. In response, Sultan Selim III promulgated a decree in 1801, also disseminated through Qina's and other provincial shariʿa courts, commanding the Muslim inhabitants of Upper Egypt to pardon the Copts who had supported the infidel French. The decree implored religious dignitaries, laypeople, and peasants to treat Copts with dignity and respect, indicating the belief that they had only cooperated with the French out of fear and the desire to protect their families and properties. The sultan asserted that the Copts had followed and obeyed the French only by force. He stipulated that they must return to their homes in peace and resume the tranquil life they had enjoyed before the political turmoil:

> A *ferman* from his majesty Sultan Selim, may God give him victory ... to the authorized court deputies [local judges] ... and the country shaykhs ... [decrees] that during the French infidels' seizure time, the Copts coercively followed the French infidels in order to protect their honor [*aʿaradahum*, i.e., families] and fortunes. Even if what they did was not accepted, they shall return to their home places and live in their houses in comfort and safety as they were in the past. Because they are in all cases the subjects [*raʿiyya*] of our Sublime state and they petition for protection against all matters. From now on, nobody should intrude upon them because of their support of the French. They should buy and sell and take and give [freely] as they used to do in the past.[105]

The Ottoman Empire's attempt at establishing hegemony would fail just a few years later, when the rising empire of Muhammad ʿAli Pasha (r. 1805–48) took control of the entirety of Egypt.

TWO

The French, the Plague Encore, and Jihad

1798–1801

In 1798, when Napoléon Bonaparte's army landed in Egypt, its declared goal was to liberate the country from the despotic rule of the Ottomans. Granting freedom to the country's minority of Orthodox Christians, the Copts, was the second task of the French colonial troops. Upon arriving in Egypt, the soldiers advanced from Cairo into the south, Upper Egypt, where the Coptic population was concentrated. As expected, Christian inhabitants received the French with admiring eyes and tender hearts. The Copts provided the French with extensive logistical support until the French triumph over the tyrannical Mamluks—the Turkic ruling elite appointed by the Ottomans. An Egyptologist who accompanied the troops to the south, Vivant Denon, depicted scenes in Qina Province of passionate Copts aiding the French, crying at the sight of their forces leaving for the battlefields. Of one incident, Denon wrote, "I was struck with the sincere interest which the sheik [chief Copt] expressed for our fate, who, believing that we were marching on to a certain death, gave us the most circumstantial advice, without concealing from us any of the dangers to which we were exposed, advised us with great judgment on every particular which could render the encounter less fatal to us, followed us as far as he could, and parted from us with tears in his eyes."[1]

Nevertheless, after the French won the wars and established a colony in Egypt, the romantic image of supportive natives awaiting their liberators was soon shattered. The Copts, in fact, were manipulating and exploiting the French for their own interests. As soon as the new administration hired them to run the taxation system, Coptic accountants controlled the colony's finances and denied the French access to files. Copts were not the only native group that acted in this manner or that manipulated the French with false impressions of welcoming locals. Many Arab tribes, as oppressed by the

Mamluks as the Copts had been, similarly showed a friendly, hospitable face and supported the French troops during the battles. They later excluded the colonial administrators from local governing councils and denied them access to decision-making institutions in villages.[2]

The French Empire's campaign in Egypt was a conspicuously failed attempt at colonization in the Middle East that lasted for only three years. In 1801, Napoléon's troops were defeated by British troops allied with the Ottomans, and the French were soon forced to depart from Egypt. However, this chapter argues that military misfortune was not the reason behind the rapid failure of the French Empire. Rather, it was a crisis of images. Before and during the campaign, French experts on the Orient forged one image of inferior and oppressed natives waiting for an enlightened nation to liberate them, and another image of the colonial self as exactly this liberator. Moreover, the colonial self was imagined as a competent exploiter of the colony's immense resources, which were allegedly underutilized. As the troops encountered the harsh reality on the ground, these images were demolished, putting the empire in deep crisis.

Upper Egypt, especially Qina Province, was a distinct site where this plight was exposed. The population of the south consisted mainly of two groups that the revolutionary French Republic came to liberate: Copts and Arab tribes. These two groups both deliberately perpetuated the discursive construction of false images in order to take advantage of the French. When the truth was revealed, it was too late for the confused colonizer to escape. As this chapter recounts, the French faced a fierce holy war of Jihad launched by local and regional Arab insurgents and had to reinstall the very ancien régime they had originally come to depose. Shortly afterward, the failed empire brought about environmental destruction to the south: a massive wave of the plague swept Upper Egypt.

Postcolonial theory pays much attention to the issue of image making within contexts of modern imperialism. The colonizer—who was in the position of controlling knowledge production—created reductionist visions of the colonized in order to simplify the process of imperial hegemony. This is the problem of "representation," as theorists of the field refer to it, where voices from the empire authoritatively described silent natives and presented simplifying categorizations and stereotypes that assisted in the domination of the colonized. Postcolonial theory largely presumes that representation was a unilateral process in which the colonizer solely controlled the production of images and imposed them on the represented natives.[3] Nonetheless, this chapter shows how image making was a bilateral process to which the natives equally contributed through deceit and manipulation of the empire. The encounters between the French and the Copts and Arab tribes in Upper Egypt during Napoléon's campaign are but one illustrative case.

Edward Said's *Orientalism* is one of the canonical texts that established the concept of representation in postcolonial theory. Said relies on Michel Foucault's vision concerning the inseparable relationship between knowledge and power to argue that European experts on the Middle East created a body of knowledge—in the form of reductionist stereotypes of Arabs and Muslims—that directly or indirectly served imperial ends. "Such 'images' of the Orient as this are images in that they represent or stand for a very large entity, otherwise impossibly diffuse, which they enable one to grasp or see," Said writes.[4] He asserts that imperialist Europeans controlled the production of these images with almost no interference from the natives. "The scientists, the scholar, the missionary, the trader, or the soldier was in, or thought about, the Orient because he *could be there,* or could think about it, with very little resistance on the Orient's part," Said asserts.[5] Thus, Said grants the natives a minimum role in creating these stereotypical representations.

In the case of Upper Egypt, the natives did play an important role in making the stereotypes: the inhabitants of Upper Egypt perceived Europeans as naïve, and sometimes foolish, foreigners and potential subjects of exploitation. This is precisely what created a crisis of images in the French Empire's colonial propaganda in southern Egypt and generated other military crises that undermined the empire's allegedly liberationist endeavor. As the holy war of Jihad and the epidemic of the plague in Upper Egypt—and particularly in Qina Province—indicate, the French campaign proved to be an environmentally scarred endeavor of a trapped empire.

IMAGE MAKING, DECISION MAKING

During the two decades that preceded Napoléon's campaign, a number of French "experts" visited Egypt to explore the country and produce scientific knowledge to aid in potential colonization. Their published records presented detailed recommendations to the old and new governments, or the ancien régime and the revolutionary French Republic, about how to use the agricultural and commercial sources of northern and southern Egypt. More importantly, their writings served as a foundational tool in an ongoing process of

Colossi of the Plain at Thebes, and Luxor beyond.

FIGURE 3. Luxor Temple and plain.

image making about the oppressed, barbarian native and the enlightened, liberating self. These writings portrayed an intelligent Frenchman who was able to go anywhere on earth, quickly learn the culture and investigate the resources of this place, and cleverly develop those resources. These foundational texts served as trusted authorities and propaganda pieces in the process of decision making, inside the French Republic's government and Parliament, concerning dispatching the military expedition to the Orient.

French travelers visited Egypt and reported about it centuries before Napoléon's arrival, especially after it became an Ottoman province in the sixteenth century. Since early travelers were mostly Christian pilgrims passing through holy places in Egypt and Palestine, they mainly sent back to France romantic accounts about biblical and holy sites. In the eighteenth century, the age of European secular enlightenment that glorified pre-Christian legacies of Western civilization, French travelers paid extensive attention to Greek and Roman relics in Egypt and romanticized Egyptian ancient sites. They were also sure to comment on the flourishing trade of this country, especially in Upper Egypt, which brought exotic luxuries of the Indian Ocean to Cairo and the Mediterranean.[6] Finally, by the end of the eighteenth century, in the age of European imperial ambitions, French accounts mixed this romanticized view of ancient times with strategic geopolitical and economic observations. More than simple pilgrims or travelers, French visitors to Egypt were increasingly scientists, philologists, archaeologists, and the like, some of whom were officially sent by the French government on formal missions to explore the possibility of creating a colony in this resource-rich land.

M. Savary probably presented the first systematic account of France as the needed liberator of the Egyptians from the Ottoman despots and their installed military regime of foreign Mamluks. Savary explored Egypt in 1779, nearly twenty years before Napoléon's Egyptian campaign. His published *Lettres sur l'Égypte* was a blunt proposal for colonialism. In the eyes of contemporary Europeans, Savary was a true scholarly expert. An English literary journal commended his "erudition and capacity" and asserted that he "has shown himself well versed in ancient and modern writings concerning Egypt and its antiquities."[7] With an informed tone, Savary indicated that Egypt was a country of immense resources, but it was unfortunately inflicted with the "ignorance" of the native Egyptians and the "tyranny" of the Mamluk rulers. Turks, Arabs, and Copts were all "barbarians" neglecting great potential sources of wealth and paying no attention to magnificent monuments. Only an enlightened nation that appreciated art and cultural history, such as France, could restore the riches of this land and return it to its ancient glory after centuries of backwardness.

In Qina Province, Savary formed the most important colonial argument, asserting that the occupation of the south would bring about French control over global trade. He observed that Qina's Red Sea port of Qusayr was a meeting point of Indian, Arabian, East African, North African, and Egyptian commerce but lamented how Mamluk despotism and Bedouin raids had reduced the port city's traditionally robust trade. He advocated using Qusayr to turn Egypt into "the center of commerce in the world," uniting Europe and Asia.[8] Savary even suggested digging a canal between Qusayr and the city of Qina—the seat of the province that was a southern Nile port and entrepôt—in order to connect the Red Sea to the river and ultimately the Mediterranean. In the late eighteenth century, caravans had to spend three days carrying Indian and Arabian commodities from the eastern desert to Qina. In ancient times, there had been a canal connecting Qina to Qusayr, but the Turks neglected it and let it dry out. Savary proposed to revive this canal—almost a century before another Frenchman proposed digging the Suez Canal for similar goals:

Were Egypt subjected by an enlightened people, the route to Cosseir [Qusayr] would be safe and commodious. I even suppose it possible to turn an arm of the Nile into this deep valley, over which the sea formerly flow. Such a canal appears not more difficult than that which Amrou cut between Fostat and Colzoum [Cairo and Suez], and would be much more advantageous, since it would abridge the voyage of the Indian shipping a hundred league, and through a perilous ocean, across the farther and narrow part of the Red Sea. The cloths of Bengal, the perfumes of Yemen, and the gold dust of Abyssinia would soon be seen at Cossier; and the corn, linen, and various productions of Egypt, given in return. A nation friendly to the arts [i.e., France] would soon render this fine country once more the center of commerce of the world, the point which should unite Europe to Asia.[9]

Upper Egypt was an important region for Savary's colonial proposal to develop the agriculture of the country, again after liberating it from despotism. He lamented that twelve thousand years of Arab and Turkish rule had degraded Egyptian agriculture. Whereas ancient Egypt had fed millions in the Roman Empire, the annual produce of the country was decreasing due to the ignorance of the present government, which neglected cultivation, just as it did trade. The Egyptian peoples themselves, Savary sympathetically added, were suffering from the rule of foreigners who were not farmers themselves; they endured arbitrary taxes and lacked means of subsistence. The poor peasants had to sell their machines to pay taxes.[10] However, he did not look highly upon those peasants he sought to liberate. The Arabs, he opined, had lost their good faith under the tyrants. Copts were not much different. Despite being the descendants of ancient Egyptians, Copts had lost the sciences of their ancestors but had kept a "vulgar" ancient language.[11]

In 1780, only one year after Savary's visit, King Louis XVI officially dispatched C. S. Sonnini, an engineer in the French Navy and a prominent scientist, on a mission to Egypt. Sonnini's observations were published in the voluminous *Travels in Upper and Lower Egypt Undertaken by Order of the Old Government of France*. During his journey, Sonnini encountered difficult situations, in which he faced Mamluk dictators as well as "superstitious and ungoverned barbarians"—both Arabs and Copts—but he managed to compile his recommendations on creating a future French colony in Egypt.[12] With an unmistakable tone of superiority, Sonnini proposed various possibilities for colonial exploitation of Egypt's underdeveloped commercial and agricultural resources. Sonnini depicted in detail the colossal Pharaonic monuments of Upper Egypt and said that in this region, and under French governance, Egypt could recover its lost glory. More importantly, he forged images of the Arab tribes and Copts of Upper Egypt as potential allies of the French would-be liberators. These two groups, however, viewed things quite differently.

In Qina Province, Sonnini's vision of developing trade at the port of Qusayr was almost identical to Savary's. Sonnini maintained that Qusayr and Qina could be turned into international centers for Indian and Asian commerce, and he also proposed reviving the ancient canal between Qusayr and Qina. He similarly and romantically asserted that the possession of this commercial area would render France in de facto control of Indian Ocean and Arabian Gulf trade, which would certainly be a great victory against Britain, France's rival. Interestingly, he indicated that Qusayr was particularly important for the Parisian coffee drinkers who cared about getting pure mocha—imported from the Yemeni port of Mocha via the Upper Egyptian port city: In Qusayr and Qina one could find the best Yemeni coffee, a product that was typically adulterated several times with American colonial coffee before reaching Paris. Sonnini explains:

> [Qusayr] is the track the caravans pursue, which transport into Arabia the commodities of the Egypt, and which carry thither the coffee of Yemen. The greater number of these caravans deliver to *Kous* [Qus]. Some also go to *Kenné* [Qina], and others to *Banoub*. If you wish to be supplied with excellent coffee, you must go to one of these three places to find it. When once it arrived to Cairo, or had crossed the Nile, it was no longer pure. Merchants were waiting there to mix it with the common coffee of America. At Alexandria it underwent a second mixture by the factors who forwarded it to Marseilles, where they did not fail again to adulterate it: so that the presented Mokka [Mocha] coffee, which is used in France, is often the growth of the American colonies, with about a third, and seldom with a half, of the genuine coffee of Yemen.... When I was in *Kous* an hundred weight of this coffee, unadulterated, and of the first quality, cost ... one hundred and five franks.... How is possible to believe that they should have real Mokka coffee at Paris at the rate of five shillings a pound?[13]

Moreover, Sonnini elaborated on the immense fertility of land in Upper Egypt. The land of all Egypt was rich, but "this uncommon fertility is still more brilliant to the south than to the north." The south might be hot and dry, but its soil was "infinitely more fruitful than the moist soil of the Delta."[14] Then he added similar observations to those of Savary about the backwardness of cultivation in the region, because the natives were "ignorant and lazy" and the Mamluks were careless, and the need for the enlightened

French to reform it. The hot weather in Upper Egypt might deter the French from inhabiting the future "colony," but Sonnini affirmed that it was still a proper environment to live in.[15]

Liberating the Egyptians and achieving these great economic goals would entail the collaboration of internal allies, and Sonnini envisioned the Arab tribes and Copts of Upper Egypt as qualified candidates. Proud of their honorable lineages, the Arab tribal leaders were constantly rebelling against the Caucasian Mamluks, while they were hospitable and generous with Sonnini. The Copts, although not Catholics, were fellow Christians. Nonetheless, two encounters that Sonnini had with an Arab leader and a Coptic merchant reveal that there was a serious misunderstanding on the part of the French expert. Sonnini the physician assumed cultural superiority with the Arab leader, when the latter clearly perceived him as another servant. Sonnini trusted the Coptic merchant, when the latter obviously thought him a naïve, foolish foreigner who would be taken advantage of. Suffering the illusions of supremacy, Sonnini created fatal misrepresentations that the troops of his country would pay for later.

While in Qina Province, Sonnini was hosted by Shaykh Isma'il Abu 'Ali, the Arab governor of a district. Upon his arrival by boat in Luxor, Sonnini heard that the Arab prince was there inspecting his tax farms, so he quickly crossed the river to meet the man of great power. Sonnini described the prince as an ugly, dirty old man, "disgusting," but he had a clear and intelligent mind. Sonnini witnessed him running administrative matters in a governing council with noticeable justice: "A concourse of Arabians and of the inhabitants encircled him; he listened to them with attention whilst he was dictating to his secretaries; he issued his orders and gave his dictions with surprising distinctness and regard to justice."[16] When the shaykh finished this case, he looked with disinterest at the Frenchman—who was patiently waiting at the door of the tent—and asked with a "voice sufficiently dry" who he was. Sonnini came close and gave him a letter from Murad Bey, the Mamluk ruler in Cairo, recommending him for the job of private physician. The ill shaykh hired him, gave him some instructions, and resumed his affairs. Sonnini sat under some trees outside the tent, unaware that he was now considered another one of the shaykh's servants. The next morning, the shaykh woke up and did not find Sonnini by him, so he shouted, Where is the doctor? Where is the doctor? *(Fen hakim? Fen hakim?)*. Sonnini was in Luxor then, so the shaykh sent him a message ordering him to come back and stay at the prince's disposal: "He dispatched a messenger after me to say, that

Mourat Bey having sent me to his assistance, I must not think of quitting him, and that from that period I was *his physician*. This message was concluded with an order to hold myself in readiness the next day, to accompany Ismain in his journey."[17]

Another Arab tribal chief, the shaykh of Luxor, gave Sonnini orders "with much polite condescension," as Sonnini put it. Sonnini knew that his importance among Arab shaykhs was derived from his medical skills rather than his white race or civilized manners, so he sometimes lied in order to maintain his position. He pretended to know the cure of illnesses when he did not. The mayor shaykh of Gurna, for instance, "was afflicted with a disorder which could not be cured except by a difficult operation. I [Sonnini] took care not to tell him that this cure was beyond my skill; I gave him some medicine which could do him neither good nor bad."[18]

While conducting himself in this unprofessional manner, Sonnini stated that "it is impossible to depict the customs of a degraded people, of whom barbarism has taken entire possession, without interference of ideas so dishonorable to humanity, ideas of crimes and robberies, which blend in the picture, and constitute the greatest part of it."[19] At any rate, Sonnini's general impression of the Arab shaykhs throughout his journey in Qina Province implied that those dark leaders were generous, powerful, and just and that Frenchmen could be good allies. He suggested that inciting the Arabs to revolt against the Mamluks could be a fruitful strategy, proposing that "the various tribes . . . perhaps ought to be disposed for revolution rather than attacked as enemies."[20]

Sonnini similarly viewed Copts as barbarians whom the French had no choice but to count on as fellow Christians. The Copts of Upper Egypt, in fact, harbored bitter sentiments against European Christians, because Catholic missionaries were spreading throughout the region and denouncing the native Orthodox faith. European monks were not successful in converting Copts to Catholicism, but they surely disturbed their lives and earned their hatred. Sonnini explained,

> The name of *Frank,* which in the East denotes all Europeans of whatever country, held in esteem among Turks, despised in the cities of Lower Egypt, was considered with horror by the inhabitants of the Said [Upper Egypt]. This hatred is instilled by the Cophts, who are more numerous here than in those districts farther to the north. They felt sore at the arrival of some missionaries, who came from Italy purposely to preach against them, to expose them openly as heretics and dogs, and do damn them without pity . . . . These pious

FIGURE 4. An Upper Egyptian Coptic priest.

injuries had perhaps merit in the view of theology; but they were extremely prejudicial to commerce and the increase of knowledge.[21]

In the city of Qus, just north of Luxor, Sonnini met a wealthy Copt by the name of Muʿallim Boqtor, a highly respected merchant. Although a Catholic convert himself, Boqtor did not hesitate to take advantage of Sonnini, who wanted to embark on a journey to the port of Qusayr. It was a harsh trip of three days in the eastern desert and required special arrangements, so Boqtor offered to take Sonnini there safely. Boqtor kept taking money and gifts from Sonnini under the guise of preparing for the trip. Time passed and the journey did not take place. In fact, the Copt colluded with a Turkish merchant to rob as much money and other luxuries as possible from the conceited Frenchman, and the pair eventually informed him that the trip was delayed for security considerations—for fear of Bedouin attacks. Then they asked him to leave his luggage with the Turk if he still wanted to go. Foreseeing their intention of robbing his belongings, Sonnini refused, cancelled the trip, and demanded his payments back. They first refused to refund him, but they did when he threatened to complain to his master, Shaykh Isma'il.

Sonnini concluded that the Coptic merchant was just another of Egypt's many thieves and added that the Mamluks were better than the dark native Egyptians: "Mu'allim Boqtor, who had so often promised to see me conducted to *Cosseir* . . . was like all his fellow citizens, nothing else but a traitor. . . . I here feel it incumbent on me to say, that for the most part I have had better reason to applaud the conduct of the Mamelucs than the natives of Egypt. . . . [Mamluks] possessed a certain pride and blunt harshness . . . whilst the Cophts, dark and designing, insinuating and deceitful, distinguished himself by the cringing and submissive deportment of the most abject slave."[22] Nevertheless, Sonnini still insisted that the Copts needed Europeans as enlightened liberators. He condemned the way Copts were treated in Egypt, "a country where the name of Christian merely is a crime." Copts enjoyed prestigious government positions and wealth, but the Mamluks arbitrarily confiscated their properties. Copts needed to understand the difference between missionaries and other Europeans who went to Egypt to assist rather than insult them, said Sonnini.[23]

During the mid-1790s, the images that Sonnini and similar experts constructed fed into the ideological underpinnings on which Paris based its decision to colonize Egypt. Political cleavages in the French Republic broke out in debates about the importance of France's imperial expansion overseas, especially after losing many colonies in the Americas. Historian Juan Cole indicates that there were two competing ideological trends with regard to colonialism: liberalism and conservatism. Discussions between them were heated in the legislature and the Directory—a council of five men elected from the legislature. The original revolutionaries, the Jacobins, were against colonialism and called both for ending it and slavery. Another group of politicians argued that it was imperative for France to obtain external colonies in order to "prosper." Colonizing Egypt for its trade and sugarcane cultivation and, above all, to weaken the British Empire in India, were all key rationales that many French imperialists contemplated. The conservative camp eventually triumphed, and the concept of "satellite republics" was born. Colonies were to be turned into republics modeled after France, liberated from old oppressive regimes and enjoying democracy and freedom of the press, but controlled by Paris. The French would seek to create such satellite republics worldwide, starting with weaker areas in Europe, such as Italy.[24] In 1798, echoing Savary and Sonnini, one legislator by the name of Joseph Eschasseriaux argued that Egypt was "half-civilized" and easy to conquer. Cole quotes Eschasseriaux as saying, "What finer enterprise for a nation which has already given liberty to Europe [and] freed America than to regenerate in every sense a country which was the first home to civilization . . . and to carry back to their ancient cradle industry, science, and the arts, to cast into the centuries the foundations of a new Thebes or of another Memphis."[25]

The revolutionary ideologues of the late 1790s condemned European conquests as a crime against humanity but still assumed they were embarking on a civilizing mission *(mission civilisatrice)* in backward societies, where they sought to introduce "progress." Through creating dependent democracies, they aimed to deliver freedom to oppressed nations and rescue them from backwardness. The same vision, ironically, maintained that all human beings were equals—brothers—and that one nation should not subjugate or exploit another. Human civilization, according to French revolutionaries, followed one universal path toward progress, and Europe was at the top of this line. The Occident should be a model for other nations to imitate, with French conquerors introducing the sciences and laws of human rights to the world's backwaters.[26] Thus, from the outset, the French imperial ideology was based on assimilating natives into the colonizer's culture—as opposed to the British ideology of administration from above. In order to spread the values of the Republic, the French preferred direct rather than indirect rule, and they intended for the colonized to adopt their customs and habits.[27]

As for Napoléon Bonaparte himself, his decision to invade Egypt was based on a belief in the essential role of the military in achieving Republican goals. He called for the spread of French liberties in the world, despite his criticism of democracy and the masses' participation in government. As Cole asserts, "[Napoléon] was already a critic of liberal democracy . . . . He complained of the impossibility of a republic made up of thirty million persons, all with different values."[28] In Napoléon's speech to soldiers before they set sail from Malta—which he had captured first—to Alexandria, he condemned the Mamluk tyrants who oppress the Egyptians and favored British merchants over the French. He swore to eradicate them within a few days of arriving in Egypt. On the other hand, the soldiers in his army were well indoctrinated with imperial propaganda. According to Cole, "The enthusiasm of the French troops and officers who joined Napoleon's army was very much shaped by the revolution and by the ideology of the early republic.... Republican rhetoric deployed 'liberty' as its refrain.... Bonaparte in his communiqué clearly conveyed the idea that the Republican army incarnated the virtue of liberty, and was now exporting it to an exotic locale."[29]

Inspired by the texts of previous travelers and their leaders' speeches, these troops carried romantic visions of Egypt derived from ancient Pharaonic, Greek, Roman, and Ptolemaic times, and their fantasies were charged with scenes from such narratives. As their ships sailed to Alexandria, the French soldiers were thinking of Napoléon as another Alexander the Great, and they imagined Cleopatra's Egypt waiting for them to restore her glory.[30]

CRISIS OF IMAGES AND JIHAD

The French fleet, *l'armée d'Orient*, landed in Alexandria in July 1798. Bloody confrontations with the inhabitants of the port city immediately erupted, and afterward the army proceeded to Cairo, where it defeated the Mamluks in several decisive battles. The French finally advanced to conquer Upper Egypt a few months later, in 1799. Experts who accompanied the troops continued to reproduce the same images of barbarian natives, but the locals now were taking an active role in shaping those images. The Arab tribes and Copts in Upper Egypt indeed did welcome their self-appointed saviors and formed faithful alliances with them, but only to take advantage of the invaders, who appeared to be exploitable. Moreover, whereas the experts still articulated a vision of the administratively competent self and the backward other, military leaders were hit hard by reality, as well as by Jihadists, and produced a completely different discourse.

Upon arriving in Cairo, Napoléon disseminated a long proclamation in broken Arabic. He asserted that the emancipating campaign was undertaken in the name of God: French soldiers were Muslims who believed in and obeyed the one God of Egyptian Muslims. Napoléon threatened that if the French were not met with full obedience and submission, the natives would face devastating punishments. The voices of Savary and Sonnini were heavily present in this document, especially in Napoléon's recounting of the ancient glory of Egypt that had declined due to the Mamluk foreign military elite and in his mention of vanished commerce and ruined canals:

> In the name of God, the Merciful, the Compassionate. There is no God but God.... On behalf of the French Republic which is based upon the foundation of liberty and equality, General Bonaparte, Commander-in-Chief of the French armies makes known to all Egyptian people that... this group of Mamluks, imported from the mountains of Circassia and Georgia, have acted corruptly for ages in the fairest land that is to be found upon the face of the globe.... I have not come to you except for the purpose of restoring your rights from the hands of the oppressors and that I more than the Mamluks, serve God—may He be praised and exalted—and revere His Prophet Muhammad and the glorious Qur'an.... Formerly, in the lands of Egypt there were great cities, and wide canals, and extensive commerce and nothing ruined all this but the avarice and the tyranny of the Mamluks.... The French are also faithful Muslims.... Blessing on blessing to the Egyptians who will act in concert with us, without any delay.... But woe upon woe to those who will unite with the Mamluks.... Every village that shall rise against the French army, shall be burnt down.[31]

Ironically, from the beginning Napoléon did not insist on liberating Upper Egypt: he was content to rule it through the old Mamluk despots. As the army of freedom was losing numerous souls to the insurgency in the north, Napoléon secretly negotiated with Murad Bey—the chief Mamluk leader who fled from Cairo to the south—in order to allow him to govern Upper Egypt in return for payment of annual taxes. A month after landing in Egypt, Napoléon sent a neutral envoy, the Austrian consul, to Murad in order to propose a peace treaty stipulating that France would not pursue the occupation of the south and that Murad would rule it in the name of the Republic. The Austrian consul, a legal deputy of Napoléon, was entitled to sign the agreement immediately if Murad agreed to its conditions—regardless of what the natives of Upper Egypt thought. Receiving the news of some defeats of the French fleet in the north, Murad refused the proposal and offered Napoléon, with an insulting tone, money to go back to France and save the blood of his soldiers. After the negotiations failed, Napoléon had no choice but to send General Désaix and his troops to colonize the south.[32]

The situation in Upper Egypt was much more complicated than what the French expected. The final, key battles to conquer the south took place in the towns and villages of Qina Province. Murad Bey and Arab peasants launched what they called a holy war of Jihad against the French in Qina. Napoléon's allegations that he and his soldiers were Muslims did not work. The insurgents where fighting the French "infidels" in the name of God, in response to the Ottoman sultan's consecutive decrees that he sent from Istanbul to Qina Province's courts, such as the town of Isna's court, addressing Arab notables and commoners.

Deploying religious rhetoric in these decrees that cited Qur'anic verses and the Prophet Muhammad's tradition, the sultan asked his Muslim subjects in every province in Upper Egypt to defend the religion of Islam. The ultimate goal of the French atheists and disbelievers in God *(kuffar)*, said the sultan, was to destroy the Muslims' places of worship in Mecca and Medina and kill off the Muslim population of these two holy cities. He particularly addressed the Arab tribes, saying that they were not regular believers but by lineage were the cousins of the Prophet Muhammad and had greater responsibilities to defend the Islamic faith. He warned the Arab tribes against French wicked promises and means of manipulation and added that whoever followed them would be committing apostasy and should be killed and robbed by other faithful Muslims.[33] Interestingly enough, the sultan asked Muslims to take care of Copts and treat them as they treated the ruling elite of commanders and the nobility: "They [Copts] pay the legal poll-tax [*jiziya shar'iyya*] and they have what we have and are obliged to what we are obliged to," the sultan asserted.[34]

The calls of Istanbul for Jihad reached Arabia, and the army of the prince of Mecca, Sharif Hasan, soon crossed the Red Sea to the port of Qusayr and from there to Qina Province, in order to fight for Islam. Religious propaganda aside, Sharif Hasan joined the effort because his commercial interests and grain provisions that shipped from Upper Egypt through Qusayr to the holy places in Hijaz (Mecca and Medina) would be severed by the French occupation. The prince was also responding to Murad Bey, who successfully mobilized many Red Sea locations on the Arabian Peninsula for Jihad. The Arabian holy warriors—or *mujahidin* and *ghuza,* as the sultan called them— included the ruling Arab family of Ashraf that claimed lineage back to the Prophet Muhammad, as well as the supreme jurist consult *(mufti)* of Medina, a notable Moroccan family that settled in the port of Jeddah, and many merchants whose trade was harmed by the occupation. They organized a large fleet well equipped with guns, swords, and food provisions for the *mujahidin* who were poor and could not provision themselves. According to French estimates, the number of Arabian volunteers reached six thousand or seven thousand.[35]

Along with other thousands of native Arab peasants, the Arabian volunteers united with the army of Murad Bey against General Désaix. Arab and

Mamluk Jihadists fought in Qina Province's villages and town's, including Samhud, Isna, Abnud, Abu Manna', and Qift. When Désaix seized the seat of the province, Sharif Hasan led Hijazi knights and eight hundred Arab peasants to restore the city. The peasants attacked French Battalion No. 61 and forced the soldiers to withdraw. It was an enormous defeat, with extensive losses on the French side. The victorious Jihadists plundered ammunitions and weapons from the French ships and used them in later battles. In the battle of Abnud, the French committed an unprecedented massacre, burning houses in the town and slaughtering Hijazis and natives. The streets of Abnud were filled with the corpses of local inhabitants and Meccan volunteers.[36]

Amid these bloody scenes, the French experts who accompanied the troops in Upper Egypt still perpetuated the false image of the proficient colonial self that Savary and Sonnini had articulated. The French acted as intelligent surveyors, certain that quick visits to houses and gazes at the inhabitants would suffice for them to understand native peoples, classify them, figure out their problems, and decide how to reform them into free citizens. Brief observations of the Upper Egyptians were, in vain, thought to be enough to grasp the culture and economy and enable the colonizer to take over. Thus, scientists went into villages, recorded descriptions of women and children, food, diseases, superstition, medicine, and more.[37] In this context, France was depicted with a glory equal to that of the Roman Empire, with its enlightened soldiers respecting and valuing the ancient monuments more than the native savages.[38]

Likewise, French experts perpetuated old, false images about the natives. But it was not entirely their fault: deceptive natives misled them to such conclusions. Vivant Denon, an Egyptologist who joined the troops to draw sketches of and write about the Pharaonic monuments, was an eyewitness of the battles that took place in Qina Province and recorded them in meticulous detail. Heartily believing that his compatriots were emancipators, he thought that Copts and some Arab tribes sincerely welcomed and adored the French, as they provided the troops with significant logistical assistance during the holy war.[39] Denon was under the illusion that a romantic, tender relationship emerged between Copts and the French. In one incident, Copts pretended that they liked the civilized French, giving the title of "the Just" to General Désaix because he treated them equitably. The head of the Copts provided the French with all the information they needed, and he tenderly cried as they were departing for the battlefields, as recounted by Denon:

Their zeal induced them to come and give us all the intelligence which they had been able to collect ... the sheik [chief of Copts] ... followed us as far as he could, and parted from us with tears in his eyes. Defaix had before been a week at Kous [Qus], and he had seen much of the sheik; and the tender interest which the latter showed for us, was the natural result of the favorable opinion which he must have formed of the frank and communicative disposition of our leader, and of that mild and unvarying equity which afterwards obtained for him the title of the *Just;* the most honorable appellation which could be obtained by a conqueror and a stranger, arrived in an enemy's country on purpose to make war.[40]

In another incident, the French attacked a Mamluk fortress in a village, resulting in a bloody battle in which dozens of the Republic's soldiers were killed. Coptic bishops sided with the French against the Mamluks in this battle, and the Mamluks later punished those Christians with imprisonment.[41] Denon showed how rich Copts, accustomed to Mamluk raids and plunder, were surprised to see that the French paid for everything they took from them. Denon was proud of his fellow citizens, who behaved with the Copts in an extraordinary way that superseded African and Asian habits: "Armed men, with power in their hands, who paid!"[42]

Similarly, Denon thought that some Arab tribes were fully loyal to the French. After one battle in which the Mamluks were fiercely defeated, the 'Ababida tribe realized that they were insufficiently equipped to resist, so they went to Qina in order to make peace with the French. The 'Ababida provided the French with extra logistical support—camels and guidance in the desert—for a battle in Qusayr. "We entirely gained their friendship," said Denon, "by exercising with them in mock charges, and showing so much confidence in them, as to accompany them all day at a distance from Cosseir, and riding with them at the rate of a league in less than a quarter an hour.... We were ... preceded by our Arab friends, to whom the desert seemed by right to belong."[43] Before the French entered Qusayr, The 'Ababida preceded them to inform the other Arab inhabitants about their arrival, and the tribal shaykhs in the port returned with the 'Ababida envoys to the French with abundant gifts and offered accommodation. The hospitable 'Ababida welcomed the French into their tents. After the final victory over Qusayr, the French went back to Qina Province, where they supposedly were received with much hospitality by more Arab tribes.

Denon noticed that whereas elite Arab inhabitants largely sided with the French, the lower classes joined the Jihadist army of the Mamluks.

Upper-class Arabs were used to being dispossessed by the Mamluks, he opined, so they greeted the French as victors. In Qina Province, wealthy Arab shaykhs—especially merchants who sought protection for their caravans during the war—showed obedience and paid tribute to the new rulers. Denon was naïvely happy with this, so he pointed out the good will *(d'étquité charma)* of those Arabs and wrote, "[This] gave me hopes that, for the future, we might promote at the same time the happiness of the natives and the interests of the colonists."[44] On the other hand, poor peasants where easily deployed in Murad Bey's holy army. The French Republic supposedly had come to extend rights and equality to these lower classes, but they did not respond gratefully because, Denon guessed, they were accustomed to obedience and the Mamluks seduced them with religious propaganda.[45]

Facing harsh reality, French officers perceived the inhabitants of Upper Egypt in a different light than that of the dreamy scientific and cultural experts. Gradually realizing that some Arabs and Copts were deceiving them and pretending to be loyal, French generals expected treason at any moment and mercilessly punished native allies whom they were suspicious of, as revealed by correspondence between the generals in Upper Egypt and the central command in Cairo. The letters of General Menou, the second commander in chief to succeed Napoléon, ordered the army in the south to keep peace with the Arab tribes but treat them cruelly if they denounced their peace truces.[46] Friendly Arab tribes assured Boyer, a battalion commander, that they were eager to meet the army of Murad Bey quickly in order to prove their loyalty. Members of these tribes worked as informants, following the movement of the camps of Jihadists and carrying the French officers' mail to Cairo. Two hundred Arabs accompanied Boyer in an expeditionary mission in the desert to look for the Mamluk camps. Boyer, nonetheless, was anxious about his allies' concealed intentions. When he grew suspicious that a certain shaykh was a double agent, he immediately placed him under detention. In addition, Boyer followed a policy of divide and rule with the Arab tribes, using tribes' past animosity and disputes to play the groups against each other. When he expected betrayal from one tribe, he incited an enemy tribe against it.[47]

The French generals believed that the fate of the occupation of Upper Egypt depended only on the demonstration of military might to the Arabs. Therefore, in Qina Province, the troops destroyed the villages that refused to give them provisions and harshly punished their Arab shaykhs. In one incident, after waiting for four hours for bread to arrive from some villages and realizing that the towns' "dogs" (i.e., inhabitants) had refused to send provisions, the French soldiers beat the villages' Arab shaykhs with a hundred sticks. Furthermore, the French requested submission of the cash tax within three hours and the grain tax within six days. When one village tried to escape the grain tax by claiming there was low Nile inundation and water shortage that year, Commander Boyer imprisoned the shaykhs of this village until they paid. Villages delivered camels, horses, and sheep and surrendered their weapons to the French troops. Boyer also once seized a large herd of sheep from an Arab shaykh who did not submit his dues to the French. The shaykh's sheep were only returned when he paid what he owed.[48]

As the months passed, Denon's misinformed presumptions of friendship between Copts the French in Upper Egypt proved untrue. Educated Copts had held the positions of finance ministers and treasury accountants in Egypt for centuries since the Islamic conquest, and they had developed the complicated *qirma* script for Arabic letters and figures in bookkeeping. Copts maintained these positions under the Ottoman/Mamluk regime until the arrival of the French. The French had no choice but to use Coptic services to decipher the coded, complex land survey and tax system in both the north and south of Egypt and so hired Copts in the same jobs that they held previously, as *mubashir*s. Copts resumed their work, only to immediately take advantage of the ignorant colonial regime. Napoléon instated Jirjis al-Juhari as the minister of finance—a position that elite Cairene Copts had held under the Mamluks—and al-Juhari was commissioned to hire local Coptic accountants in villages and towns throughout Egypt. Napoléon apparently did not trust the native employees, probably affected by the narratives of Sonnini about the Coptic merchant who deceived him. Thus, he hired French agents to monitor each accountant, in order to audit their registers and learn the language of the system.[49]

In Upper Egypt, Copts were not particularly pleased by the French overseeing the work they had done for centuries. The French hired local Coptic accountants in the south starting in February 1799, after they fully completed the conquest of the region. When local peasants refused to pay taxes, the French had to bring back the old Coptic tax collectors to help. Muʿallim Yaʿqub, a prominent Upper Egyptian Copt who formed an army to fight with the French, was the general accountant of the south, or *l'intendant général de la Haute-Égypte*. From the beginning, local accountants forced the French to deal with them as a collective group, through the Coptic minister of finance in Cairo who acted as their head. This way they managed to maintain their autonomous unity against the French, despite the monitoring system that Napoléon put in place. Copts were extremely careful not to give away the secrets of their profession or to furnish complete information about the sources of revenue. It was difficult and implausible for the French to learn how to calculate the time of the Nile inundation and the withdrawal of the flood, how to survey the size of land cultivated after the flood in each village, and how to estimate the revenue of each piece of land. As Nasir Ibrahim, an Egyptian historian, puts it, it was a knowledge/power battle between the French and the Copts, in which the latter controlled information as well as revenue.[50]

Daily conflicts broke out between the Copts and the French auditors, as the former were deliberately imprecise in the information they submitted to the latter. The Copts kept in mind the potential defeat of the French and return of the old Mamluks, with religious retaliation, so the Copts did not grant full loyalty to the French. The Coptic minister of finance, Muʿallim al-Juhari, centralized the land survey and tax collection system and archived all registers in his Cairo office, and he did not allow the French access to local records. His office was the only place that issued tax reports, and, hence, he was in full control of the financial information passed to the French. In Upper Egypt, when the French demanded records from the Coptic accountants in villages, they only delivered vague and ambiguous data. This raised anger and suspicion among the French officials during times of hardship, when the troops were in dire need of Egypt's income. More importantly, in the villages of Upper Egypt, Coptic tax collectors embezzled the revenue of villages that they purposely did not list in the French official registers. Tired of the Copts, General Kléber, the first commander in chief after Napoléon, gradually reduced reliance on them and formed a committee to review their files. In a state of hopeless anger, his successor, General Menou, eventually decided to marginalize them.[51]

Supposedly friendly Arab tribes excluded the French from administration of Upper Egypt on another front as well. Leaders of Arab tribes traditionally governed daily affairs of villages and towns through democratic councils (*majalis ʿarab*). Shaykhs and peasants regularly gathered in these councils to manage cultivation and irrigation matters and to resolve local disputes between individuals or villages. The tribes resumed this governing method after the end of battles with the French in order to discuss the demands of the new colonial regime, but they did not invite the French, who did not even speak the local language, to attend and participate in decision making.

Obviously very impressed with it, Denon drew a huge sketch of one of these councils in Qina Province and wrote the following about the meeting: "It is not in my power to give the particular deliberations of this council, but I was informed that no innovations were introduced without previously consulting with the will of the inhabitants, to whom every possible encouragement was promised.... The consultation was not about arbitrary impositions, but the best means of promoting the public welfare."[52] Denon asserted that the council functioned the same way as it had during the golden age of Shaykh al-'Arab Hammam, the former autonomous Arab ruler of Upper Egypt. Denon proudly credited the French for restoring this system of democracy that allegedly had vanished after Hammam, despite Sonnini's elaborate description of similar councils' presence in Qina only a decade earlier.

Immediately after the holy month of Ramadan in 1800, an exceptionally large Arab council issued a decree to resolve a major dispute among several villages, revealing a high degree of social and religious equality. The session was evidently unattended or overseen by French official representatives. The shaykhs of disputing villages came to Isna Court in order to register this decree and make it legally binding for all involved parties, and the shaykhs recorded equal treatment of Copts and individuals from every social background—even less honorable tribes such as the Jamasa, who were notorious for their lack of morals and ethics. As the court record states, "All the shaykhs of ... [named villages] agreed and consented to that whoever transgresses by hitting, robbing, or committing any action that generates chaos in the market or elsewhere must pay the governor of the locality four bags of 24,000 silver coins. That is the oath they all took. This condition applies whether the attacked was Muslim *ra'iyya,* Christian, Jamasi, guest, or native resident."[53]

TURN TO DESPOTISM AND "IMPERIAL PLAGUE"

With the French colonial image of the self as liberator being dramatically smashed by both the natives' Jihad and deceit, the panicking French Republic soon reinstalled a despotic government. The French hired Murad Bey himself to serve as the autonomous governor of Upper Egypt. The letterheads of official correspondence between the French generals supposedly governing the south and their supreme chief in Cairo always carried the emblem of "Liberté, Égalité—République Français" (Liberty, Equality—the French Republic). Nonetheless, the Republic brought back to rule over the south the same

Mamluk tyrant that Sonnini had condemned and that French troops had fiercely fought and defeated. The French self-perception of being quick and efficient developers of the crops and commerce of Upper Egypt similarly faded away, replaced instead by a desire for a rushed seizure of resources by means of oppression. Finally, the environmental destruction that the new despotic government generated brought about an unprecedented wave of the plague in Upper Egypt.

After the conquest of Upper Egypt, the colonial regime regularly retaliated against the manipulative natives. General Menou ordered his officer in the south, Donzelot, to lie and pretend that his decisions, even if they did the opposite, were in the best interest of the natives. In one incident, the French troops collected horses and camels from Upper Egyptians but later realized that they no longer needed them. Instead of returning the animals to their original owners, Menou, with a spirit of revenge, ordered Donzelot to burn them and tell the people that this was an action of grace for their benefit. "Some practices of charlatanism are always needed with those people" (Il faut toujours un peu de charlatanerie dans ce monde), Menou affirmed.[54]

The French placed great emphasis on coercive control of grain, which the troops needed desperately. Storing 100,000 *ardabb*s of wheat and 150,000 *ardabb*s of beans, barley, and lentils was necessary to sustain the army for the year of 1800, so General Kléber ordered that these provisions be collected from the Upper Egyptian provinces and sent for storage in Cairo. Kléber ordered the boat captains of Upper Egypt to ship only the grain of the French Republic and prohibited them from transporting the loads of any native peasants or merchants. The boat captains disobeyed and secretly carried the people's grain. They filled only part of their boats with the French grain and saved the rest of the space for the people's crops. When the French found out, the Food Committee issued a decree to confiscate any grain that did not belong to the Republic on these boats in Cairo ports and to force the boat captain to pay a fine in addition to the regular customs and tariffs for confiscated commodities. Military officers inspected the grain boats and protected them from people's attacks.[55]

Kléber later hired private French companies instead of native boats to carry this grain. The company of Livron et Hamelin was responsible for collecting the Republic's grain and transporting it to Cairo. The remaining grain was not to be left for the people but was sold and its revenue sent to the colonial treasury. French agents in the provinces of Upper Egypt were ordered to prepare daily registers of the current prices for each kind of grain in the markets of towns and big villages and to send the information to the general financial manager. The same private company was ordered to sell this grain in Upper Egypt on behalf of the Republic. The sale took place in return for cash, and the two capitalist businessmen, Livron and Hamelin, received a handsome commission of up to 5 percent for their commercial services.[56]

The second resource that the occupation hastily attempted to seize in Upper Egypt was the commerce of Qusayr and Qina Province. Instead of developing it proficiently, the French ruined this trade in the brief period of their stay. Upon the arrival of French troops in Qina Province, Denon described the robust trade from India, Arabia, East Africa, North Africa, and Turkey, contradicting the negative assessments made by Savary and Sonnini. Denon asserted that Qusayr was the best-known port on the Red Sea and the point of connection between Asia and Africa. Highly amazed by what he saw, Denon depicted the lively trade scene in Qina:

> We ... arrived at Keneh [Qina], where we found a number of merchants of all nations. By encountering the natives of very foreign countries, remote distances seems closer. When begin to reckon the days required for the journey, and the necessary means of affecting it, the space to be passed over ceases to be immense. The Red Sea, Gidda, Mecca, seemed like neighboring places to the town where we were; and India itself was but a short way beyond them. In the opposite direction the oases were actually no more than three days journey off us, and ceased to appear to our imagination as an undiscovered country.... The journey to Darfur may be accomplished in forty days, a hundred more are required to reach Tombuctoo. A merchant whom I found in Keneh ... had often been in Darfur, where the caravans arrive from Tombuctoo.... Here we also found many Turkish, Meccan and Moorish merchants, come to exchange coffee and Indian cottons for corn.[57]

However, Denon still maintained the fundamental view of his predecessors, saying that the Mamluk tyranny had ruined this trade.[58]

The colonial actions that followed brought Qina's commerce into a state of chaos. General Menou and his officers in Upper Egypt paid much attention to the Yemeni coffee and Sudanese commerce, including black slaves, and attempted to control the flow of goods through direct correspondence with the rulers of these places. Menou sent envoys to the sultan of Darfur in order to resume trade with his territory, and he received in return a gift of three black concubines. After reconciliation with the sharif of Mecca, Menou assured him that the French would send the holy places in Hijaz their regular shipments of grain and asked the sharif to send the regular shipments of coffee in return.[59] Nonetheless, more than a year after concluding the invasion of Upper Egypt, the French failed to control the region's trade, let alone develop it. Commerce in the Qusayr port was interrupted, and the volume of shipping on the Nile decreased daily. In December 1800, the commander of the French Navy informed Menou that "slowing and hindering trade in Qusayr hurt agriculture and navigation in Upper Egypt."[60] Furthermore, Denon lamented that the French troops were randomly killing innocent merchants, who were mistaken for Meccan Jihadists, and raiding their caravans:

> The soldiers who were sent out on scouting parties, frequently mistook for Meccans the poor merchants belonging to a caravan, with whom they fell in; and before justice could be done them, which in some cases the time and circumstances would not allow, two or three of them had been shot, a part of their merchandize either plundered or pilfered, and their camels exchanged for ours which resulted from these outrages, fell invariably to the share of bloodsuckers of the army, the civil commissaries, Copts, and interpreters; the soldiers, who sought every opportunity to enrich themselves.[61]

Eventually, the failing French restored the tyrannical regime in Upper Egypt in order to contain this chaotic situation. As mentioned earlier, Napoléon had not been able to conclude a peace agreement with the Mamluk leader Murad Bey, but General Kléber succeeded. An agreement was signed in April 1800, and according to its conditions Murad Bey was granted an independent authority over Upper Egypt in return for taxes and military support of the French in Cairo. The French threw their ideological claims about liberating Upper Egypt into the Nile. According to 'Abd al-Rahman al-Jabarti, a prominent contemporary Egyptian chronicler, Murad Bey—a blond with a great beard and a scar from a battle on his face—was oppressive, reckless, arrogant, and conceited. Murad married the widow of his former Mamluk master and shared power in Egypt with Ibrahim Bey, with whom he occasionally disputed over the sources of revenue. Murad led a luxurious life in his many vast palaces located outside Cairo, and he coercively collected taxes to sustain his lavish lifestyle and hefty military. He built a great arsenal and a navy, for which he hired a Greek Christian commander.[62]

The agreement between Murad and Kléber initiated an alliance between the French and the Mamluks against the Ottomans. Thus, Murad split from his former master, the Ottomans, and happily ended the Jihad. Murad's influential wife, Nafisa, mediated between the two parties to reach a satisfying treaty for both. Under its conditions, Murad became a vassal of France, or a tributary to the French Republic, and the Upper Egyptian provinces from Jirja to Aswan—including Qina—were allotted to him. He was granted the title of Prince Governor for the French Republic, and he was not allowed to keep but a few hundred knights from his former army. The treaty compelled him to submit an annual tribute of 20,000 *bara*s (a monetary unit) and 15,000 *ardabb*s of wheat and 20,000 *ardabb*s of other grains. This tribute was divided into four installments to be paid every three months. Murad was allowed to control the revenue of the port of Qusayr, which suggests that the French had given up on their dreams of controlling international trade through this Red Sea harbor. Murad enjoyed full authority over the administrative system in his territory without the intervention of the Republican regime in Cairo. The treaty also compelled the French to protect him against any external attacks—alluding to Meccan Jihadists, Ottomans, and the British. When Kléber was assassinated two months later, in June 1800, his successor, General Menou, maintained the agreement and ordered General Donzelot in Upper Egypt to treat Murad in a friendly and sincere manner.[63]

Murad Bey died exactly one year after his installment. In April 1801, he was killed by the massive plague epidemic that struck Upper Egypt under the French occupation. Murad was infected and died in the city of Suhaj, where he was buried. The official gazette of the Republic in Egypt, *Le Courier d'Égypte,* published the news of the death of a "great man," and Menou granted his widow, Nafisa, an annual salary of sixty thousand pounds.[64]

In fact, it was the French who killed Murad—albeit indirectly. The French troops carried the plague to Upper Egypt. It was a wave of "imperial plague." Contemporary European physicians affirmed that the south of Egypt had been immune to outbreaks of the plague for hundreds of years under Mamluk and Ottoman rule. European observers largely reported that the healthier and hotter air of Upper Egypt made it difficult for the plague to infiltrate the south, whereas Cairo and the Mediterranean coast of Egypt were more susceptible.[65] A French physician asserted that the plague was a natural phenomena "almost unknown" in Upper Egypt.[66] "It was well known that there was a line of demarcation which cut off Upper Egypt, beyond which the plague never passed," an early 1800s British report indicated.[67] The plague had not visited Upper Egypt for five centuries, ever since the great epidemic of the 1300s had spread throughout Egypt and most of the Mediterranean world. But in the last few years of the 1790s, imperial interventions by the Ottomans led to the spread of this disease from Cairo and the Delta to Upper Egypt, and then the French Empire introduced a second wave of this imperial plague.[68]

The great numbers of French soldiers transmitted the disease. They, along with the fighting Mamluks coming from the north, contaminated the environment of Upper Egypt. The plague broke out first in Cairo and the north in February 1801 after the Nile inundation, and later it had a devastating impact in Upper Egypt.[69] Al-Jabarti, a well-informed eyewitness, chronicled the epidemic's repercussions using a letter that he received from his friend Shaykh Hasan al-'Attar, who was at the time residing in Upper Egypt. Dated May 1801, al-'Attar's letter asserted that it was an enormously sweeping wave of disease, "never heard of." It started in mid-March and ended in mid-May. "Plague raged in all Upper Egypt," he wrote, "but especially [in] the city of Asyut, where more than 600 persons died every day. Such a scourge has never been seen in the memory of man. I think the country lost two-thirds of its population. The streets are deserted; friends or relatives only learn of the death of those near to them long after the event for everyone is absorbed in his own family's misfortunes. Corpses remain in the houses for days on end, for only after a great deal of trouble can one find biers, washers, and porters."[70]

In addition, Sir Robert Wilson, a contemporary British general who came to Egypt with his country's troops, reported that one of the unusual characteristics of the disease was that "persons who remained stationary were liable to it, and that those who passed rapidly through various currents of air escaped."[71] The French troops passed through northern Egyptian lands and communicated in the most intimate manner with the natives in Alexandria, Cairo, and the villages of Lower Egypt, where numerous natives were afflicted with the epidemic and died. The soldiers then landed and settled in Upper Egypt with their contaminated bodies and luggage. Around 60,000 inhabitants perished during this wave of plague, out of the estimated 750,000 population of Upper Egypt. Whole villages were wiped off the face of earth. The French administration attempted to treat the plague by applying lime, draining off all stagnant waters, whitewashing the walls of houses, paving city streets, using coal fire to burn objects, and using burnt brick instead of mud in building. Nothing worked to stop the devastating epidemic.[72]

In the wake of this massive environmental destruction, and by the time the French troops departed from Upper Egypt, any images that the French had of themselves as liberators or competent managers of other countries' resources had vanished. In a similar vein, any images of the natives as inferior barbarians awaiting liberation and progress had become, painfully, much more complex. The French Empire's occupation of Upper Egypt, as proven in Qina Province, was a relationship of mutual manipulation between the colonizer and the colonized, in which the former suffered the illusion of intelligently and correctly representing the latter and being a clever administrator. Other world empires would continue to fall prey to the same mistake for the following two centuries, until the present day.

THREE

The Pasha's Settlers, Bulls, and Bandits

1805–1848

Between 1820 and 1824, a series of unprecedented revolts erupted in Upper Egypt, all from Qina Province, aiming to overthrow the regime of Muhammad 'Ali Pasha. Throughout the long, rigid forty-year reign of Muhammad 'Ali (d. 1848), Egypt had never witnessed such outbreaks, in either the country's north or south. Ahmad al-Salah, an Arab shaykh, led the first and largest revolt, mobilizing about forty thousand followers for his cause, including peasants and Arab tribal shaykhs. From his home village of Salimiyya, al-Salah emerged as a Sufi mystic and self-proclaimed messiah and declared a holy war against the pasha, claiming that he had received orders from the Ottoman sultan to execute his mission. He seized the local government's treasury and storehouses and hired his own administrators to rule over Qina for two months. A British eyewitness to this revolt, J. A. St. John, recounted, "The composition of the revolters, their hopes and the grounds of them, were eminently characteristic.... At their head was a Sheikh, who, having assumed the title of a prophet, promised them victory in the name of heaven.... It appeared, nonetheless, that they were by no means dazzled by his divine pretensions. They did not believe him to be inspired; and regarded the miracles related by his enthusiastic companions as so many pious frauds. Taxation, however, pressed heavily upon them; and what was wanting in credulity was compensated by discontent."[1]

Muhammad 'Ali soon sent an army from Cairo to bring an end to the separatist state. Under the command of a young Turkish officer, the soldiers burned villages, destroyed houses, displaced women and children, and exterminated the rebels. Al-Salah fled, crossing the Red Sea to Hijaz, where nobody heard from him again.[2] Two subsequent revolts followed, emerging from adjacent villages in Qina, and were similarly crushed.

Muhammad 'Ali Pasha—originally an ambitious viceroy of Ottoman Egypt—built a short-lived empire, carving away from his sultan's territories to expand into the Sudan, Arabia, Yemen, and Syria. This chapter argues that in the empire of Muhammad 'Ali in the Near East, Upper Egypt was the "first colony." Before invading other territories, the pasha first fought fierce wars for many years to incorporate the south into a unified Egyptian state. As in other world cases of "internal colonialism," such as that of Ireland in Britain, the pasha's rising empire depended on the economic exploitation of the internal colony to support further external expansion. This process involved the implantation of imperial settlers and the creation of vast plantations in the colony. As his extended empire began to collapse, the pasha's hegemony over the south also waned. Upper Egypt constantly simmered with both separatist revolts and acts of resistance in daily life, championed by peasants, women, laborers, slaves, and, most importantly, ever-ruthless bandits.

Given the dominant position of nationalistic perspectives in the historiography of Egypt, the theory of internal colonialism has not been considered as a way to understand the place of Upper Egypt under Muhammad 'Ali. Prevailing Arabic and English narratives alike traditionally assume that the pasha was the founder of modern Egypt or the creator of an Egyptian nation-state. He modernized the army, established bureaucratic state institutions, reformed legal codes, introduced European industries, restructured the agricultural organization, sent students to Europe, and so on, all of which allegedly contributed to the formation of a unified nation that encompassed the north and the south.[3] Khaled Fahmy, a leading Egyptian historian, attempted to undermine these nationalistic narratives in his groundbreaking works, including *All the Pasha's Men*. Studying the modernized army that Muhammad 'Ali built based on conscription of native peasants and laborers, Fahmy used archival evidence to show that the pasha's military institution was far from being a nationalist one working to develop Egyptian "citizens" in a "nation-state" per se.[4]

There is no doubt that Muhammad 'Ali introduced fundamental "modern" reforms to Egypt, but he was never able to build this alleged nation-state. Fond of copying modern European methods of governance, the pasha learned from the experience of several contemporary Western empires that used internal colonialism to create centralized states before embarking on external expansion. The experiences of Britain in Ireland, France in Brittany, and Spain in Catalonia were either recent or still ongoing during the pasha's time. In his book *Internal Colonialism: The Celtic Fringe in British National*

Development, Michael Hechter asserts that the political and economic expansion of the British Empire followed the internal colonization and exploitation of the Irish, Scottish, and Welsh regions. The empire made these peripheral cultures representatives of British national interests and then deployed them to expand its power.[5] Muhammad 'Ali followed a closely similar path in southern Egypt.

For many centuries, from Mamluk to Ottoman times, Upper Egypt was an autonomous state governed by a native tribal regime. Economically, it was a prosperous region, not only due to its commercial production of cash crops such as grain and sugarcane or its lucrative industries in sugar and textiles, but also, more important, because of its integral role in the Indian Ocean world economy. This was the hegemonic global economic system up until the mid–nineteenth century. The Upper Egyptian Nile and Red Sea ports in Qina Province were a thriving link in a regional market that encompassed East Africa, the Arabian Sea, and the vast ocean beyond. When Muhammad 'Ali came to power, the independent state of Upper Egypt had recently fallen to the Ottomans, and it was under the chaotic rule of some Mamluk factions (see chapter 1). For the ambitious new viceroy of Egypt, conquering and annexing the south meant supplying his treasury with immense economic resources and paving the imperial road to neighboring colonies in the Sudan and Arabia.

Thus, Upper Egypt serves as another important example in world history of a failed attempt at internal colonialism. Qina Province's enormous Arabic archival records reveal a problematic and unstable relationship between the central government in Cairo and the colonized peoples of the south. Daily correspondence between the province's bureaucrats and the pasha *(sadir mudiriyya)* as well as registers of the general inspector of Upper Egypt *(sadir mufattish 'umum qibli),* subaltern petitions (*'ardhala*s), shari'a court records, and more depict a clear case of an internal colony boiling with persistent unrest.

Muhammad 'Ali's internal colonization of Upper Egypt went through various phases. Before turning to this, a few words are due about the chronology of the rise and fall of his empire in order to place his actions in the south in context. The pasha came to power in 1805, but he conquered the south six years later in 1811. Only one year after that, he embarked on a successful campaign to conquer Hijaz and terminate the authority of the Wahhabis and the Saudi family from Arabia. In 1820, he sent his troops to invade the Sudan and established full control over it. His vicious army helped the Ottomans crush Greek rebels in 1821, but he did not colonize Greece, instead returning it to the sovereignty of the sultan. In 1831, he took hold of Syria and the entire Levant. The next year the pasha's army humiliatingly defeated the troops of the Ottoman sultan in the battle of Konya and almost invaded Istanbul itself. He established authority over the important port of Mocha in Yemen in 1837. As Muhammad 'Ali was planning to finally declare independence from the Ottomans, his wild imperial ambitions came to an abrupt halt. Great Britain supported Istanbul in achieving this task. The imposition of the 1838 Anglo-Turkish free-trade treaty rolled back the pasha's commercial monopolies—the main source of his economic power—and the 1841 London treaty forced him to relinquish all conquered territories, save for Egypt and the Sudan, back to the sultan. The sultan awarded Muhammad 'Ali Pasha hereditary rule over these two countries as compensation.

In Upper Egypt, the process and dynamics of internal colonialism varied between the early and the late days of the empire, and so did the modes of subaltern resistance. The pasha began his subjugation of the south in a traditional, or Ottoman, mode, coupled with the coercive transfer of resources to Cairo in service of external expansion. This period ended with the revolts of the early 1820s in Qina Province. After crushing the rebels, the pasha introduced a settler, plantation-based, and industrializing model of colonization, in which imported Sudanese bulls played a crucial role. He also adopted methods of modern-state hegemony, through institutions and manipulative discourse rather than coercion. As widespread revolts failed to take off during this period, subaltern rebellion took novel forms, sometimes using violence, devised by the audacious bandits of Qina's mountains.

"WHAT THE MONGOLS DID": SUBJUGATION AND REVOLT

Upon assuming power in Cairo, Muhammad 'Ali Pasha embarked on a long six-year war to conquer Upper Egypt, which was in the hands of military Mamluk groups. In 1811, the pasha's eldest son and army leader, Ibrahim, finally conquered all of the southern provinces after winning the decisive, last battles in Qina Province—where the Mamluks maintained their seat. In the holy month of Ramadan in the same year, Muhammad 'Ali rewarded his victorious son by appointing him the governor of Upper Egypt, calling the region Wilayat al-Sa'id just as the Ottoman Empire had, in an indication of its independent status.[6] Upper Egypt was, in fact, the lucky start of Ibrahim's military career as his father's imperial conqueror—later he would grow into the vicious victor of all the pasha's wars of expansion across the region.

Ibrahim settled in Qina Province, and he rapidly transferred the economic resources of the new colony to Cairo. In the meantime, he maintained the position of minister of finance in his father's regime.[7] Once the governor of Upper Egypt, Ibrahim "did to the peoples of the south what the Mongols did when they invaded countries. He humiliated the nobility and behaved in the worst manner with the people, robbing their harvests and money, taking their cows and sheep . . . and imposing unbearable taxes on them," recounted the contemporary chronicler 'Abd al-Rahman al-Jabarti.[8] Ibrahim was younger than twenty years of age, and besides winning battles, his father taught him only one value: to extract as many taxes from the south as he could by any possible means. According to al-Jabarti, "He [Ibrahim] imposed enormous amounts of money [taxes] on them [the Upper Egyptians] that was impossible for them to pay, and urged them to pay soon. When they failed to pay, he applied different means of torturing, beating, hanging, and burning to them. . . . He once tied a man's feet to a long board of wood that two other men held from the two ends and they rolled him over fire like *kabab*. . . . He humiliated the people of Upper Egypt and disgraced them."[9] When Ibrahim received his post, the size of cultivated land in Upper Egypt exceeded that of the Delta by at least 200,000 acres, so the taxes he extracted from the wealthier south exceeded those of the north by more than 150,000 pounds.[10]

The first thing that Muhammad 'Ali ordered his son to transfer north was the famous grain of Upper Egypt that had sustained Istanbul's imperial granaries for centuries. Ibrahim forcibly confiscated this crop, and the pasha exported it to a desperate Europe during the Napoleonic Wars at inflated prices. A few months after the invasion, the pasha established a monopoly over the southern grain trade: a decree issued in 1812 forbade local merchants from participating in this trade. Grain was also seized from peasants, even what they had stored for their own sustenance. The pasha's officials broke into the peasants' homes, seizing as little or as much grain as they found, without paying, claiming that this would be deducted from the following year's tax bill. The pasha's gigantic ships, built especially for shipping grain purpose, then carried the crop down the Nile to Cairo.[11] In 1816, al-Jabarti observed one of these annually recurring scenes: "Ships from Upper Egypt come to Bulaq and Old Cairo ports. They unload huge cargoes very high into the air and then the ships come from the north to take them [the cargo] to Alexandria and in the morning you would not find any of it left at the site."[12]

Within only a few years, this very grain made Muhammad 'Ali "the richest Pasha in the Ottoman Empire," in the words of a French consul.[13] The Ottoman ships now came to Alexandria in order to carry the Sublime Port's grain, which Istanbul had received regularly for the previous three centuries. But these Ottoman ships returned empty, while British ships harboring adjacent to them were heavily loaded with Upper Egyptian wheat and setting sail to Europe. The sultan's complaints did not stop the ambitious viceroy from accumulating immense capital.[14] Europe was in dire need of wheat during the Napoleonic Wars, so the pasha sold it at exaggerated prices. Historian Fred Lawson writes that "these sales generated considerable income for the central treasury.... Sa'idi [Upper Egyptian] wheat was being exported for between sixty-two and eighty piasters per *ardabb* at the beginning of 1811, a price some five times that in the local market; nevertheless, British buyers were not dissuaded from increasing their purchases."[15]

The wheat of Qina Province, particularly, sustained the troops of Muhammad 'Ali during his invasion of Hijaz. The process of transferring wheat to the army was easy because Ibrahim's base as the governor of Upper Egypt was in Qina, and from there he crossed the Red Sea to Hijaz. John Bowring, a British official, reported the impressive quantities: "Keneh [Qina] has gradually sent large quantities of wheat to Arabia; sometimes as much as 200,000 *ardabbs*, or a million bushels per annum."[16] One of the main tasks of the appointed Turkish governor of the towns of the province was to ensure a regular flow of grain shipments and secure them on their way to Ibrahim and his fighting soldiers in Arabia. Harsh punishment awaited any governor who did not fulfill this crucial duty. In their itinerary from Qina to the Red Sea port of Qusayr, these grain shipments were frequently raided by local Arab tribes and did not make it to the military camps, which greatly angered the pasha.[17]

The equally famous sugar of Upper Egypt was the second resource to be transferred to Cairo and sold at high price, solely for the benefit of the pasha's treasury. For centuries, significant shipments of this sugar also used to be shipped to Istanbul. Al-Jabarti reported that Ibrahim established a monopoly over the southern sugar trade as soon as he completed his conquest. Within a few years, he was already in control of all the sugarcane harvest and sugar mills of Upper Egypt. To expand the industry, he advanced credit to private sugar refineries and shared profits with them, which led to a tremendous increase in both the size of sugarcane fields and the number of mills. He established a large, new refinery near his vast plantation in Middle Egypt, and Upper Egyptian cane provided it with continuous supplies. To consolidate his monopoly, Muhammad ʿAli later restricted sugarcane cultivation to Upper Egypt, issuing decrees prohibiting its cultivation in Lower Egypt.[18]

Impressed European observers reported how the pasha's huge and ever-growing capital gained from southern harvests, especially grain, inspired him to invest in "modern" reforms. These are the same famous military, administrative, agricultural, and industrial reforms that made the pasha a celebrated figure in Egyptian and world history. "The next step of accumulating this capital was to invest it in projects that would increase the acreage of land under cultivation and increase production as well as introduce new money-making crops," a French consul reported.[19] Before the decade ended, Muhammad ʿAli universalized the abolition of tax farming; consolidated his agricultural monopolies; constructed new canals, dikes, embankments, and so on; modernized the army; founded textile factories and imported in European expertise; sent students for education in Europe; and, above all, introduced long-staple cotton to Lower Egypt.[20]

Furthermore, the pasha appropriated Qina's regional Red Sea market and established monopolies over its commerce. Along with Upper Egypt, the conquered areas of the Sudan, Hijaz, and Yemen formed one uniform market, and capturing them put the pasha in control of the Red Sea trade routes and ports that had helped sustain the Cairene economy for centuries. Qina's Qusayr port, on the Red Sea, was the first of those important trade centers, and Ibrahim also used it as a point of logistical support during his military campaign. Muhammad ʿAli appointed Ibrahim as the governor of the new southern colonies, along with Upper Egypt, a move that helped maintain the commercial unity of this market for a time. Dreaming of conquering the rest of this traditional market in East Africa, the pasha named Ibrahim the governor of Abyssinia without actually invading the area.[21] Muhammad ʿAli did not waste time in establishing monopolies over Yemeni coffee and other commodities of Indian Ocean trade that came from the ports of Mocha and Jeddah through Qusayr to Qina Province. He also monopolized the Sudanese slave trade and East African commodities that came to the province both through its Nile ports of Isna and Farshut and the overland caravan routes.[22]

Moreover, by controlling the Red Sea market, Muhammad ʿAli appropriated Qina's textile trade in East Africa and Arabia, which had functioned for hundreds of years based on the exportation of large quantities of textiles produced by the province's women and Coptic weavers.[23] Muhammad ʿAli founded three modern textile factories in Qina Province, in the towns of Isna, Qina, and Farshut, and he commanded the provinces of Upper Egypt to expand cotton cultivation. To further monopolize the industry, in 1820 the pasha issued a decree banning the operation of any private weaving and textile mills in Egypt, leaving no room for the female and Coptic textile weavers of Qina to carry on their traditional profession. Muhammad 'Ali even paid his Sudanese soldiers partly in cotton clothes, in order to consolidate state control of the market.[24] The pasha's three factories in the province were successful and worried British textile merchants operating in East Africa and Arabia. Lamenting the inability of British textiles to compete with Qina's garments, John Bowring's report stated, "The cotton manufactory at Keneh is on a large scale, and carried on in a building erected for the purpose. There are nearly 1,000 persons employed in it.... [The produced pieces] are very readily disposed of, and, in fact, this species of goods is to be found in the bazaars of all towns in Egypt.... Though there would seem to be no difficulty in the fabric, it would appear we have not succeeded in imitating the articles in England, and that the native article is much preferred."[25]

In order to ease the transfer of these resources to Cairo, Ibrahim developed a new system of administration immediately following the conquest that was applied for the first time in the pasha's government—and was afterward extended to the Delta. Ibrahim reversed the Ottoman laissez-faire political economy and instituted heavy state interventionism. He started out by surveying the land of Upper Egypt, using the expertise of local Coptic accountants, and then he modified the tax tables accordingly. He abolished tax farming and confiscated land from large Arab tax farmers, including the remaining leaders of the Hawwara dynasty, rendering them powerless and humiliated. He also confiscated the sizable, previously untaxed farms endowed for religious establishments, the *waqf* lands, from local shari'a law scholars.[26]

In Qina Province, Ibrahim distributed seeds to every peasant in the beginning of every season and forced them to farm an assigned parcel of land, which sometimes exceeded the capacity of what the peasant and his family could till. To this end, the government built numerous state storehouses to distribute seeds to villages and later to store the collected harvest.[27] Ibrahim also established a system to punish those who left any of this assigned land uncultivated or did not pay tax revenues. "If you leave any wasteland this year, I will collect four times as much tax from it," Ibrahim swore in one of his firm decrees.[28] Some peasants did not work because they simply did not have enough cattle to help them farm the land, or so they told Ibrahim. Thus, Ibrahim extended state funds for the purchase of animals; but in order to first ensure that the peasants had told him the truth, he imprisoned and tortured them.[29]

At the end of a long decade of subjugation and exploitation of the first colony, three revolts finally erupted in Qina Province and spread across Upper Egypt. These revolts emerged from various villages in the province between 1820 and 1824. Uprisings were rare under the harsh regime of Muhammad 'Ali, and those of Qina were the only massive rebellions that Egypt witnessed during his reign, aside from two minor insurrections of Arab tribes in the Delta.[30] When the first revolt broke out, Ibrahim had already resettled in Cairo, where he lived as a great imperialist, owning several affluently decorated palaces with vast gardens and mills serving his court and wives.[31] But even in Ibrahim's absence, Qina was still enduring the coercion of several other Turkish governors who followed him. The three widespread revolts have captured the attention of many historians who seek to analyze their causes and social composition. Some perceive them as a rural insurgency of peasants attributed to overtaxation, corvée labor, and army conscription. Others insist that they were workers' revolts that erupted when Qina's textile weavers and merchants lost their market to the pasha's modern factories.[32]

In the first and by far largest uprising, Ahmad al-Salah, an Arab shaykh, mobilized about forty thousand angry peasants in an attempt to overthrow the government of Muhammad 'Ali. Luckily, the tragic events of this revolt were meticulously recorded by a British eyewitness, J. A. St. John, who happened to be in Qina during the outbreak while he was traveling up the Nile. Al-Salah called himself al-Mahdi, or the long-awaited messiah, and preached to villagers, who soon elected him their commander. Despite al-Salah's religious rhetoric, he was originally a merchant with no shari'a training except for acquired mysticism. He was one of the many long-distance merchants hurt by the pasha's monopolies over Red Sea commerce, and he started his political career when, returning from Mecca with shipments, he refused to pay taxes to the pasha's duty officers at the port of Qusayr.[33] Al-Salah came from the village of Salimiyya, whose peasants eked out a living with subsistence farming of wheat and beans. His movement spread quickly and, when the number of rebels expanded to tens of thousands, he proclaimed a coup d'état. Elite Arab shaykhs in towns soon joined, and the pasha's Turkish governor fled the province after surviving an attempt on his life.[34]

Al-Salah installed himself as the governor of Qina and Qus. He claimed that the Ottoman sultan had delegated this holy mission to him, saying that "he had an order from God and the Grand Signor to dethrone Muhammad Ali Pasha," according to St. John's account.[35] Al-Salah immediately seized the government treasury and storehouses and established a new administration for a separatist state. His original plan was to expand his government down the Nile to encompass all of Upper Egypt as far as the province of Asyut. As for the majority of his followers, the wretched villagers of Qina, St. John recounted that they apparently were not fooled by al-Salah's alleged spiritual revelations, but heavy taxes pressed them to join the rebels.[36]

In spite of al-Salah's messianic pretensions, he appeared to be a skilled statesman who knew how to build internal alliances and accommodate existing foreign relations. He maintained religious rhetoric while carefully limiting the side effects that religious fanaticism might generate. When some of his zealous followers proposed decapitating the Coptic population of the province, he promptly halted the action against the native Christians. Aware of Ottoman foreign relations, al-Salah neither preached nor led aggressive actions against Europeans in the province, especially the British, who were then the sultan's allies against the French. When a group of rebels held a meeting in the village of Armant to plan the murder of the Englishmen in the area, al-Salah condemned and stopped the action, as recounted by St. John:

> During his audience, some of the Prophet's more zealous followers handed in a requisition to be allowed to decapitate all the Copts, to which the saint answered by an exhortation to general forbearance, urging the propriety of not injuring any one unless compelled. "If you are attacked," said he, "you may kill, but not otherwise." . . . He solemnly declared "that the English were his friends, and that he was their friend, and would protect them." Nay, more, he swore by the Koran and the sword, "that if any one robbed an Englishman, even of the cord of a camel or an ass, he would restore them a camel or an ass in its place." . . . Two men came from Erment, where there had been a large public meeting, in which it had been proposed to murder the Englishmen. The Prophet however, severely rebuked the person who advised the sanguinary proceeding; and so far from giving it any countenance, sent us a letter assuring us of his friendship, and promising us protection.[37]

Barely two months had passed with al-Salah in power when Muhammad 'Ali sent a large body of troops with gunpowder cannons to Qina to crush the rebellion. It had already been a hard year for the pasha, with an outbreak of the plague in Cairo and conflict with separatists in Greece; however, he still managed to send a great number of soldiers to the south from his newly modernized army. Under the command of Ahmad Pasha, a young Turk no less aggressive than Ibrahim, the troops advanced to Qina, terrorizing the inhabitants of villages and forcing women, children, and men to flee their homes and seek refuge in the Pharaonic temples or in the nearby mountains. Ahmad Pasha tried to persuade the rebels to return to their villages by promising to exempt peasants from the next year's taxes. As persuasion failed, a bloody war began.

Through many battles and rounds of victory and defeat, Ahmad Pasha and the troops burned entire villages, destroyed houses, and displaced thousands of women and children. In one village, they put "every soul they met—man, woman and child—to the sword."[38] Interestingly, there were natives of these very villages among the disciplined soldiers of the pasha's modern army. Finding themselves ordered to kill their own fathers or kin, many of them decided to desert and join the rebels.[39] The village of Qammula was turned into a symbolic place of resistance: it was where the former independent ruler and last Arab dynast of Upper Egypt, Shaykh al-Arab Hammam, had died from grief and had been buried after his defeat by the Mamluks of Cairo a few decades prior. One morning, al-Salah recruited thousands of his followers and advanced to Qammula, where he fiercely attacked one of the pasha's garrisons, achieving a great victory over Cairo's soldiers. But this was only one victory among repeated defeats. Although al-Salah still claimed to be fighting with support from the angels and the Prophet Muhammad, his followers questioned his heavenly powers. Realizing his inability to expand north to the province of Asyut—his original plan—he told his followers that he had not received the orders to do so; it is not clear whether these orders were expected to come from God or the sultan.[40]

Finally, the followers of al-Salah were ruthlessly crushed. Concluding the mission, Ahmad Pasha offered a handsome price for the life of every mutineer. Volunteer Bedouins searched the mountains for fugitive rebels; they came back with heads and received the handsome reward. St. John recounted a disturbing scene of Ahmad Pasha buying the heads of the decapitated insurgents: "The Bedouins in his service scoured the mountains, with considerable success, in search of victims, whose heads were brought down and sold according to the tariff established by the youthful Ahmad." As for al-Salah, he fled to the Qusayr port and from there to Hijaz, where nobody heard from him again.[41] The leaders of the two successive uprisings also carried the name of Ahmad, and these new rebels were brutally crushed in the same manner. By 1824, Muhammad 'Ali's Upper Egypt was free of armed rebels and was ready for a new era of colonization à la European style.

SETTLERS AND BULLS FOR HEGEMONY

Upon putting down the rebellions, Muhammad 'Ali sent an urgent decree to all the Turkish governors of the districts and subdistricts of Upper Egypt. "It is imperative," read the promulgation, "to organize the lands that will be cultivated this year. Bring what they need from machines and cattle, erect waterwheels and everything else. . . . [I have] appointed a special official to work with you [the governors] on this matter. . . . Lands should be assigned in accordance with the number of their inhabitants, and village shaykhs should be urged to serve the crops and erect waterwheels, and registers should be kept."[42] This was the first decree of its kind to reach Qina Province. To adjust to the realities of southern discontent, the pasha changed his methods of internal colonialism, applying European models that were particularly used in the Americas. He colonized by sending settlers and creating plantations; imposing heavy central planning and government intervention in the economy; and maintaining close control of the environment and energy sources. He also created modern institutions of hegemony to allow the political participation of the subjugated populace, though the south nonetheless endured taxation without representation.

An ever-increasing influx of Turkish settlers from Cairo arrived in Qina Province to assume positions as government bureaucrats and, more important, to establish state and private plantations. Their plantations followed a model similar to what European empires devised in the Americas: they forcefully enclosed large plots—hundreds or thousands of acres—cultivating them with one cash crop, especially grain or sugar, and employing slaves or forced local labor to till them. To establish their social prestige and separate themselves from the natives, Turkish settlers carried the titles of *agha* and *bey*, referring to their status within the bureaucratic hierarchy as governors of provinces, directors of districts, or managers of subdistricts. Their sweeping presence in Qina altered the socioeconomic composition of a province historically inhabited by Arab tribes and native Copts, as these Turks purchased large houses in the urban centers of the province and brought their families from Cairo to take up residence in them. On a daily basis, they sent meticulous reports to Muhammad 'Ali about all incidents, big or small, on every plantation they ran. Back in Cairo, the pasha responded to these reports personally, with equally detailed orders dictating how to handle both important and minute affairs on the plantations and in the province at large.[43]

FIGURE 5. An Upper Egyptian village street.

To allow these state and private plantations to take form, Muhammad 'Ali introduced fundamental legal reforms in the landownership system. He issued a civil laws that introduced three new types of agricultural properties: *ab'adiyya, 'uhda,* and *çiftlik*. The *ab'adiyya*s were private plantations—originally vacant arable land that the pasha granted for reclamation to bureaucrats, army officers, and co-opted local elite and that was fully or partially exempt from taxation for a number of years. In 1836, the pasha legally transformed these holdings into semiprivate properties that the owners were then allowed to pass down to their heirs and white slaves. By 1842, he fully converted them to private properties. The *'uhda*s were state-owned plantations—originally the confiscated land of runaway peasants who fled their plots after failing to pay overdue taxes or to escape army conscription or corvée labor. The state seized whole villages from fleeing villagers, transformed them into plantations, and assigned their management to Turkish bureaucrats. The plantation manager was obliged to pay the state overdue as well as new taxes. The *çiftlik*s were royal plantations—privately owned by Muhammad 'Ali and his family, exempt from taxes, and administered by Turkish bureaucrats. The pasha annexed vast lands from villages that failed to pay overdue taxes and added them to his swiftly expanding collection of personal properties.[44]

These legal reforms were introduced in the Delta and Upper Egypt alike. Whereas they did not bring fundamental social change to the Delta, as that region was already accustomed to the intensive presence of Turkish landholders from the Ottoman period, they did alter the face of life in Upper Egypt. The south witnessed for the first time the rise of a foreign white elite. In Qina Province, numerous Turkish *agha*s expanded private, state, and royal landholdings every year.[45] In 1837, when ʿAli Agha, the director of the subdistrict of Farshut, received an *abʿadiyya* plantation in one village, he turned a part of it into a family endowment untaxed by the state, with full ownership accruing to the family. The revenue of the plantation would be passed down to his offspring forever and, after they died, to the offspring of the *agah*'s freed black slaves.[46] After accumulating substantial capital, Turkish settlers started expanding their plots by purchasing small and big parcels from the local farmers, in addition to purchasing cattle and machinery.[47] Given the hot weather of Qina Province, many of the new elite administered their duties from luxury Nile boats furnished as dwellings. Nonetheless, Turkish settlers were not able to move within the province without armed guards—black slaves and Turks—to protect them against potential attacks from the native inhabitants, which apparently happened frequently.[48]

The new settler elite formed an indispensable alliance with segments of the old native elite, whom the empire co-opted. Among those co-opted groups were local judges hired in shariʿa courts, village shaykhs serving the plantations, merchants whose boats transported the pasha's monopolized goods, and Coptic merchants and accountants administering provincial finances. The new and old elite quickly intermarried and became business partners. Turkish bureaucrats married the daughters of upper-class Arab families, and rich Arab men married the daughters, sisters, and sometimes divorcées of *agha*s.[49] The settler and native elite founded commercial companies that traded in grain, Sudanese slaves, textiles, and more. Turkish partners entered those companies only by contributing shares to the principle capital or extending credit, or sometimes they were fully involved in the business with their own Nile boats and employees.[50] A business contract concluded in Isna's shariʿa court, in 1836, reveals these new colonial realities in Qina Province. Hijjo Agha, working for the office of the city governor, appointed Shaykh Ibrahim al-Fawi, the chief of the merchants' guild in the city of Isna, as his legal agent to buy, on his behalf, a share in a commercial boat and its equipment from the company of Khalil Ibrahim the Copt and Hajj Ahmad ʿIsa al-Asyuti. The Turkish bureaucrat, the Copt, and the Arab ended in each owning one-third of the boat, which could carry up to 13,400 liters up and down the Nile.[51]

The new plantations hired Qina's peasants as seasonal labor and the plantations also used slaves. Laborers were also rented out to local farmers through sharecropping contracts. The slave trade in the Sudan continued to be a significant commercial sector in Upper Egypt during this period, but now local merchants and Turkish settlers collaborated closely in the buying and selling of slaves in order to secure more laborers for the plantations.[52] Many families of enslaved laborers ran away from the plantations to escape oppressive treatment.[53] Similarly, seasonal local labor fled the land to escape the repression of a foreign colonial elite. When it was reported that a peasant from the royal plantation of Armant ran away, taking with him his animals and properties, the orders of the Turkish provincial governor were strict: to arrest him with everything he had and send him back to the manager for punishment and probably to resume forced work.[54] Ironically, even tenants or sharecroppers deserted their plots and fled to hide in other villages, resenting the high taxes collected from them in-kind and in cash.[55] In service of the plantations, village shaykhs collected corvée laborers, who spent months at public work sites away from their home villages. These laborers had to dig canals, construct dikes, and build bridges, and many ran away to escape unpaid, compulsory duties.[56]

Turkish settlers were not always efficient or rigorous managers of the plantations, which allowed native sharecroppers to take advantage of their overseers at every possible opportunity. One of the largest royal plantations in Qina was in the area of Armant, which mainly produced grain and sugar. The sharecroppers in Armant occasionally bargained with the Turkish administration to increase their percentage of the harvest. Before the beginning of the winter grain season of 1835, realizing the vulnerability of the state in matters concerning grain, the sharecroppers sent a petition to the Turkish governor of the province asking for an increase in their share from one-sixth to one-third of the harvest. Apparently the request took an aggressive form and a crisis mounted inside the plantation between a weak Turkish manager and the sharecroppers. The governor eventually decided to increase their share to one-fourth; nonetheless, two years later, the same sharecroppers refused to pay their dues to the weak manager. Moreover, they proposed to administer the plantation themselves. Information reached the general inspector of Upper Egypt that this manager was inefficient, ignorant of state laws, and, more important, not on good terms with the farmers, who in turn exploited his weakness by refusing to submit the product of their labors and delaying their work. The governor declined the farmers' proposal to administer the plantation and instead replaced this manager.[57]

Aside from administering the plantations, the Turkish bureaucrats applied Muhammad 'Ali's new colonial system of heavy state intervention in the economy and close control of the environment. They took charge of enforcing the pasha's new laws and orders pertaining to land assignment to small peasants, water and irrigation organization, industrialization, and allocation of sources of energy. In Qina Province, the Turkish bureaucrats controlled the process of assigning native peasants small plots of land for compulsory cultivation and forced them to till this land and pay its annual dues in-kind and in cash according to a set timetable that matched the harvesting seasons. Bureaucrats hired village shaykhs to keep these farmers working on their plots, collect taxes, and hunt down runaway peasants who deserted their land and fled their villages after failing to pay taxes. In water organization, the bureaucrats were assisted by modern chief engineers (*bashmuhandis*), who arrived from Cairo to supervise the building of new dams and the digging of new canals, while village shaykhs collected corvée laborers to work for extensive periods on these public projects. In addition, Turkish bureaucrats managed the lucrative state textile, sugar, and gunpowder factories in the province. They applied the pasha's strict policies in order to regularly provide the factories with animals to run the machines, recruit local workers, undertake occasional maintenance works, and so on, and they brutally punished native supervisors and workers alike for laziness or negligence.[58]

The creation of the Department of Sudanese Cattle was the epitome of the new colonial realities of heavy central planning in this plantation-based and industrializing economy. The pasha's regime sought to secure sources of energy for farms and factories, so in 1833 the pasha founded a special department for the importation and distribution of Sudanese bulls, cows, and camels, giving it the name of Maslahat al-Mawashi al-Sudaniyya. One of the main tasks of the appointed Turkish collector of cattle in Halfa, a Sudanese Nile port, was to oversee the transportation of these cattle so none of them would die en route; he received direct orders from the pasha in regard to this important duty. Qina's Nile ports played a central role in the function of this department: on a weekly basis they were the first to receive the imported cattle, take some of them to local state factories and royal plantations, and send the rest north to be allocated to state-owned enterprises in other provinces. The Department of Sudanese Cattle was large, with an immense budget, and it employed hundreds of laborers in the province every year, including camel drivers, shepherds, guards, foremen, scribes, and more, who worked along with modern veterinarians dispatched from Cairo in the gigantic state barns prepared to receive the cattle. The peasants of Qina were ordered to provide the barns with tons of grass, hay, and fava beans to feed the precious bulls and cows all year long.[59]

Feeding the bulls of Isna's textile factory seemed an important personal concern of the pasha. He sent harsh memorandums to the Turkish director of the district urging him to regularly supply the factory with maize and beans for the bulls, and he demanded that receipts of delivery be sent directly to him in Cairo at set dates to ensure the enforcement of his orders. "If you are later than the due date, you know how you will be punished. If I do not receive statements [of delivered hay] with the director's signet, I will find my way with you," the pasha swore, alluding to his system of corporal punishment that ranged from lashing to beheading.[60] Similarly, Turkish administrators of the royal plantations in Armant and Ruzayqat in Qina Province received extensive correspondence directly from the pasha about the handling, feeding, and use of the Sudanese cattle. Village shaykhs took responsibility for distributing the amount of hay stipulated by the pasha's decrees to every individual bull or cow in the plantations. Even cattle that died during transport were addressed in the orders of the pasha, with their skin to be used in certain factories in the province.[61]

To maximize the taxed agricultural produce, the colonial regime distributed some of these cattle to peasants for use in plowing the plots that the government forcibly assigned to them. The Turkish director of the Department of Sudanese Cattle in Qina Province sold the cattle at subsidized prices to the province's farmers, who received them only after state approval and signing of receipt—probably to inspect them afterward and ensure that they followed the state orders in employing the cattle. At the different stations where the cattle stopped in their long journey, the sick and weak ones were sold off to local communities after making sure that the animals were incapable of serving at the local factories and plantations or continuing on the road to serve in other provinces. Prices varied according to size and health. Impoverished peasants of Qina Province, in turn, sold these cheaply purchased bulls and cows to make some money, which infuriated Muhammad 'Ali. He sent a memorandum to the assistant collector of cattle of the towns of Qus and Isna, in which he firmly insisted that "those cattle are brought from the Sudan for the development [*i'mar*] of the countries and welfare of the populace [*rafahiyyat al-ahali*]. We found out that the people buy the cattle from the government and sell them in the markets, and this is against laws and regulations. You must prohibit the people from doing so."[62]

With Turkish settlers and central planning, Muhammad ʿAli introduced his modern institutions of hegemony to the internal colony—yet also kept it peripheralized. In the 1820s, Muhammad ʿAli revised his rhetoric and system of government to adopt modern European methods that manipulated his subjects rather than directly repressing them. In his orders and memorandums, the pasha propagated his own imperial interests as the "greater good." Instead of addressing his population as inferior subjects, using the old Ottoman term *raʿiyya,* he adopted the new respectful and compassionate term *al-ahali,* meaning "the populace" or "citizens" in a French sense, and declared that the goal of his policies was the "welfare of the populace," or *rafahiyyat al-ahali*.[63] More important, the pasha founded three separate state institutions: a legislative council, a modernized bureaucracy, and a reformed shariʿa court system.[64] In Upper Egypt, these government bodies marginalized the internal colony: they produced a situation of taxation without representation. In other words, the peasants and laborers of the south were overtaxed and submitted their dues in-kind and in cash to hundreds of colossal state storehouses (*shunas*) that were spread out in almost every village and town, but they enjoyed no representation in the pasha's modern institutions—in dramatic contradistinction to the north.

Muhammad ʿAli founded the Council of Consultation (Majlis al-Mashura) in 1824 and delegated law-making authority to it, but the council was also extensively involved in administrative affairs. Its members were mainly Turkish officials, and the pasha expanded it in 1829 and appointed village shaykhs, thus opening the door for native representation in his legislature.[65] Qina Province was not represented in this council; neither were any of the Upper Egyptian provinces south of Asyut. Whereas all of the Delta provinces were handsomely represented, Muhammad ʿAli did not grant a single seat to any of the shaykhs of Upper Egyptian villages.[66] Nonetheless, the council frequently intervened in every aspect of Qina's economic life, such as organizing land cultivation, digging canals, building dikes, erecting state storehouses, hiring laborers, managing state-owned factories, and placing limitations on private grain merchants. Due to the lack of Upper Egyptian representation in Cairo, the number of public works that the central government decided to undertake in the south noticeably decreased. The council had to summon a few southern shaykhs to draft the section on Upper Egypt in the principle statute it issued for agricultural organization, *La'ihat Zira'at al-Fallah*. In this code of seminal importance, the conditions in the Delta set the norm while Upper Egypt was defined as the remote exception.[67]

The second institution of the pasha's hegemony was a modernized bureaucracy. The Syasatname, or the comprehensive law that the Council of Consultation drafted for the pasha to promulgate in 1837, crystallized the structure and function of this new administrative system. Muhammad 'Ali again asserted that this law aimed to improve "the prosperity of the country and the welfare of the people and the provinces."[68] The bureaucracy in Qina Province was highly centralized: all ranked officials were Turks appointed from Cairo. While the general inspector of Upper Egypt undertook basic supervising duties, the provincial governor and district and subdistrict directors were in charge of detailed executive affairs. Officials at all levels in Qina reported directly to Muhammad 'Ali, who closely followed their work.[69] When the pasha applied a new, yet limited policy to incorporate native Egyptians into the high-ranking bureaucratic offices, native Upper Egyptians were excluded from the process. The pasha promoted several notable shaykhs from villages in the Delta to the position of district director and then further to provincial governor. Qina's shaykhs were not considered for minor or major offices within the centralized government, and, once again, the province was excluded from representation.[70]

The third institution of the pasha's hegemony was the reformed court system. Muhammad 'Ali integrated Qina's shari'a courts into the state apparatus and made them a part of the administration. The judges of the province's local courts were officially appointed by the state, and their *sijill* registers were used to notarize official transactions between bureaucrats, village shaykhs, and Coptic accountants, on the one hand, and peasants, factory workers, camel drivers, and Nile boat captains, on the other—in accordance with both shari'a law and civil legislation.[71] Qina's local scholarly community of shari'a jurists was excluded from participating in these developments, unless they changed the school of law they adhered to. The majority of Qina's shari'a law scholars belonged to the Maliki school of law, but Muhammad 'Ali decided to make the Hanafi school the official and only shari'a law applied in the province's courts. The state worked on gradually transforming the legal system until, in 1839, the Turkish governor of the province sent a letter to the Maliki jurisconsult *(mufti)*, in Isna indicating that it was now state policy that legal opinions *(fatwas)* only be issued by the official Hanafi *muftis* sitting inside the court when both litigants and defendants were present before the judge. By this decree, the pasha prohibited informal legal practices from taking place outside his state courts and restricted the application of laws other than his own Hanafi codes in the province, which further marginalized Qina's majority of Maliki scholars.[72]

BACK TO REBELLION

Settlers, taxation, and peripheralization did not go without resistance in the southern colony. After Qina Province's three revolts of the early 1820s were crushed, no other massive rebellion took place in Upper Egypt for as long as the pasha was alive. Horrific news of the modernized imperial army of Muhammad 'Ali—with disciplined soldiers and gunpowder weaponry—defeating troops in faraway lands in Europe, Asia, and Africa certainly served to deter any separatist thoughts in the south. However, rebellion escalated in many other forms; it turned into daily-life resistance championed by oppressed women and men. Peasants fled plantations and corvée work sites, escaped taxes, and deserted the plots that the state forced them to till. Workers in government factories were no different, as many of them ran away from their production lines and fled taxes. Other types of laborers who were forcibly employed and highly taxed, including camel drivers and Nile boat captains, similarly sought to escape government tasks and taxes. The colonial regime was forced to coin a new term to describe all of these runaways: *mutasahhib*s. Out of these fugitives finally emerged the largest and fiercest resistance in the province: the bandits (*falatiyya*) who opted to avenge their losses by violent means, upsetting the security and political stability of the south.

Before resorting to violence, the peasants of Qina sometimes resisted the colonial administration simply by deliberately neglecting the pasha's orders, and when interrogated they fabricated excuses.[73] But when fed up, they vandalized government buildings and bloodily attacked Turkish bureaucrats and other government employees. For instance, a group of villagers from the town of Farshut assaulted the postman transporting some treasury funds; they cut his bag and stole the money that was in it. At receiving the news, Muhammad 'Ali was furious, as this was not the first time that news of such offenses reached his ears.[74] In another incident, a revolt almost broke out when a large group of villagers not only refused to pay their dues to the treasury but also attempted to kill a Turkish bureaucrat. In 1836, after rejecting the collection of the imposed tax, the peasants of Ballas attacked the state official as he tried to gather corvée laborers for public works projects in the canals. Upon learning about the insurgency, the pasha immediately sent troops to the village and they captured the shaykhs who had plotted with the peasants against the government.[75]

In 1844, the peasants of the village of Ruzayqat, where a vast royal plantation existed, destroyed the dam that diverted irrigation water to the plantation, away from their own thirsty lands.[76] Three years later, the situation dramatically escalated again in the same village, when the farmers murdered many Turkish bureaucrats and soldiers and injured others. The entire village of Ruzayqat united in this act against the bureaucrats, and even the shaykhs helped hide the murderers.[77] In the same year, a less violent incident took place on another plantation, again in the village of Ballas. Two laborers by the names of Ahmad and Isma'il attacked the tax collector of a state-owned plantation, managed by a Turk, Mustafa Bey. They succeeded in taking back the eight hundred piasters that the tax collector had levied earlier.[78]

Highway robbery evolved into a common act of resistance in Qina Province, creating a serious security dilemma for the imperial regime. Gangs of highway robbers were often the product of an alliance between two oppressed groups: peasants and Bedouins from settled Arab tribes. Some Bedouin communities sheltered rebellious farmers who fled their home villages to escape taxes or army conscription and built special dwellings for them. These gangs frequently targeted government officials and buildings, Coptic treasury clerks, and wealthy Muslims and Copts.[79] Coming from three different villages, Farraj Ahmad, Muhammad Rayyan, and Muhammad 'Awad joined forces to form a gang that attacked travelers on roads. They committed various crimes, from theft to murder, until they were finally arrested and brought to court. Personally concerned about this high-profile security case, the Turkish general inspector of Upper Egypt had the gang swear an oath on the Holy Qur'an to quit criminal actions and repent. He warned them that shari'a punishment awaited them should they break the oath and return to their sins; he threatened them with crucifixion, lashing, or amputation of their hands and legs.[80]

Women often used legal channels of resistance against corrupt Turkish bureaucrats and oppressive village shaykhs. They raised petitions (*'ardhalas*) or took their cases to court. Umm Muhammad, of the village of Hamidiyya, volunteered on behalf of the inhabitants of her village to petition against the local shaykhs, who had attacked the peasants with the collusion of a resident bureaucrat. With the dispute simmering and escalating to a crisis in the village,

Umm Muhammad hurried to address a petition to the general inspector of Upper Egypt, where she informed him in detail about the shaykhs' and bureaucrat's coercive actions and requested an investigation. The inspector responded by issuing orders to examine the incident and identify the transgressing parties, but apparently the case did not reach a satisfying closure.[81] A woman from Nagada, by the name of Amina, raised a petition against Shaykh Hasan, who had seized the palm trees that she had inherited from her mother. Her petition was passed down to the Turkish district chief and the shari'a judge, and the two requested that Amina bring certain documents to prove her claim. She had to travel to Qus, crossing the Nile by boat with her son, to bring the required documents with the signets of many shari'a authorities. Eventually, she failed to submit the demanded evidence and lost her palm trees to the shaykh, who was well connected within the bureaucracy.[82]

Running away from one's village in order to escape plantation work, overdue taxes, factory production lines, corvée labor, or army conscription became one of the most common acts of resistance in Qina Province during this period. Such flight, known as *tasahhub,* was not new in either Qina or Egypt as a whole, but it noticeably increased with the growing colonial repression in the south. Entire families of peasants carried their animals and small properties, fleeing to hide in other remote villages as fugitives of the government. One of the main tasks of village shaykhs was to keep registers of the original inhabitants of each village, monitor the arrival of mysterious strangers, report them, and, if they were runaways, send them back to their home villages to pay their taxes or conclude their duties. The wives and children of escaped peasants were first carried back by force to their original villages, in order to pressure the hiding breadwinner to return. The governor of Qina Province also kept detailed registers that included the names of runaways, dates of their flight, reasons for deserting the village, and suggestions for resolving the problem.[83]

Interestingly, fleeing sometimes turned into a method of negotiating with the government to improve one's conditions. During the first few days of the holy month of Ramadan in 1844, several workers ran away from the state's textile factory in Isna and from other government jobs. The factory workers fled unjust treatment—they were paid small daily wages and state taxes were directly subtracted from these wages. Most puzzling to the workers, these taxes often exceeded their wages. Thus, a few days after the workers fled, and probably also inspired by the generous spiritual atmosphere of Ramadan, the governor of Isna decided to raise the daily wages of workers, "for their comfort," and to end the problem of flight. Furthermore, the governor decided to reform the entire system of payment regulations, obliging only workers who served for twelve months and ten days to pay taxes and levying a tax equal to the wage of only one month. The governor had to make such a decision when the factories needed to recruit more workers from villages.[84] This was not the first or last incident of workers running away in which the officials responded by raising their wages; the Nagada runaway laborers were granted the same benefits when the district chief decided to modify their taxes in accordance with their wages.[85]

Finally, the *falatiyya* (bandits) emerged in Qina Province during this period, carrying out the most radical and audacious form of resistance. They formed small lawless groups in almost every village and town in the province to attack government bureaucrats, disturb the province's security, and prevent the colonial ruling elite from enjoying their wealth. One of the most prominent topographical characteristics of Qina is that mountains border its villages and towns along the eastern and the western coasts of the Nile. Where the village ends, mountains begin, and it was in these mountains that the bandits found refuge and planned their operations. Bandit communities were fed by the fugitive peasants and factory workers who had escaped to hide in the mountains, where no village shaykh could capture them and return them by force to do the work they had run away from.

One night in 1846, a gang of bandits attacked the house of a tax collector and his brothers and stole government treasury money along with the property of the attacked family. The house was in the center of Samhud East, a big town located close to the western mountains with a large elite community and a weekly market. The gang killed one person, and some villagers were injured by accident in the process.[86] Meanwhile, the *falatiyya* of Karnak made the state-owned plantation managed by Salih Bey their constant target. They took advantage of the Luxor area's geography, which included Pharaonic temples and people's dwellings located in the heart of the mountains. This made it easier for people to vanish through the labyrinthian alleys of ancient ruins and houses and to disappear in the mountains after their attacks on the plantation. For public safety reasons, the plantation's watchmen were ordered to shoot at the gang only after sunset in the caves where they hid.[87] Some bandits from Qina even joined forces with fellows from other Upper Egyptian provinces and co-plotted operations against bureaucrats outside their own localities. This was the case when the state-owned plantation managed by Hasan Bey and the house of the tax collector in Asyut were attacked by a gang from Qina and elsewhere in the southern provinces.[88]

Because bandits were a high-profile security matter of utmost urgency, in 1846 the regime had all the governors, department heads, district chiefs, shaykhs, and other bureaucrats of Qina Province sign a pledge in shari'a court. It legally bound them to shoot the *falatiyya* and arrest them wherever they were found, dead or alive. The pledge exempted the signatories from the blood money, owed according to shari'a law, to the murdered bandits' families. If caught alive, the bandit was to be crucified or sent for hard labor to Alexandria, and those villagers who granted them refuge were to receive the exact same punishment.[89]

For many dark years, Haridi al-Rujayl, or Haridi the Petite Man, posed the most disturbing threat to the province's officials with his armed group of dozens of bandits, who largely targeted the properties of Turkish bureaucrats. Haridi gathered his group of rebels and felons in an audacious fashion: whenever he passed by corvée laborers doing public work, he would call out and take a few of them before the very eyes of the village shaykhs. In this way, he added about thirty-five men from different villages to his group, largely from the village of al-Samata, and equipped them with guns. He was often seen with his armed fellows, and he stole cows and donkeys from villages and sold them in the north to purchase the guns. Village shaykhs feared his name and did not dare to approach his men to capture them; they could only inform the Turkish governor of the province that his power was increasing. Wherever he went, Haridi was followed by orders from the vice general inspector of Upper Egypt for his arrest. Haridi once claimed that he met with Muhammad 'Ali Pasha himself during his visit to Isna and that the pasha pardoned all his old crimes, exempted him from any obligations toward the government, and gave Haridi continued permission to do whatever he wished in the province. This was a fabricated story that the vice general inspector furiously rejected, still insisting on his capture.[90] In 1846, Haridi and his gang mounted a big operation against Muhammad Agha, a bureaucrat working for the state plantation in the village of al-Samata, home of many of Haridi's men. At night, they attacked the bureaucrat's house, stole furniture, weapons, money, and more. Upon reporting the incident, the government summoned Haridi, his younger brother, and five of their fellow bandits for interrogation.

Haridi defended himself. He started by thanking and praising God and Muhammad 'Ali Pasha. Then, he asserted that, first of all, his brother was too young to be involved in such a crime. He again repeated the fabricated story of meeting with Muhammad 'Ali Pasha, who pardoned his old crimes, and confessed that this was one of these old crimes that he had already repented of and the pasha had already forgiven. He admitted that he did go to the village of al-Samata with the five bandits to steal things from houses, but they did not target the bureaucrat's house on purpose and did not realize that it was among the raided places. He added that they had already sold everything they stole and nothing remained to return. He concluded his confession by thanking God again for redeeming him from old sins and Muhammad 'Ali Pasha for forgiving him. Only one month after the interrogation, Haridi and fifty to sixty armed men from Qina, Isna, and Asyut attacked the local market of Dishna, which was a large urban center where many state enterprises existed, and extorted tributes. The district chief had to go himself to the market to restore security. In a troubled colony, Haridi the Petite Man's name continued to show up in government papers in disturbing ways, where he remained the ultimate undefeatable threat to the province's settler and local elite and the government of Muhammad 'Ali Pasha.[91]

For Muhammad 'Ali Pasha, Upper Egypt was no more than a perfectly exploited, yet well peripheralized, colony. It was indeed a part of a centralized government, but it was never a component of a homogenous state—a fact to which its massive rebellions and daily actions of subaltern resistance testify. After the pasha died, his successors kept the south in the same marginalized position. In the following decades, as hegemonic Europeans arrived in the scene, Qina Province's discontent expanded.

FOUR

A *"Communist" Revolution*

1848–1882

In 1864, a massive Egyptian revolt once again erupted from Qina Province. Ahmad al-Tayyib did what his father had done forty years earlier during Muhammad 'Ali's reign: he led tens of thousands of peasants in an attempt to overthrow the government. The rebels attacked the steamboats of European merchants, Turkish plantation owners, and rich Copts and, more important, called for the redistribution of wealth. Originally from the village of Salimiyya, al-Tayyib, like his father, was a Sufi mystic and self-proclaimed messiah. He used religious rhetoric to mobilize the rural masses who were discontented, this time, over foreign commercial activities, massive land losses, and forced labor. An English traveler, Lady Lucie Duff-Gordon, was staying in the province to recover from an illness at the moment the revolt broke out and recorded the event:

> [A] Prussian boat had been attacked, all on board murdered, and the boat burnt; then ... ten villages were in open revolt.... A crazy darweesh has made a disturbance.... He did as his father likewise did ... by repeating one of the appellations of God, such as "ya Lateef," three thousand times every night for three years, which rendered him invulnerable. He then made friends with a Jinn, who taught him many other tricks.... He then deluded the people of the Desert [the mountain *falatiyya* bandits], giving himself out as "El-Mahdee" [messiah] ... and proclaimed a revolt against the Turks. Three villages below Kiné [Qina] ... took part in the disturbance.[1]

The Englishwoman described al-Tayyib as "a communist." Military steamships soon arrived from Cairo to terminate the rebels, chopping their bodies with the very axes that the rebel leaders had used as weapons.[2]

Many world historians describe the mid-nineteenth century as a period of "informal" imperialism. Without military colonization, Great Britain imposed its hegemony over vast territories of the world in the name of modernity, a main component of which was the market economy. The informal empire embarked on a mission to replace traditional economies with modern ones. It introduced free trade, private property, and foreign experts to lands that were eager to taste the trappings of civilization. Despite their fundamental disagreement on matters of global imperialism, liberal and Marxist theories agree on one presumption: the empire's market was a success. It altered peoples' lives, for better or worse, in the dominated regions long before the advent of armed occupation.[3] This chapter argues that empire's modernity did affect people's lives in Upper Egypt, but only because it failed. For the subalterns of the south, the success of the market during this period is a mere myth. Trade liberalization, reformed landownership codes, and foreign investments proved incompetent at achieving their professed goals in the south of Egypt. Moreover, they generated sweeping subaltern rebellion against any symbols of market modernity.

Liberal historians of British imperialism endorse the concept of informal empire and largely use it to praise the efficiency of English domination over the world economy. Niall Ferguson differentiates between "direct" and "indirect" rule of an imperial polity over other territories and asserts that Britain imposed successful indirect control in many parts of the world in the mid-nineteenth century and, thus, grew into an informal empire.[4] British liberalism assumed supremacy primarily through market means, in particular through free-trade agreements that it signed with subordinate polities.[5] Marxist theorists endorse the concept of informal empire, but for an entirely different reason: the critique of European capitalism. Marxist historians of the twentieth century adopted the notion of imperialism of free trade, ever since Ronald Robinson published his 1953 article that carried that title. Giovanni Arrighi—a Marxist and world-system theorist—asserts that in the mid-nineteenth century Britain was the sole world "hegemon," and its most successful imperialist strategy was trade liberalization.[6] Dependency theory also has long asserted that free-trade treaties were the essence of European capitalist domination. Unequal exchange took place between Western industrial cores and peripheral suppliers of raw material, resulting in the economic dependency and underdevelopment of the latter.[7]

Historiography of the mid-nineteenth-century Egypt asserts that the country fell under the hegemony of an informal British Empire, in a clear case of unequal exchange between an industrial core and an agricultural periphery. British textile industrialists sought raw cotton from Egypt and demanded that the regime in Cairo allow laissez-faire trade in order to open the Egyptian market to their manufactured commodities. To meet these demands, Cairo promulgated new laws and regulations to promote commercial agriculture and facilitate movement of European merchants in the north and south. It also invited foreign experts to manage or invest in modern ventures, including the Suez Canal and some coal-mining projects. This situation of dependency started when Britain subjugated Muhammad 'Ali to the Anglo-Turkish free-trade agreement of 1838. The succeeding regimes of Muhammad 'Ali's dynasty—the governments of Khedives 'Abbas (r. 1848–54), Sa'id (r. 1854–63), and Isma'il (r. 1863–79)—applied policies of economic liberalization under similar imperial pressure.[8]

Whereas these important arguments are true for Cairo and the Delta, Upper Egypt has a different story to tell in this context. An informal empire never achieved full domination in the south, and its failure brought about a great revolution. This chapter tells six stories about a dysfunctional market and resented imperial modernity in Qina Province. These stories revolve around steamers, plantations, and coal mines and how these major players in market change devastated the lives of the province's subalterns. The protagonists of these stories are the peasants, laborers, and women of Qina Province. The village of Salimiyya—where the 1864 revolt broke out—is the stage where they mostly take place.

STEAMSHIPS ON THE NILE

The first aspect of market modernity that Qina Province encountered was free trade. From his first month in office, Sa'id Pasha—son of Muhammad 'Ali—showed a faithful commitment to opening Egyptian markets to European merchants. Sa'id generally embraced liberal economic policies and applied them extensively in all aspects, but he started with commerce.[9] He urged his government officials across Egypt to strictly apply existing free-trade treaties and facilitate the activities of foreign businesses. In July 1854, immediately after assuming power, the pasha issued the following decree to his bureaucrats: "Despite the obligation of free trade as stipulated by the treaties, ... problems arose in transactions in some districts that violated freedom and principles. From now on, it is [your] duty to ease transactions and [to prevent] dishonesty and difficulties between the buyer and the seller."[10]

Carried on their modern, fast steamships, European merchants quickly found their way to Qina Province in the age of open global markets. While passenger steamers carried tourists and mail past Qina every fortnight, commercial steamers uploaded and offloaded cargos all week long.[11] European merchants turned the province into a big vendor of one main cash crop: grain. They also traded in the commodities of the Sudanese caravans that arrived in the province. British, French, Austrian, and American consuls and consular agents spread out through Qina's towns and villages to carry out their commerce, and they usually hired elite Copts to assist them. A community of Europeans soon settled in the towns of Luxor and Qus, where they bought large houses and employed cheap local laborers.[12] Greek merchants were the largest foreign community in the province, to the degree that they received special attention from the state; Cairo sent endless decrees to the governor of Qina to ensure their security and safety.[13]

The government exerted every effort to facilitate foreign business, while repressing the natives of Qina. When provincial officials were recruiting corvée labor for public works, they also recruited cheap workers to provide private services to the European consuls and consular agents. In one incident, a consul sent a request to the governor of Qina for four laborers to construct his ships. The governor responded immediately. He only had to confirm that the consul, not the treasury, would be responsible for paying their wages, lest those workers confuse this job with government tasks and turn to him for payments. Similarly, officials granted another European merchant a number of camel drivers for his trade with the Sudan. While European merchants enjoyed all the financial benefits that came with hiring cheap local labor, these laborers did not enjoy any financial privileges from employment by foreigners. Their wages were no higher than those paid by government or local employers, because their payments were determined by the existing local rates. The agent of the French consul hired workers from Salimiyya and other villages for his businesses, and, apparently due to low wages, they were late in paying their taxes to the government. The guild chiefs and shaykhs of the laborers' villages were held responsible for collecting these overdue taxes.[14]

Similarly, European consuls and consular agents paid unfair prices for the grain they collected from the province. Thus, wholesale merchants sometimes organized strikes to negotiate fairer deals. In 1858, a huge dispute erupted between the agent of the French consul and the town of Farshut's grain wholesalers, who refused to load his ships. In the local markets of the town, the agent had made a business deal with the wholesalers to collect the grain of surrounding villages, but they discovered that he had paid them a very low price and they refused to send the grain to his waiting ships at the nearby port. The agent insisted that the local merchants did not have the right to strike because local business customs specified that the payment made in the market at the time of the purchase should be irreversible. The local merchants still insisted that they had not received what they deserved.[15]

At times, exporting grain resulted in severe food shortages, which forced the Egyptian state to violate free-trade agreements and apply strong interventionist measures. In 1853, the government issued a decree that prohibited the export of grain to Europe when there was need for it inside the country. The decree stated that the people had recently suffered from grain shortage and a radical increase in prices because most of the harvest had been shipped to Alexandria to be exported. Thus, the decree banned European consuls and their citizens from purchasing any grain, either from the provinces or Cairo's markets. The governors of provinces were ordered to prevent activities of European merchants in their respective areas of jurisdiction.[16]

The Egyptian state, in fact, was in fierce competition with European merchants for Qina's grain. The state collected taxes from the province in cash or in the form of grain submitted to the state's numerous storehouses in the province. The government relied on this grain for different purposes, including sustaining the supply to Cairo and the Hijaz and as partial payment of labor wages. Prohibited from pricing grain by the Anglo-Turkish free-trade agreement—as this went against the principles of the market economy—the state closely followed the rise and fall of prices in Qina's local markets by preparing lists every ten days. The government attempted to encourage peasants to submit their grain as taxes instead of selling to Europeans by buying it at market prices. In other words, peasants used their grain to pay taxes because the government paid the rather high market prices, which covered a significant portion of the peasants' tax burden but left them with little of the food staple.[17]

This competition between the Egyptian state and European commercial steamships over Qina's grain did not benefit the peasants of the province. Coptic and Muslim wholesale grain merchants profited from credit arrangements with the peasant farmers: the merchants usually extended credit to peasants and collected the harvest at the end of the season, two to four months after the advanced payment. According to shari'a law, this type of credit was permissible through *salam* contracts. Therefore, in most cases profit went to the moneylender rather than the peasant.[18] At this time, grain was almost the peasants' only cash crop in demand at a decent price in the global market, so they sold grain despite needing it for their own sustenance. The households of Qina were emptied of wheat, and wheat bread became precious—offered to guests as an expression of generosity—and baking a loaf of bread with a handful of wheat became a source of pride for affluent families. An ever-increasing number of peasant women sued their husbands in shari'a court for not providing the family with enough staple foodstuffs.[19]

Political resentment soon grew in the province against the presence of foreign merchants. Raids on European steamships occurred almost every day. Some *falatiyya* bandits specialized in raiding the commercial boats of Greek merchants that shipped the grain of the province to the north. In one case from 1859, at midnight some Nile bandits shot at the commercial boat of a Greek *khawaja* by the name of Georgie Anton (at the time, *khawaja* was a title used for Europeans). They attacked the boat crew and stole money and goods from them.[20] Similarly, as soon as it arrived at the town of Isna, the loaded commercial boat of another *khawaja* was raided on its way from Aswan to Qina.[21] Nile boat captains, who lost their businesses to the steamships of European merchants, turned into *falatiyya*, raiding plantations of the upper class and stealing from government bureaucrats. At the coffeehouse of a freed slave in the city of Qina, a bandit by the name of 'Uthman stole the attire and purse full of cash of a bureaucrat. 'Uthman was a member of a gang of bandits who had been committing robbery and escaping from jail for years. He was, in fact, a former sailboat captain who apparently had lost his business in Nile transportation due to the dominance of steamers.[22]

In 1858, an uprising led by *falatiyya* broke out in Isna and forced Sa'id Pasha to reform the entire administrative system in the province. The bandits apparently threatened or directly attacked many Europeans, who reacted by randomly shooting at the inhabitants. As usual, after completing the operation the rebels escaped to the mountains, where they hid from the government. The police failed to arrest them, and the governor of Isna lost his job for such incompetence. Sa'id Pasha became so concerned about political unrest in Qina that he reformed the province's administrative system by merging Qina and Isna Provinces under one governor and replacing all Turkish district chiefs with Egyptian ones. To ease his task of inspecting for disobedience inside the newly created province—extending in great length along the two banks of the Nile—the new governor was granted a steamship for his own personal use. In addition, a special army was brought from the north and put under the new governor's command. Sa'id Pasha affirmed that the primary task of the new governor was ensuring the safety of Europeans and guarding public security. As for Europeans who might commit crimes, such as shooting at the province's inhabitants, the pasha added that they should be handled gently and escorted to their respective consuls.[23]

The story did not end here. The pasha's new system would not entirely succeed at subjugating the rebels. Subaltern resentment against European merchants would continue, reaching its peak moment in the 1864 revolt.

PRIVATE PROPERTY, LOSING PROPERTY

The second pillar of the alleged market modernity that Qina Province encountered was the reformed law of private property in agricultural land. The advent of these modern codes in the province only helped elites to win property rights, while peasants lost them. The codes expanded the propertied class in Qina to include Turkish and native government bureaucrats, Europeans, Coptic agents of European consuls, village notables, and shari'a law scholars. These beneficiaries accumulated vast plantations at the expense of thousands of dispossessed peasants, who were in the process turned into seasonal laborers on these plantations. The village of Salimiyya, where the 1864 revolt later erupted, fell under the grip of many prominent members of the growing propertied class.

Sa'id Pasha promulgated the new land code of 1858, presenting it as a great step toward the country's modernization. Before this law, the lands of all villages were theoretically the property of the state. After Muhammad 'Ali died, and under the idle, decentralized regime of his grandson 'Abbas Pasha, provincial bureaucrats seized state-owned lands from peasants and grew as a new class of large landowners.[24] Sa'id's law, known as al-La'iha al-Sa'idiyya, was the product of internal pressures by provincial bureaucrats and village notables to consolidate and legalize their properties, coupled with the empire's advocacy of private property as a sign of modernity.[25] In drafting the new law, Sa'id Pasha, in fact, consulted with the governors of Upper and Lower Egypt and with high-ranking bureaucrats, who were mainly interested in consolidating their new properties. The law was finally issued, regulating ownership of three main categories of land: *kharajiya,* or common peasants' land; *ab'adiyya* plantations, or the previously uncultivated state-owned land leased to government officials for reclamation at a reduced tax rate; and *'uhda* plantations, or land that the state confiscated from runaway peasants who had fled after failing to pay taxes or to escape corvée labor.

The new legal code finally granted the bureaucrats absolute property rights to the *ab'adiyya* plantations. It also opened the door for sales of more of those plantations to government officials, Europeans, and whoever could reclaim them and pay taxes on them. Public auctions were held all year in Qina Province to lease or sell *ab'adiyya* plantations, and bureaucrats won thousands of acres by outbidding peasants. In one auction in the village of Salimiyya, the governor of Qina won a plantation of about two hundred acres. Some peasants in the village bid against him, claiming that this land was originally theirs, but they lost the auction to the influential governor.[26] More important, the new law gave bureaucrats and village shaykhs property rights to the *'uhda* state-owned plantations seized from runaway peasants. It decreed that if a peasant was proved absent from his land for three years, he would lose his property rights, and whoever held and cultivated it for five years would gain the right to keep it. Peasants returned to their villages to find their lands confiscated and registered under other people's names, usually state officials. Whole villages were transformed into *'uhda* plantations, and the new code gave the administrators of those plantations absolute ownership rights to them.[27]

The governor of the city of Isna, 'Abd al-Ghafur Effendi, owned three plantations of hundreds of acres each. The effendi maintained a religious and pious lifestyle, as he "abstained from mundane matters and sought charitable deeds" by funding the construction of the great mosque of Qus. Nonetheless, he was a corrupt official who took advantage of his position to employ local laborers and use slaves without paying them wages and also to delay, or completely avoid, paying taxes. For instance, he drafted slave workers from the neighboring gunpowder factory, owned by the state, to perform temporary jobs on his land.[28] Furthermore, he acted as a moneylender, giving out loans to peasants and subsequently appropriating their lands and evicting them when they failed to repay their debts. Outraged by such actions, the farmers of Karnak, who had mortgaged four hundred acres to the effendi and had already paid back part of their debt in cash and in-kind, raised many petitions to the central government to stop his attempts to illicitly evict them. Other peasants avenged their lost properties by less legal means; Farshut peasants released their cattle and sheep to graze in the effendi's fields and damage part of his harvest.[29]

As the owner of several plantations of thousands of acres, Bishara 'Ubayd, a Copt who was the agent of the French consul for many years, was without a doubt the wealthiest person in the province. His medium-size and large plantations expanded in almost every village in Qina. In public auctions of only one year, 1862, Bishara purchased 1,654 acres in Qus, followed by another 1,166 in seven different villages. The village of Salimiyya strongly felt Bishara's presence, as he purchased more than 500 acres there. State officials in the province authorized him to appoint new mayors (*'umda*s) for the villages where he owned most of the land. The mayors' primary job was to force the peasants to evacuate and deliver their plots to the new landlord. In Salimiyya, Bishara hired laborers to work the plantations for low wages, insufficient even to pay for their taxes. Furthermore, Bishara established control over a significant share of the province's trade, as he owned commercial boats and collected grain from wholesalers to ship north.[30]

A small number of Europeans owned vast plantations in Qina and enjoyed immense authority in the province. The French administrator of the sulfur mine of Qina, *khawaja* Monier, was probably the largest foreign landowner in the province. In 1862, Monier bid at auction for a 3,318-acre plantation in a district rich in sugarcane fields. He paid a very low price of only three piasters per acre. He also made a small purchase of another 11 acres from the peasants of the same district, but he had problems with this transaction. The peasants apparently complained to the government that he forced or tricked them into selling the land. The state declined the peasants' claim and deemed the Frenchman's property deed valid.[31] Monier resided in a palace in the city of Luxor, to the north of his plantations, and he appropriated a piece of land in the same city to build storehouses, horse stables, a garden, and a waterwheel. He drafted local construction workers and artisans to erect these buildings without paying them wages. Some of the city's inhabitants disputed his possession, asserting that the land was their property. Investigations revealed that he had obtained a permit from local state officials. In the middle of the dispute, Monier contracted an illness and had to travel north to receive treatment. Probably happy with receiving this news, the inhabitants of the city thought that he had gone back to his country to die there, but he soon returned to the province to buy more land.[32]

The new law also allowed native village notables, particularly mayors and shaykhs, to join this new class of large landowners. As the village shaykhs and mayors seized the land of absent peasants and actively participated in public auctions, winning medium-size plantations, they also extended credit to peasants as an indirect way to eventually seize their plots when the chances came.[33] The village of Salimiyya witnessed one of the most acute cases of conflict over mortgaged lands between creditors, who were village rulers, and indebted peasants. The village mayor, Hasan 'Abd Allah, and his father and uncles held 337 acres that peasants mortgaged to them for cash and grain. The heirs of the owners now claimed their right to the land, as they were ready to pay back the mortgage. The mayor not only refused to return the land but also petitioned for guaranteed government support in his case.[34]

Shari'a scholars also constituted a new class of medium-size landowners in this process. The regime rewarded them for their collaboration, after the government issued new shari'a law provisions and *fatwas* supporting the new civil land code and bestowing legitimacy upon it.[35] The same year the land code was promulgated, in 1858, Sa'id Pasha granted Shaykh Muhammad Abu Shanab, a Hanafi jurist following the state's school of Islamic law, a plantation of one hundred acres in Qina Province. Another shaykh, Shaykh 'Uthman Taha, owned thirty-seven acres in Farshut that he rented to peasants.[36] Corrupt shari'a judges, particularly in Qina Province, were rewarded for their collaboration with the provincial bureaucracy because they registered new land titles in the Islamic court, as it was the only place to obtain property deeds.[37] The wealth of shari'a judges in the province was second only to that of bureaucrats, and when the judges died they left their heirs great fortunes.[38]

The plantation owners managed their land by using dispossessed peasants as tenants or seasonal laborers. As tenants, these peasants held sharecropping contracts that stipulated that they give a set percentage of the harvest every year to the landlord, who sometimes provided them with capital and machinery.[39] Also, hundreds of landless farmers in each village gathered every season, sought jobs on plantations near and far, and then returned to their villages with their small wages. The peasants in the village where Husayn Bey, the vice chief of the district of Qus, had his plantation, boycotted the temporary jobs he offered because he frequently annexed their trees, waterwheels, and pieces of other farms around his properties. Thus, his plantation manager had to recruit seasonal laborers from nearby villages to work on the plantation. The peasant laborers tilled the land and also worked in the sugar mills attached to it. Some worked for the whole year, while others worked for only one or two seasons. The plantation manager paid them their wages in wheat, maize, and beans and in small amounts of cash, which they needed to pay the state dues. The cash wages the peasant laborers received never provided them with enough capital to save and buy back their lost lands.[40]

MINES, *KHAWAJA*S, AND WORKERS

Foreign experts and capitalist enterprises also quickly found their way to Qina Province, carrying the dream of modernity to the south. But their utter incompetence and inefficiency were only equaled by the misery they inflicted on the laborers of the province. The liberal market created by informal imperialism again failed here, breaking down the legend of an ever-successful European capitalism in the nineteenth century—a myth that many prominent economic historians present as conventional wisdom.[41] The globalization of the informal empire pressed the Egyptian regime to search for sources of energy to operate new technologies, such as steamships, railways, modern factories, and much more. It was the age of coal. It was also the age of "trust" in "foreign experts" to deliver modernity.[42] The coal mines of Qina Province were essential sites of venture capitalism, where European experts were entrusted with the passage to the modern. As the resistance of Qina's oppressed workers in the mines mounted, the venture rapidly failed.

In 1820, Louis Michel, a French scientist, suggested to Muhammad 'Ali Pasha that he should search for soft coal in Upper Egypt. When Michel had come with the French expedition to Egypt more than a quarter of a century earlier, in 1798, the scientist had heard that there were potentially soft coal deposits there. At the time, Muhammad 'Ali powered his modern manufacturing only with oxen imported from the Sudan, so he welcomed the idea. The pasha hired Michel as the chief commander of a search mission in the deserts of Qina Province and supported him with the facilities needed to launch mining. Initially, the project was rather limited, as Michel was sent to the excavation sites with only one assistant. The project did not yield fruit for many years, yet it continued to receive the state's support through more funds, miners, and tools. Some Austrian engineers came to join the project but they were discouraged from journeying to Upper Egypt by the excessively hot weather. The state kept hiring one French commander after another with no satisfying results, until the pasha died without ever seeing one good piece of soft coal from those mines.[43]

In 1858, the project gained new momentum that brought it to life again under Sa'id Pasha. Rather than merely hiring foreign experts to manage the mine, Sa'id made the *khawaja*s (Europeans) the state's business partners.[44] The purpose of the enterprise was to search for soft coal in the eastern desert between the province of Qina and its port of Qusayr. Employing about one hundred people, including foreign experts, clerks, mining workers, camel drivers, and water carriers, it grew into a relatively big enterprise for its time and place. *Khawaja* De Francis was the state's main partner, but he stayed in Cairo and hired a deputy miner, *khawaja* Barbarous, to manage the site. Although the terms of the contract of this "company" are not clear in the records, it seems that De Francis contributed only his expertise, without a share of the capital. The state granted a small steamship to De Francis so he could go to Qina Province to inspect the mine. The workers were recruited from the villages and towns of Qina, and the chief camel driver, Shaykh Zayid Khamis, was responsible for hiring camel drivers to deliver laborers to the excavation site in the desert. The governor of Qina was officially the highest authority in the enterprise, as he allocated all the needed funds and resources to the mine from the storehouses of the province.[45]

The taxpayers of Qina Province carried the financial burden of this costly enterprise. All the provisions were supplied by Qina's storehouses, where peasants, artisans, merchants, and other social groups had to submit their dues to the state treasury in-kind or in cash. The mine administrators requested their daily provisions from the governor of Qina, who ordered them from the reserves or collected them from the people of the province according to strict deadlines. Such provisions included bread, butter, lentils, baskets, mining tools, wood, water skins, cash for wages, transport fares, and so on.[46] Camel drivers regularly carried shipments of provisions to the mine and were paid twelve piasters per qantar. A group of camel drivers had to write a petition to the governor of Qina in order to receive allowances of food supplies for the trip in addition to their wages. The governor agreed to this request but subtracted the food they received from their wages or from the transport fares the state paid.[47]

Qina residents formed the workforce at the mine. Although the number of workers in the mine at any given time did not exceed a hundred, the mine affected the lives of thousands of laborers throughout its years of operation. A system of regular replacement substituted new laborers for fatigued ones, making it almost impossible for the laborers of the province to escape serving in the mine. Through forced conscription builders, blacksmiths, carpenters, and water carriers were all sent to the mine. They received wages along with food and transportation supplies. Each subdistrict in Qina had to contribute its share of laborers. Conscription took place through the guild chief, or *shaykh al-ta'ifa*. For example, when there was a need for carpenters, the chief carpenter, or *shaykh al-najjarin,* in each subdistrict was officially ordered to send an assigned number of carpenters from the area under his chiefdom.

Individual artisans in each guild were registered by name in the official state files, area by area. This meant that each artisan was requested by name when it was his turn to serve in the mine. According to the applied labor law, workers in state enterprises and public works had to be replaced every given period, usually a fortnight, before they lost their energy and became too fatigued to work. Workers in the mine were replaced at regular intervals, but not all at the same time. Some workers preferred permanent wage labor at the mine and expressed their wish to stay for full-time jobs, which they were mostly permitted to do.[48]

After the guild shaykh conscripted him, a mine worker had to undertake a long, hazardous journey to reach the excavation site in the middle of the eastern desert, carry out the assigned tasks, and, if he was lucky, return home safely. First, he had to carry his own work tools, if required, and deliver himself to Hamad Muhammad, the camel driver of the mine from the ʿAbabida tribe, who was officially responsible for delivering him and was acquainted with all the routes in the desert due to his Bedouin origins. The worker was provided with food for the road, namely one qantar of crackers (*buqsumat*). He had to sign a receipt upon receiving this snack in order to have it deducted from his wages. When the worker arrived at the mine, the camel driver handed him to the chief miner, who then would send a letter to the governor of Qina confirming the delivery. The chief miner then assigned the newly arrived worker his tasks at once. After that, there were two possible scenarios: he either stayed to finish the job and, in rare cases, liked it and applied to be hired full-time, or he ran away. Running away was a fatal decision if it was not arranged with secretive help from an expert camel driver. It was easy to get lost and die in the vast desert. Even the most skilled camel drivers sometimes got lost in the desert on their way to or from the digging site. If the worker had enough luck, he would be replaced after a reasonable period before his physical condition deteriorated. Eventually, he returned home to his family with his small wage in hand.[49]

In one incident, workers protested the irregularity of their pay. Wages were suspended on some days because of long pauses in digging. It was not possible for the miners to find side jobs to make up for the lost wages; there was nothing around them but desert. Thus, they complained and requested that they get paid for all weekdays regardless of the current state of work. The governor of Qina affirmed that it was the responsibility of the enterprise to find them tasks to do on a daily basis and to pay them regular wages. He established new rules for regular payment and sent them to the *khawaja*. The rules entailed paying wages for all weekdays, except for the weekly holiday, Friday. Eventually, the mine's administration decided to pay the workers on a monthly basis, probably to discourage them from running away.[50]

As at all mining sites in the world in the nineteenth century, safety measures were a crucial problem. Rates of injury and accidental death were high among mine workers. In Qina's coal mine, the foreign miners chose a specific point to excavate and they trained the workers to carry out the digging. One day, a disaster almost happened when the walls of the pit collapsed on the workers. Luckily, nobody was injured. This accident disturbed Sa'id Pasha, and he issued strict orders to the *khawaja* to find a safe method of digging. Interestingly, the *khawaja* was asked to study the issue with the workers in order to reach the best technique. He was ordered to agree with them on a secure method for their own safety as well as for expediting the work. The governor of Qina directed *khawaja* De Francis to "think with them [the workers] about the appropriate technique until you reach an easy one . . . that will not delay the course of work or cause any harm to the workers."[51] They decided to build wooden walls for the pit during the digging process to prevent the collapse of the sand walls. De Francis confirmed to Sa'id Pasha that the construction of such walls was the best method reached by his deputy, Barbarous. European mines commonly applied it during this period. Wood was shipped from Cairo to Qina's storehouses specifically for this purpose, with firm instructions to Barbarous to use it for ensuring workers' safety.[52]

As time passed with no signs of progress, Sa'id Pasha showed his dissatisfaction with the work of De Francis, who was asking for more time and state support to finish the search for soft coal. A few weeks after the collapse of the pit's walls, and without waiting for the work at the site to be finished, the *khawaja* began digging another pit. The governor of Qina requested an explanation for the waste of resources. The difficult search for coal eventually failed to yield any fruit. Sa'id Pasha finally issued a royal decree giving De Francis a deadline: before the beginning of the holy month of Ramadan of 1858, he was directed to present satisfying samples or terminate the search. The decree stated that the government would neither accept the allegations of De Francis and his accompanying Egyptian miners that soft coal existed in the province, nor respond to their request to continue the search at the state's expense.[53] The venture was closed down six months after the pit collapse incident. The only losers in the entire venture were the people of Qina Province, who had to pay for the failure of foreign experts and the wrong decisions of a liberalized state.

The coal enterprise was not the only failed capitalist enterprise in Qina. The Egyptian state ran a sulfur mine in the mountains close to the Qusayr port, and the product of this mine was processed in the four state-owned gunpowder factories in the province. This mine was also managed by European experts, namely the notorious Monsieur Monier, who owned large plantations in Qina's villages, jointly with Italian miners. Foreign experts were state business partners and, according to the company contract, they enjoyed the right to a quarter of the mine's revenue. The sulfur mine also hired Qina's local laborers, who endured hazardous conditions similar to that of their fellow workers in the coal mine and who resented these conditions just like them. In the late 1860s, when the sulfur mine project showed signs of failure, European consuls and newspapers harshly attacked it because its product lacked quality. The failed Italian miners gradually deserted the site and returned to their country.[54]

A "COMMUNIST" REVOLT

As the discontent of peasants and laborers in Qina Province accumulated, a massive revolt broke out in the province. In 1864, one year after Sa'id Pasha died and Isma'il Pasha came to the throne, the uprising erupted. Although the revolt seems almost identical to the 1820 revolt that had occurred under Muhammad 'Ali, particularly in having religious leaders who used spiritual rhetoric to mobilize the subalterns, it had completely different conditions and causes.

Two new conditions in the global market galvanized the uprising. First, the years of the American Civil War (1861–65) tremendously increased British demand for Egyptian cotton. Sa'id and Isma'il both capitalized on this opportunity to maximize their profits in European markets. The war raised cotton prices in Alexandria, and exports surged to 2.5 million qantars in 1865. As a result, the state placed its focus on cotton cultivation in the north, the Delta, and economically marginalized Upper Egypt in the process. Although Qina Province was traditionally a cotton producer, the cultivation of this cash crop shifted to the Delta due to the latter region's proximity to the world's hegemon in Europe.[55]

Second, wheat, the other main cash crop of the country, which largely came from Upper Egypt, was facing fierce competition from the rising producers in Europe and the Americas. The grain of Europe and the Americas generally witnessed a boom due to the application of modern technologies in agricultural machinery, including steam engines used in irrigation. More important, despite preaching laissez-faire policies, Britain and other unhappy European countries applied protectionist policies instead to rescue their agricultural producers from outside competition.[56] Thus, many European governments, including Britain, introduced so-called Corn Laws that closed the door to grain imports.[57] 'Ali Mubarak, the Egyptian statesman and chronicler, lamented this reality: "Farming in European, American, and other countries advanced and their grain production grew. They fulfilled their needs and their demand for Egyptian wheat decreased ... which would harm the people of Upper Egypt."[58]

Before the outbreak of the 1864 revolt, unrest in Qina Province simmered in various forms. In the year of the revolt, attacks against foreigners increased, leading an American merchant residing in Luxor to demand that the government enhance security in the town. Apparently he raised the issue after an assault took place in the area where foreigners lived. He complained that the watchmen (*ghafirs*) in the areas surrounding the town were insufficient, both in number and in effectiveness, to protect the inhabitants. The Supreme Court in Cairo—functioning also as a legislature—had issued a decree ordering provincial governors to assign capable watchmen and to have village shaykhs and watchmen sign legal documents making them fully responsible for maintaining public safety. The American resident called for a rigorous application of this decree.[59]

Some villagers refused to vacate their land and give it over to new landlords—bureaucrats and foreigners—who bought it in auctions.[60] Refusing to pay rent to the new landlords also became a common practice among peasants, so landowners resorted to asking the government's help to collect rent.[61] Another common practice was to block irrigation water from reaching the lands of the new landlords, especially Europeans or agents of European consuls, by damaging dikes and embankments. The peasants of the village of Marashda, for instance, blocked the canal that carried water to the land of the agent of the Prussian consul, so his land missed its turn in receiving irrigation water that season and remained fallow. The consul complained to the governor of Qina, who ordered peasants to open the canal, but it was too late.[62] In addition, armed *falatiyya* gangs raided the houses of village shaykhs to steal cash, clothes, jewelry, and the like, and they did not hesitate to shoot at the shaykhs and their family members.[63]

The governor of Isna Province, the notorious 'Abd al-Ghafur Effendi, faced aggressive resistance from peasants. The peasants of a village where one of his plantations was located attacked his land to prevent the seasonal laborers he brought from other villages from farming it, and some of them damaged the crops. After Abd al-Ghafur died, the peasants of Karnak seized back their lands from his plantation and even refused to sign a lease and pay rent or enter into a sharecropping agreement. Moreover, they refused to pay the remaining taxes. The manager of the plantation had to ask for the help of the chief of the district of Qus to deal with this situation.[64] In another case, peasants let their cattle and sheep graze on Bishara 'Ubayd's land in order to ruin his harvest. He lost the produce of eight acres this way in the village of Faw.[65]

The coal and sulfur mines produced severe discontent among Qina's families. Many workers did not come back from the mines, and their families never heard from them again. They either died of fatigue in the mines or got lost in the desert while attempting to run away. One way these families reacted was by filing lawsuits against the guild or village shaykhs who had recruited the workers. The brother of Ahmad Isma'il, from the village of Kalahin, disappeared after he was drafted to work in the sulfur mine. Ahmad heard rumors about the death of his missing brother, so he sued his village shaykh in the Supreme Court in Cairo. The shaykh argued that this worker in fact had run away only two days after his arrival at the mine, and an intensive search for him had not yielded results.[66]

The four state-owned gunpowder factories in the towns of Qina Province did not escape the wave of revenge, not only for their connection with the sulfur mine but also for oppressing workers. To make things worse, the gunpowder factory of Karnak was close to the plantation of Abd al-Ghafur Effendi. The angry landless peasants surrounded the factory, and some of them were made wage laborers at the factory. The workers frequently ran away, but the government always brought them back if they had not gone far and forced them to continue working. The government's promises to pay their belated wages or even actually make payments did not always succeed in encouraging the workers to stay: many found a way to run off again despite all the efforts of the factory manager to monitor them. The factory was also the target of other forms of villagers' revenge. The cousin and land partner of the factory's chief donkey driver—who ran a group of five other drivers—embezzled thousands of piasters, among other things. The donkey driver was arrested and jailed until his cousin returned what he had taken.[67]

On the eve of the revolt in 1864, the village of Salimiyya was simmering with political unrest. The village was already one of the growing centers of the *falatiyya* gangs that attacked the watchmen of the village.[68] The peasants of Salimiyya, who were losing hundreds of acres to high-bidding bureaucrats in frequent auctions, tried legal channels to redeem their properties without success. Murad 'Abd al-Rahim owned only one acre of sugarcane, which apparently was not enough to sustain his family. He had to find a job as a construction worker on the irrigation steam engines of a state-owned plantation. One day, after he was late to work because he was finishing harvesting and pressing his sugarcane, the Turkish manager of the plantation, 'Abd Allah Agha, ruthlessly beat him. On his way back, Murad ran into two other farmers from his village who were drafting a complaint against the same Turkish manager, protesting his numerous crimes. When the state held a public auction to rent out some of the plantation's land, this manager collaborated with other partners to seize a medium-size piece of land in the village, winning it through fraud. The manager also supported many other village shaykhs in their efforts to seize lands and harvests from peasants. In addition, he beat some peasants, stopped their waterwheels to damage their crops, and put them in jail. Although Murad himself had nothing to do with any of these cases, he decided to put his signet on the complaint to take his own revenge.[69]

Finally, the revolt erupted. From Salimiyya, Ahmad al-Tayyib declared his messianic revelations and preached rebellion. In addition to the thousands of dispossessed villagers, al-Tayyib managed to mobilize *falatiyya* from their secret hiding places in the mountains. Like the 1820 revolt, this one deployed religious rhetoric and took on a spiritual tone, yet its aims went beyond alleviating high taxation or overthrowing Isma'il Pasha in Cairo. Rebels developed an angry discourse against the propertied class and foreign commercial domination, which is why Lady Duff-Gordon, the English eyewitness, suggested it was a "communist" uprising.

Unfortunately, Duff-Gordon's account is the only full record of the revolt available. One must note that the Lady's friends in Luxor were Turkish bureaucrats, an affluent shari'a law scholar, and a rich Copt who was a British consular agent, so she received and delivered a rather unsympathetic, and somewhat simplified, account of the revolt. 'Ali Mubarak, the state's chronicler of the period, also provided a politically biased and brief account. He characterized Ahmad al-Tayyib as a sinful, subversive man who led people to disobey God. He transgressed shari'a law, Mubarak suggested, because he disobeyed the "imam" of Muslims, that is, the khedive. He added that God had already punished the inhabitants of the village of Faw, who followed him, for their sins—when Ismaʿil Pasha sent soldiers and Turkish officers to kill most of them, destroy their houses, and confiscate their money.[70]

The revolt arose, Duff-Gordon recounted, from one incident involving a rich Copt and then spread throughout the province. Because Copts usually worked for Europeans, the poorer population commonly perceived rich Copts in a negative light. The story goes that the Copt in question owned a Muslim slave girl, who read the Qurʾan and was pious herself, and he wanted to take her as his concubine. She resisted because shariʿa law forbids a non-Muslim man to own a Muslim woman; and she went to Ahmad al-Tayyib, who offered the Coptic master money for her. "He refused it and insisted on his rights, backed by the government whereupon Ahmad proclaimed the revolt," wrote Duff-Gordon.[71] The rebels then attacked a boat that belonged to Greek merchants, but nobody was hurt, although Duff-Gordon asserted elsewhere that a party of forty rebels plundered the boat and killed the steersman. The state sent Fadl Pasha from Cairo by a fast steamship with an army to crush the rebels. Most people thought that al-Tayyib was killed in the battle, but in fact he managed to flee to the desert to take refuge with the *falatiyya*.

Duff-Gordon recorded the public opinion of different social groups about the rebellion. On the one hand, her friend who was the shariʿa law scholar, Shaykh Yusuf, visited Salimiyya and returned critical of the rebels: "Shaykh Yoosuf returned from a visit to Essalimeeyeh last night. He tells me the darweesh, Ahmad et-Teiyib, is not dead; he believed that he is a mad fanatic and a communist. He wants to divide all property equally, and to kill all the Ulama and destroy all theological teaching by learned men, and to preach a sort of revelation or interpretation of the Koran of his own. 'He would break up your pretty clock," said Yoosuf, "and give every man a broken wheel out of it; and so with all things.'"[72]

On the other hand, villagers were already expressing great discontent because Ismaʿil Pasha regulated the price of wheat, bringing about a famine in the province in the same year of the outbreak. Furthermore, Duff-Gordon explained, "only Cairo could do anything, and everything is done to please the Cairene at the expense of the Fellaheen [peasants]."[73] In irrigation, the use of steam engines and their coal was only for the rich: "The great folks get steam-engines, but the laborers work with no better implements than their bare hands and a rush basket, and it takes six men to do the work of one who has good tools."[74] Thus, even though some ordinary villagers did not participate in the revolt, because they believed that al-Tayyib was a madman, they supported the rebels' cause and spoke up about all forms of injustice. As Duff-Gordon recounted,

> One Mohammad, a most respectable, quiet young man, sat before me on the floor the other day, and told me the horrible details he had heard from those who had come up the river. "Thou knowest, O our lady that we are people of peace in this place; and behold, now, if one madman should come, and a few idle fellows go out to the Mountain (desert) with him, Efendeena will send his soldiers to destroy the place, and spoil our poor little girls, and hang us: is that right, O lady? And Ahmad-el-Berberee saw Europeans with hats in the steamer with Efendeena and the soldiers. Truly, in all the world none are miserable like us Arabs. The Turks beat us, and the Europeans hate us and say 'quite right.' By God, we had better lay our heads in dust (die), and let the strangers take our land and grow cotton for themselves. As for me, I am tired of this miserable life, and of fearing for my poor girls. Mohammad was really eloquent . . . he threw his meláyeh over his face and sobbed.[75]

As a fugitive exiled in the mountains, Ahmad al-Tayyib joined the *falatiyya* in their hiding places. His followers visited him there to listen to his speeches and receive instructions. Duff-Gordon affirmed that Isma'il Pasha himself came with steamboats and soldiers to terminate the uprising. The steamers were also supposed to evacuate all Europeans if things got out of control. Al-Tayyib's brother, Muhammad, and his father's father-in-law were taken prisoner. The pasha confiscated the properties of all suspected rebels, including innocent villagers. A village shaykh assisted the government in capturing the rebels. In 1865, Fadl Pasha, a Turk, perpetrated a massacre where he "had the men laid down by ten at a time, and *chopped* with the pioneers' axes." The Fadl Pasha murdered at least sixteen hundred men, women, and children. Upon crushing the revolt, every man, woman, or child related to Ahmad al-Tayyib by blood was taken in chains and jailed in the city of Qina.[76]

NO LAND FOR WOMEN

The revolt was crushed, and market modernity readily resumed undoing the lives of Qina Province's subalterns. It was women's turn. European Orientalists argued that modernization would improve the lives of oppressed women in "traditional" patriarchal societies, but this was not the case with new legal codes of private property. In 1869, Isma'il Pasha promulgated a new landownership law that deprived women of the right to inherit land, a right that shariʿa law had granted them for centuries. This law was an imitation of the contemporary British inheritance codes. Western legal modernity in the nineteenth century was paternalistic in nature, and when it made it to Qina's villages, this law severely hurt thousands of women who owned modest properties, sometimes as small as a fraction of an acre. After losing their parcels, women expressed resentment against their male relatives by various means.

With increasing British domination in northern Egypt and the consequent expansion of cotton cultivation, the Delta families involved in commercial agriculture ascended politically. They constituted the main political unit in a growing paternalist regime. Through the alleged political liberalization process, the male heads of plantation-owning families not only constituted the incumbents of the regime but also became the lawmakers in modern legislative institutions, namely the Council of Rules and the Parliament.[77] These men pressured the state to issue laws depriving women of land inheritance rights in Egypt. Copying the British code of primogeniture enshrined in the "family settlement" law,[78] the male landed elite of Egypt helped to promulgate a series of similar laws between the 1850s and the early 1880s. Ismaʿil Pasha's law of 1869 was the most oppressive to women.

The legal system had begun to turn against women from the time of Saʿid Pasha. During the first year of Saʿid's reign, before the pasha's 1858 land code was issued, women enjoyed full rights to land inheritance according to shariʿa as well as state civil laws. Many women from Qina Province were able to dispute attempts to disinherit them, and the state courts supported their claims. For instance, a woman named Fatima took control of the five acres her deceased husband had left to her, their three daughters, and son. She leased the land to farmers who cultivated it and paid its taxes to the government. When a cousin of her children attempted to assert his control over the parcel, she submitted a petition against him to the general inspector of Upper Egypt. The inspector supported her right to keep the land, provided that it was cultivated and its taxes were paid, and Fatima complied. In similar cases, the local officials always consulted the applied civil land code, which obliged them to grant land to widows.[79] Only a few months before the 1858 law was issued, Siʿda, a widow from the village of Samhud, asserted her rights and those of her two daughters and son to the land of her deceased husband, in a case she won against two male villagers. She went to the shariʿa court with her son to sue the two farmers who attempted to build a waterwheel on her land. The dispute was resolved and the family retained its property.[80]

The 1858 code began to dismantle this system of justice, as it allowed women to inherit land but deprived them of the right to control their plots. The Council of Rules (Majlis al-Ahkam), which issued the law, functioned both as the Supreme Court and legislature, and its members were males from local elite families, high-ranking Turkish bureaucrats, army and police officers, the state *mufti,* and eminent shari'a law scholars. From Qina Province, for example, Ahmad Bey Muhammad—a member of an upper-class landed family in the village of Abu Manna' and an army general—maintained a seat on the council. Provincial councils, composed of village shaykhs and mayors, were founded later in the Delta and Upper Egypt to adjudicate local disputes and refer unresolved cases to the council in its role as Supreme Court. In most cases, the promulgation of new codes or changes to existing ones took place in response to unresolved provincial cases, which allowed local male elites to enact their interests in the process of law making.[81]

Copying British inheritance laws, the Sa'id's 1858 code ruled that the land of a deceased father should be registered only under the name of the eldest male in the family who lived in the household. The law was intended to keep properties under the control of older men and prevent the division of land among heirs. It allowed women to benefit from land inheritance but deprived them of having land registered under their names. The eldest male (*arshad al-'a'ila*) was responsible for farming the land, sustaining the family, and paying the tax. He was required to keep listings of the assigned land shares of the family members, male and female, and their respective revenues. The code also compelled women who already had agricultural land titles to change the status of their properties in accordance with the new law, even if they had fulfilled their tax obligations.[82]

Finally, in 1869, the newly founded Parliament of Isma'il Pasha issued a law that completely deprived women of inheritance rights to agricultural land. In fact, the modern legislature was little more than an institution created to consolidate the power of plantation-owning families and entrench a paternalist regime. This Parliament was called the Council of Consultation of Representatives (Majlis Shura al-Nuwwab), and its members were high-ranking bureaucrats and village notables, almost all of whom were the males of elite propertied families. Qina Province's members of Parliament, for example, included Shaykh Muhammad Abu Sihli, a large landowner of two thousand acres of sugarcane in Farshut. Abu Sihli also served as the mayor of the villages of Salimiyya and Abu Manna' and the president of the provincial council. Another member from Qina, Mahmud 'Abd Allah, was the mayor of Dishna and owned sugarcane fields, a sugar mill, and a big palace in his home village. The interests of the male elite influenced the law-making process in this legislature.[83]

Some parliament members proposed a law to allow women to inherit only real estate and other properties, rendering the male members of the family the only heirs entitled to inherit agricultural land. The rest of the Parliament did not take long to discuss this law. After brief consideration, all the members who commented on the proposal and voted for the code. The rationale behind it was twofold: agricultural property in a family should be kept intact and women were not capable of farming. The Parliament members argued that this law would enhance the economic and social status of the patriarch of the family and work best for his welfare. An heiress, the eldest female member of the family, was allowed to control the land only if no male heirs were alive, and the law compelled her to appoint a male agent, such as her husband, as the farm manager. The pasha approved the proposal and promulgated this law the same year, in 1869.[84]

For many years following, the eldest male of the family that lived in the same household (*fi ma'isha wahida*) took control of land, whether he was a brother, uncle, cousin, nephew, or an in-law. It was a traditional social practice for extended families to live in one household, and the 1869 law further subjugated women in these households to male relatives. Some women in the villages of Qina Province refused to comply, but taking their cases to court only affirmed the authority of the male landholder over them. Women who tried to claim their rights faced violent attacks by their male relatives, who sometimes escalated to shooting at them. While she and her sister were sleeping in their late father's house, for example, the nephews of Sitt al-Ahl bint 'Awad shot her because she had established control over the inheritance of the family.[85]

During these dark years, mysterious cases of deaths of female peasants surfaced with unprecedented frequency in the province. Although these cases were recorded in state files as honor killing crimes, their high frequency suggests that other causes were behind them, which probably had to do with disputes over land inheritance. The state usually registered honor killings as accidents of women catching fire or drowning in a local canal, in order to close the case without investigation and leave the killers unpunished, respecting local customs that did not consider these murders crimes. During this period, in recurrent cases, dead bodies of women were found floating in canals or burnt inside their houses, and the family insisted that the deaths were accidental.[86] These women were probably killed by their male relatives in land conflicts, and their families made them appear to the state as honor killings to evade punishment.[87]

A manifest goal of Western modernity was to rescue native women from patriarchal oppression in their societies, especially if they were Muslims. Obviously, the women of Upper Egypt would argue the opposite. The market did not deliver what it claimed it came for.

BITTER SUGAR

When he expanded his numerous sugarcane plantations and founded several modern sugar refineries in Qina, Khedive Isma'il introduced more market measures to the province. By the 1870s, Isma'il had turned whole villages in Qina into the private sugarcane farms of the royal family, in order to secure for himself a place in a transforming global market. Thousands of Qina's peasants worked on those plantations, and the sugar factories attached to them employed thousands of other landless workers. The stories of daily suffering and discontent of those subalterns exposes new faces of the market reality.

After the end of the American Civil War, cotton exports in Egypt experienced a period of bust but still constituted half of the country's revenue. To compensate for losses in the cotton market, Khedive Isma'il envisioned making sugar for Upper Egypt what cotton was for the Delta, or making the economy of the south market-oriented based on commercial agriculture in sugar.[88] While Isma'il left the majority of cotton fields in the Delta to the local elite families of large landowners, the khedive established a monopoly over the sugarcane fields in the south—especially in Qina Province, where this crop was most concentrated. The plantations of the royal family annexed more thousands of acres to their existing properties in the province and constructed modern sugar mills on them. As a result, public works in Qina were in the service of the khedive's sugar.

Small landowning peasants lost more of their parcels to the khedive's plantations, called the Daira Saniyya, and many villages in the province became almost the private property of the royal family. For instance, Naj' Hammadi had 32,000 acres of the Daira land, some of which were leased out and the rest of which employed seasonal labor. The area of Farshut, meanwhile, had 12,000 acres farmed mainly by seasonal labor.[89] In 1870, the khedive's mother annexed a total of 3,531 acres in five villages in the province to the Daira plantations, and the peasants of these villages were forced to surrender their fields to the government. In the official papers, the state claimed that the farmers and shaykhs of those villages submitted a petition to the state to relinquish their property rights to Isma'il's mother, who in turn agreed to purchase the land. Some peasants accepted the prices that the Mother Pasha offered them, and others requested that she replace these plots with others elsewhere. Bishara 'Ubayd, a Copt who was an agent of the French consul and owner of several plantations, rented hundreds of acres of this land through an auction, after he outbid the shaykhs and mayors of those villages.[90]

The khedive annexed the peasants' land through legal strategies. He reissued a decree that his predecessor had promulgated about the small properties of runaway peasants (*mutasahhib*s). In 1865, that law had affirmed that *mutasahhib*s who left their lands for more than three years would lose their right to it; either heirs would take it or the state would declare it public property. In many cases the state confiscated the land from the legal heirs, declared it public property, and then annexed it to the khedive's plantations.[91] In addition, to consolidate the plantations in closer areas, the Daira exchanged fields with other large landowners. For example, Bishara 'Ubayd gave up 950 acres of his fields in Armant in return for replacing them with land in another village.[92]

Qina Province had several large-scale modern sugar factories, which were designed and run by French experts. The French factories (*fabriqas*), operated with steam engines and were fueled with coal, and the state recruited the province's villagers to construct them. The factories operated twenty-four hours a day, and the laborers worked according to a shift system and were harshly punished if they showed any negligence or were suspected of theft in the sugar mills.[93] The modern factories of the khedive hurt the traditional sugar industry of the province, which used deep and wide melting pots. The older sugar mills could not compete and gradually disappeared. The modern mills relied on the traditional sector only for supplying pottery containers (*ballas*) for the storage of molasses.[94]

The government initiated public works in Qina Province for irrigation, drainage, steam pumps, and transportation projects—all powered by steam engines—mainly in order to benefit the sugar plantations of the royal family. The only place where steam irrigation pumps and short railroads were constructed in the province was on the royal plantations, leaving the small plots of peasants to traditional farming methods. Modern engineers designed new canals, dikes, and embankment projects and the state recruited corvée labor to carry out work in the khedive's fields. In one incident, six thousand corvée workers from almost every single village in the province were drafted to finish one project in the Daira.[95] Corvée laborers had no choice. They had to do the jobs assigned to them or the state would punish them. The only thing they could ask for—through submitting petitions—was to be assigned to nearby villages.[96]

Although the years that followed the termination of the 1864 revolt did not witness any new uprisings in Qina Province, the subalterns of the khedive's plantations exhibited constant resentment over their conditions. Sabotage to the telegraph was one manifestation of resistance. For the people of Qina, the telegraph was not a sign of an advancing benign modernity. Rather, it was the disciplining machine that brought the orders to recruit corvée labor and collect taxes. Through the telegraph, workers were recruited for the khedive's plantations. In 1870, only a few days after the sugar mill in Mata'na sent orders to collect carpenters and construction workers, the inhabitants of Nagada damaged two wooden pillars carrying the wires of the telegraph line.[97] In another example of resistance, *falatiyya* gangs launched occasional attacks against the boats of European merchants who carried out large-scale commercial transactions for the khedive's plantations.[98]

In 1873, three workers from Mata'na attacked a shaykh with a knife and long, heavy sticks (*nabbuts*) before they ran away. The shaykh was collecting corvée labor with the help of a village watchman to work on the steam pumps in Armant when he was attacked. Investigations revealed that the three workers in fact had run away from jobs at the steam pumps, and the shaykh was looking for other laborers to replace them. As soon as the runaways saw him pass, they panicked, injured him, and fled again. Following the incident, the houses in the area were searched for weapons, and many knives and eight *nabbut*s were found and confiscated, to prevent similar incidents in the future.[99]

In the same year, Jahin and his three landless brothers were restless *falatiyya* bandits in the area of Mata'na, where vast royal plantations, steam pumps, and mills existed. Their story began when their village shaykh attempted to conscript them for corvée labor. They refused to go. Instead, they shot at the shaykh and fled with other villagers, forming a *falatiyya* gang and hiding in the nearby mountains. They routinely raided the sugarcane fields, beat the watchmen there, and escaped back to their hiding places. When one of the brothers was killed—apparently during a raid—Jahin carried his corpse on a donkey to the police station and accused the above-mentioned shaykh of shooting him. Jahin alleged that he and his brother had been carrying, on that donkey, a half *ardabb* of barley and were on their way to sell it to pay their tax. Once they arrived in the area of the Mataʻna steam pumps to the east of the canal, Jahin added, the shaykh killed his brother and stole the barley. The shaykh was put in jail for a prolonged period, but investigations proved that Jahin's story was fabricated; his family did not even own any land on which to cultivate this claimed barley. As the police always failed to find or arrest the bandits after their attacks, Jahin and his clever gang were never convicted or jailed for their crimes.[100]

After devastating the lives of the subalterns in the south and provoking their resistance, market arrangements in Upper Egypt failed once again. Using modern European technology and employing French experts did not help. By the end of 1870s, Khedive Ismaʻil's capitalist sugar endeavors in Upper Egypt had incurred extensive debt; bankruptcy soon followed. The Daira Saniyya and mills were all put up for sale in the next decade.[101]

In the mid-nineteenth century, Britain was far from being a successful informal empire in Upper Egypt. Britain attempted but never penetrated Upper Egypt or was in any way close to domination there. The empire's main market measures failed because the discontented subalterns of the south fundamentally resented them. Western modernity, as the empire claimed to introduce through the market, was devastating to the peasants, women, and laborers of Upper Egypt; it altered their lives only because of its incompetent pretensions of superiority. In the following decades, when the informal empire turned into a formal one in the later part of the nineteenth century and first half of the twentieth century, Qina Province's discontent continued and took on new faces.

FIVE

Rebellion in the Time of Cholera

1882–1950

In 1885, three years after the British colonization of Egypt, an incident that appeared to be an ordinary theft in a village market revealed the existence of a gang of audacious bandits. It was a period of dark, hard days in Qina Province, deep in the south of Egypt, as signs of a serious cholera breakout were spreading throughout the villages of the region. 'Ali Effendi Ibrahim—the province's Parliament member—was on his plantation when he received the bad news: money and jewelry had been stolen from his house, along with the precious state medal bestowed upon him by the khedive in Cairo. The police arrested two bandits by the names of Sa'id and Ahmad in the market of the village of Armant, where they were trying to sell the stolen goods, but the khedival medal was still missing. Sa'id and Ahmad denied the charges and insisted that they were only poor peasants. They asserted that it would have been impossible for them to reach the parliamentarian's house for a raid, as it was a long five-hour trip between their village and his town and numerous police guards fortified the road. Furthermore, they added, they did not even know where the house was. Days of investigation passed with no results, but the mystery was finally resolved: the missing medal resurfaced and provided indisputable evidence against the two bandits. They had taken it to a textile store and mortgaged it for garments. At the recently modernized legal council of Qina, they were sentenced to two years in jail.[1]

It was under colonial regimes, postcolonial theorist Benedict Anderson asserts, that myths of "national identities" were created and "nations" forged. The capitalist interests of the colonizer and the colonized elite entailed such a project, the nation-state, to emerge in different places in the world. They built it by unifying near and far local markets into what Anderson calls imagined communities.[2] This process succeeded in various regions under the hegemony of one modern empire or another, and the historiography of Egypt under the British Empire has long celebrated the birth of the nation-state during this period. Nonetheless, British colonialism in Egypt, this chapter argues, marked a period of failed empire and an unfinished nation. The colonial administration and the co-opted native ruling elite attempted to unify the Delta with Upper Egypt—the north with the south—into a single consolidated market, the basis for a modern state. However, the empire's capitalism in Upper Egypt proved utterly incompetent, faced bailout crises, and generated environmental catastrophes, including the cholera epidemic. The south was constantly simmering with subaltern rebellion, in which ruthless bandits assumed leadership roles.

When the British colonizer arrived in 1882, a modern nation did not exist in Egypt, despite the intense endeavors of several centralized governments throughout the nineteenth century. Muhammad 'Ali Pasha's and his successors' attempts to unify the south with the north—or rather to subjugate Upper Egypt to a regime based in Cairo—were met with massive separatist revolts that emerged from Qina Province. The nation lacked a unified market to assist its evolution, thanks to European interference in the northern economy. For four decades before the British military occupation, industrial Britain inflicted extensive influence on the khedives of Cairo in order to secure supplies of cheap cotton from the Delta in the north. Upper Egypt was not invited to participate in commercial agriculture, and the fact that the south was a rebellious region and relentlessly resented ventures of economic penetration by the informal empire did not help ease its growing marginalization. As soon as the British occupied Egypt, the colonial regime embarked on a new attempt at incorporating Upper Egypt, mainly through capitalist means. It would work with Cairo's elite to assimilate the south into the northern market, and hence solidify a nation.

Colonial capitalism was a great success and beneficial to the colonies, many historians of the British Empire assert. Niall Ferguson, for instance, admits the many mistakes that the empire committed but insists that the British still introduced a "good thing" to their colonies by spreading efficient capitalism that enhanced global welfare. As a liberal economic historian, Ferguson claims that "the legacy of the Empire is not just 'racism, racial discrimination, xenophobia and related intolerance' ... but the triumph of capitalism as the optimal system of economic organization."[3] For completely different ends, in fact the critique of imperialism, Benedict Anderson supports the general presumption of the success of colonial capitalism. A leading figure in postcolonial theory, Anderson says that nations were "invented" by the colonized elite, and he argues for the "primacy of capitalism" in fabricating national identities. To achieve his capitalist goals, the colonizer was heavily involved with the native upper class to unify local markets; these markets evolved into communities of peoples sharing the same imagined identity, and those communities were in turn another basic stage in the metamorphosis of modern nations. "Is Indian nationalism not inseparable from colonial administrative-market unification, after the Mutiny, by the most formidable and advanced of the imperial powers?" Anderson inquires, with a predetermined answer.[4]

Theoretical narratives about efficient imperial capitalism upon which nations were effectively constructed apply to many places in Latin America and Asia, but not to Egypt, where the story was more devastating. The prevailing historiography of late nineteenth- and early twentieth-century Egypt perpetuates the myth of a nation. Traditional accounts in Arabic and English alike conventionally presume that, under British occupation, the south was happily integrated with the north, and one modern nation was heroically struggling for liberation. The patriotic champions of liberation, they add, were the northern bourgeoisie, or the female and male large landowners and capitalist entrepreneurs in the Delta and Cairo who materialized as the official representatives of the unified nation. Nonetheless, this nationalistic literature fails to recognize the essential role that British capitalism attempted to play in assisting the northern elite invent the nation for the interests of both the British and northern elite. This chapter illustrates that capitalism was devastatingly unsuccessful in Upper Egypt, and thus this alleged nation was never born. Moreover, the conventional narrative ignores the distressing dynamics of assimilating Upper Egypt into a Cairo-led market and centralized government. Similarly, it fails to see the fierce political resistance encountered in the south, leaving the subaltern women and men of Upper Egypt invisible and voiceless.[5]

Through a microscopic gaze at the villages and small towns of Qina Province, deep in the south of Egypt, this chapter narrates an alternative story of Upper Egypt, the empire, and the nation-state. It follows how the colonial regime first peripheralized Upper Egypt, through its liberal institutional and legal reforms, and then later sought to reintegrate it through market actions. It closely investigates the presence of British capitalism in Qina in the form of a sugar company and a bank and reveals the environmental destruction generated through the cholera epidemic. Furthermore, the chapter explores the nonnationalist, nonelite rebellion of female and male peasants and laborers in the province, against both the empire and its alleged nation.

LEGALLY PERIPHERALIZED

After a short trip to the south in 1889, Lord Cromer—the British high commissioner of Egypt for a quarter of a century, from 1883 to 1907—reported that he "visited many *remote* villages of Upper Egypt in which the face of a European is rarely seen."[6] The "remoteness" of the south, or in other words its inaccessibility to foreign penetration, was problematic to Cromer. However, it was in fact Cromer's administration that persistently marginalized Upper Egypt, particularly during his first years in office. Upon arriving in Egypt from India, Cromer vowed to undermine the old "corrupt and oppressive" regime of Egypt's despotic ruler—to use his own language—and replace it with a new, liberal one.[7] But British liberalism immediately gave birth to a state that was no more than a continuation of the ancien régime it purported to replace. And in the new nation-state that was created, Upper Egypt was, legally, peripheralized.

The story of the British Empire's interaction with this divided nation started long before Cromer's arrival. In the years between 1840s and 1870s, Great Britain extended its influence over the khedives of Egypt—still viceroys of the Ottoman Empire, at least nominally—through free-trade agreements and close commercial relations.[8] As the British textile industry demand for long-staple cotton from Egypt swelled, owners of cotton plantations in the Delta accumulated agricultural wealth and emerged as a new ruling elite, with both native Egyptian and Turkish origins. Sa'id Pasha (r. 1854–63) and his successor Isma'il Pasha (1863–79) reformed the landownership legal system, which led to consolidating the agricultural properties and political power of the northern elite.[9] Left out of this new order of commercial agriculture, Upper Egypt failed to generate a considerable class of rich families to influence politics. A few large southern landowners—of sugar rather than cotton plantations—did join the ruling elite in Cairo, but only as a second-class elite.[10]

The legal peripheralization of the south began when Khedive Isma'il decided to establish a modern Parliament in 1866. This Council of Consultation of Representatives (Majlis Shura al-Nuwwab) was conspicuously dominated by Delta plantation owners, and its law-making agenda functioned mainly to serve their interests. The election law restricted the right to run for seats on the council only to males able to pay a high land tax of five hundred piasters or more.[11] Although Upper Egypt was equally represented by some of its propertied families, northern members of the Parliament held the role of council speaker and headed every important committee, and—aside from a few occasions in which southern council members spoke—their voices were the only ones heard in every session. Cotton was the most important and most frequently discussed subject, as the council concentrated its attention on solving issues pertaining to digging canals, building barrages, conducting land surveys, controlling seasonal labor, and reorganizing villages, mainly in the Delta.[12]

The formation of this Parliament was a significant moment in the rise of bourgeois nationalism in the north. Khedive Isma'il—an Ottoman, nonnative of his realm—presented and celebrated the council as a great step toward building a modern nation, or *watan* (fatherland), similar to European models. In his speech at the Parliament's opening session, Isma'il vowed that the noble purpose of the body was to benefit *al-ahali,* or citizens, of Egypt, and he mainly emphasized the Muslim majority of them.[13] The council soon became an ideal platform for the rising nationalistic rhetoric of the north, building on an existing intellectual discourse—in both press and books—of the fatherland produced by the Western-educated Cairene bourgeoisie. Cairo's regime determinedly integrated the south into the nationalist myth, no matter the south's marginalized representation in the council. "The council pleaded to the government to find a feasible method ... [to protect] cotton, and it responded.... Thus, we should thank it ... and may God keep the generous Khedive whose vision is bound for this nation and its citizens," a Delta parliamentarian once stated, and the rest of the members answered, "Amen."[14]

British troops occupied Egypt in 1882 after a debt crisis broke out in the north and the state failed to pay back its European creditors. The following year, London's liberal administration summoned Lord Cromer from India, where he had served as a finance member of the British viceroy's council, and sent him to Cairo to govern the new colony. It was not Cromer's first time in Egypt. From 1879 to 1880, he had been in charge of managing Egyptian finance after the onset of the Egyptian debt crisis and the takeover of the country's budget by a dual British-French committee. In September 1883, Cromer arrived with much confidence in his ability to replace the old, malfunctioning regime by applying the liberal recommendations of an important report—prepared by Lord Dufferin and submitted to Her Majesty the same year—concerning reform of the legal system.[15] Cromer started by abolishing the old Parliament and forming a new one. Taking a radical tone about the new election process, Cromer declared, "When we are liberal in Egypt, we do not content ourselves with half measures."[16]

Two months later, in November 1883, when the results of the elections were announced, Cromer's legal reforms brought back almost all the members of the previous council to win their very same seats. According to the reforms in election regulations (the Organic and Electoral Laws of 1 May), the minimum land tax a candidate had to pay to qualify to run for a parliamentary seat was raised tenfold, from 500 to 5,000 piasters.[17] The colonial regime evidently intended to structure itself around the wealthy class of cotton-plantation owners in the north. A glance at the list of newly elected parliamentarians shows that almost nothing changed. The council maintained its old speaker, Muhammad Sultan Pasha; its vice-speaker, Muhammad al-Shawarbi Pasha; and the same members from influential propertied families such as the Abazas, the Fiqis, the Shawarbis, and 'Abd al-Ghaffars—all from the Delta.[18]

The elections also brought no change for Upper Egypt. The colonial regime co-opted the same wealthy families that the khedive had assimilated into the old Parliament, and many of them also won back their old seats. A striking example in Qina Province is Tay' Salama, a village mayor who continuously held a seat in the council from 1876 to 1890.[19] A few months after Salama was elected to Cromer's new legislature, the people of Qus, one of the big towns in the province, raised a complaint to the Parliament asserting that Salama was an illegal, inadequate candidate. While he was a member of the previous council he had been convicted and sentenced to jail twice for violently seizing peasants' land. Many similar lawsuits were still pending. In the weeks leading to the election, people of the province had filed a petition against him with the Ministry of Interior, but they received no response. They raised another petition to the Parliament after Salama won, but the council responded that it was too late. He was already a member, and this matter was outside their realm of jurisdiction. In the end, Salama not only kept his seat but also won it again in the next election six years later.[20]

Another stunning example is Muhammad 'Umar Bey, a Parliament member from 1896 to 1901. He came from a large clan in the village of Abu Manna'; and his clan was part of the precolonial co-opted elite, clients of the deposed khedive who had served in his army and bureaucracy. Members of this family held various prestigious positions under the ancien régime, including as army colonels, members of the Supreme Court in Cairo, vice-governors of Qina and Isna Provinces, and governors of Girga and Asyut Provinces.[21] As for Muhammad 'Umar himself, he was the son of a former province governor and was heavily involved in moneylending to small peasants, forcefully confiscating their lands when they defaulted. Through this, 'Umar managed to expand the agricultural properties of his influential family. Peasants complained to the Cabinet of Ministers in Cairo about his unjust deeds and illicit representation of them, but their desperate voices met with silence on the part of the colonial regime.[22]

The reformed Parliament resumed business as usual, primarily discussing issues pertaining to cotton and agricultural development in the Delta. The laws and decrees that the Parliament passed favored the north with public projects, ignoring the south and even muting the voices of its representatives. In irrigation, for example, under the supervision of the British inspector general of the Ministry of Public Works, the government undertook extensive projects in the Delta to transform the irrigation system from the traditional basin method to the modernized perennial method during the 1880s.[23] Meanwhile, the Delta elite sabotaged calls to implement the same system in Upper Egyptian provinces, including Qina. In 1893, a representative from Upper Egypt finally raised the irrigation issue and submitted a proposal to extend public works to Upper Egypt, insisting that southern provinces were deprived of water for summer cultivation and their annual income was not anywhere near that of the cotton-producing north. The northern members not only unanimously vetoed the proposal but also decided not to inform the government about them on grounds that the state's budget would not cover the projects' high costs.[24]

Projects of modern irrigation in Upper Egypt were limited only to the plantations of the khedive and the royal family. In 1895, Lord Cromer received a report revealing the impact of the uneven irrigation policies of his regime on the peasantry of the south. The report stated, "The peasants cannot raise cotton or sugar-cane except to a very limited extent by means of irrigation by hand (shadoofs) because their lands are not embanked; they are however tantalized by seeing splendid crops of both these profitable staples grown in their neighborhood on the Daira estates [the khedive's plantations] and where the farms are embanked, and where steam pumps furnished plenty of water."[25] Cromer did not make significant attempts to improve the situation, and Qina Province was particularly neglected. In 1904, the peasants of the Isna, one of the province's towns, petitioned the government in Cairo, complaining about the lack of water pumps in their villages, which was causing great hardship for farmers and plunging their lives into misery.[26]

Another example of how the new Parliament ignored the needs of Upper Egypt in public works can be seen in the development of the railways, primarily to transport goods. While railways were widely expanded in the Delta, Alexandria, and Port Said throughout the 1880s and 1890s, Qina Province went without railroads until nearly the end of the century. From the mid-1800s on, railways were heavily used in the north to ship cotton from the Delta fields to the port of Alexandria, where it was exported to Britain by way of the Mediterranean Sea. The peoples of Upper Egypt, however, would not see this modern transportation technology for a long time. In addition to the main railways, which the government extended in the north and paid for with public funds, the Delta Parliament members promulgated a Railways Law that allowed the construction of short private railroads at the expense of the plantation owner.[27] The law meant nothing to the elite of Qina Province. They could not build their own railways, because they lacked capital—provinces like theirs did not enjoy the cotton profits that the north did.

In 1890, the Department of Railways submitted a proposal to the Cabinet of Ministers requesting 3,000 Egyptian pounds to prepare a plan for railroad lines in Upper Egypt, one of which would cross through Qina Province and its town of Luxor, another from the city of Qina to the province's Red Sea port of Qusayr. The Ministry of Public Works rejected the Qina–Qusayr line, insisting that its profits would not match its cost. The ministry thought that the Luxor line would be more beneficial, given the foreign communities that had settled in this area of heavy tourism. But in the end, the ministry also rejected the Luxor line under the pretext that more research was needed to ensure the rail line's profitability. A British-led financial committee in the Department of Railways vetoed funding this research. The project never saw the light of day.[28] Aside from a limited line for mail service, Qina Province lacked railways for many years to come. Ironically, the colonial administration approved a railway project only when a French-British sugar company proposed it for its private purposes in the late-1890s.[29]

As for taxation, in February 1886 the Parliament members from Upper Egypt proposed modifying the timetable of tax collection in their southern provinces, a proposal that was entirely ignored. According to the government's preset schedule, landowners paid the required annual tax in monthly installments, but two-thirds of it was to be collected over the three months of the winter grain harvest. The Upper Egyptian parliamentarians' proposal argued that "the situation in Upper Egypt is apparent to the public: its crops are not sufficient to fulfill the required taxes and its population lives in extreme misery and poverty. The government should consider the comfort of the people and what benefits them in modifying the tax timetable."[30]

At the same time, the Parliament members from the Delta made a similar request for Lower Egypt. The council submitted the two proposals to the colonial government, but the government considered only the Delta's and completely ignored that of Upper Egypt. It did not even refer to the southern request in its correspondence with the Parliament. A prominent Delta Parliament member, 'Abd al-Ghaffar Pasha of Munufiyya Province, attempted to justify the colonial administration's position by suggesting that it might have thought it reasonable to collect the largest portion of taxes during the grain harvest time, because this was the main crop cultivated in Upper Egypt. In the meantime, Upper Egyptian members did not persist. Six months later, the Cabinet of Ministers issued its final decree: approving the Delta's request and rejecting Upper Egypt's. Moreover, two years later, the Parliament passed a modification of Upper Egypt's tax timetable that was exactly the opposite of what Upper Egyptians had requested: doubling the amount of tax collected during the winter harvest months. It was the prominent Delta Parliament members who voted for this decree, whereas Upper Egyptian members were totally silent.[31]

While he applied these conspicuously discriminatory policies, Lord Cromer nonetheless exclaimed in his 1889 trip up the Nile about the "remoteness" of Upper Egypt and the absence of European faces there—a problem that he would try hard to fix in the following years.

A FAILED MARKET TO BAILOUT

Lord Cromer lent considerable support to the bourgeois project of creating a modern nation-state in Egypt, but one fundamental problem impeded this goal: the lack of a unified market. The early colonial administration in Egypt tolerated the nationalistic rhetoric that the northern members perpetuated inside the reformed Parliament, and Cromer himself used the term *nation* to describe the Egyptians.[32] The empire supported this project because a modern nation-state was a perfect mechanism for completely divorcing the new Oriental colony from the remaining influence of the Ottoman Empire, to which Egypt had belonged for the previous three centuries. Thus, Cromer envisioned a non-Muslim identity for this state, in the hope of cutting old ties with the Ottoman sultan and also ensuring the incorporation of foreign communities residing in Egypt. He authoritatively argued, "I stated in the last Report I wrote from Egypt that it is well for ... every nation to have an ideal. The ideal of the Moslem patriot is, in my opinion, incapable of realization. The ideal which I substitute in its place is extremely difficult of attainment, but if the Egyptians of the rising generation will have the wisdom and foresight to work cordially and patiently, in co-operation with European sympathizers, to attain it, it may possibly in time be found capable of realization."[33]

It was still problematic for Cromer that Upper Egypt was not fully incorporated into the imperial economy, receiving significant influxes of foreign capital as the north did. Only a few years after Cromer's first visit to Upper Egypt did European faces start to appear in the remotest place in the south—Qina. Europeans were brought to Qina by two enormous capitalist enterprises that had found their way to the province: an agricultural bank and a sugar company. Neither of them was a success story.

In the last few years of the 1890s, agents of the Société Générale des Sucreries et de la Raffineries d'Égypte, a joint Anglo-French sugar venture, swept through Qina's villages and towns to buy thousands of acres of sugarcane and establish large mills equipped with the latest technology for refining sugar. The Anglo-French firm purchased land from the Daira Saniyya, plantations owned by the royal family in the province, after the colonial administration forced the khedive to privatize this land in an attempt to solve the foreign debt crisis. This resulted in one of the most dreadful episodes of widespread land loss in the province's history.

In May 1898, all thirty-five thousand farmers in the villages of Armant, Maris, Rayyaniyya, and Ruzayqat sent an urgent telegram to Cromer and the Parliament in Cairo to complain about the sale of the Daira farms where they worked. The peasants insisted that this was their own land, as the royal family had confiscated it from their ancestors, reducing them to mere tenants and even turning many into landless laborers in the royal sugar factories. The farmers heard the news that the foreign company had purchased the Daira's land, which meant that their leases would be terminated. The government also sold every asset the peasants owned on this land—including their cattle, houses, waterwheels, and machinery—to the foreign company. Peasants proposed instead to purchase this land at the prices the government set, but by paying installments at a reasonable rate of interest. Cairo never responded to this proposal, and the Parliament ruled it outside its area of jurisdiction.[34] The company finalized the deal and commenced work.

The Société Générale des Sucreries built a mill in the town of Najʿ Hammadi, turning it into a rising urban center where numerous dispossessed laborers worked either for the company or in projects associated with it. The sugar company also developed basic infrastructure, financed by foreign and government capital, in order to facilitate its business. In 1897, the government in Cairo granted the company a contract to construct narrow railways to transport sugarcane to the factory's premises from surrounding farms.[35] At the same time, a Paris-based construction company worked on building a bridge over the Nile for the railroad, which later became one of the largest bridges in the province.

Landless workers from the province were employed in this bridge-building project, but the construction company's safety and protection measures were so poor that many of them were injured or killed at the construction site. In one incident, the bridge's cylinder fell on thirteen workers, killing them instantly. Unfamiliar with European laws, the grieving families of the dead workers had to hire an expensive French lawyer to sue the company for compensation. The company had paid these families only 200 Egyptian pounds, but the lawyer negotiated to add another 600 Egyptian pounds. This was still much less than what they had hoped. The French company did not respond to the high amount requested, as its lawyer argued that these were low-wage workers who were worthy of little compensation. The dispute went on for months, until a telegram from Paris offered the families a small payment. They were forced to accept the offer after Cairo's intervention and pressure.[36]

Unexpectedly, in 1905, the sugar company declared bankruptcy only a few years after its formation. The colonial administration decided to bail it out, intentionally violating the basic rule of the liberal market—that the state should not interfere in the economy. The company, in fact, was rewarded for its bankruptcy. It "was given a new lease of life under fresh auspices, with diminished charges and additional working capital," said an official report. "The Government redeemed its promise of assistance by taking over the company's railway system at a cost of 400,000*l*."[37] The colonial administration's support for a failing capitalist enterprise went on for the following decade. The government set low prices on sugarcane for the benefit of the company and at the expense of Qina Province's peasants. Suffering from poverty, food shortages, and debt during World War I, thousands of sugarcane farmers in the villages of Armant, Maris, Mataʻna, and Dabʻiyya sent a petition to Cairo demanding an increase in prices. They cried,

> Our houses are ruined, we lack the necessary food, and our debts are accumulating because of the government's oppression. We have been crying out to the government for more than a year but nobody listens to our cries.... While the prices of cotton and other crops multiplied ... we grow sugarcane and the sugar company pays us the same old price, 3 piasters per *qantar* .... The war conditions force us to purchase farming necessities at high prices. The prices of coal for the irrigation engines, oil, iron, and fertilizers multiplied three and four times. The wages of seasonal laborers and [rents of] camels multiply because the military authorities [British Army] recruited many of them for its operations. We buy the grain to feed our children at a doubled price. Thus, how could it be fair that the company purchases our sugarcane at the same price set before the war? The company insists that it is the government that presets the price and it is not willing to pay more. The truth is that the price of sugar in Egypt now is half or even a third its price all over the world.... The current price of sugarcane is not sufficient to cultivate, and we have failed to pay the taxes and the rents of the lands to their owners.[38]

The Société Générale des Sucreries was not the only capitalist enterprise working in Qina. The Agricultural Bank of Egypt was also operating in the province and bringing about similar effects. Lord Cromer founded this bank himself at the turn of the twentieth century, working closely with influential capitalists in London. When Cromer arrived in Egypt, part of the general debt crises that he had to resolve was the indebtedness of thousands of peasants to European creditors and their inability to repay their debts. Applying strict principles of the market economy, the Cromer administration refused to bail out the peasants, asserting that this was a matter of private capital in which it should not intervene; the government promised "de ne s'immiscer en aucune façon dan le réglement des affaires privées" (not to involve itself in any fashion in the regulation of private business).[39] Throughout the rest of the 1880s and in 1890s, the issue of the "indebtedness of the peasants [*fellaheen*]" continued to appear frequently in Cromer's annual reports, until he finally suggested that foreign private capital should play a role in resolving their problems.[40]

Because the debt crisis mainly originated from high-interest credit, Cromer proposed establishing a bank to give peasants new loans but at lower interest rates so they could pay off their old debts. In 1899, he tested the idea first by opening an agricultural loan department in the National Bank of Egypt, founded only one year earlier by British capitalists. In 1902, Cromer registered this department as a separate company, the Agricultural Bank of Egypt. British capitalists were the main shareholders of this company, particularly Sir Ernest Cassel, who maintained good connections with British bankers, such as the Rothschilds, and foreign bankers in Egypt, such as the Suarés brothers. The supposedly liberal administration directly intervened in the economy to assist the bank taking off. Cromer approved a government guarantee that investments in the bank would receive a minimum return of 4 percent. He also authorized the use of government tax clerks to manage the bank's branches in villages throughout Egypt.[41]

When the Agricultural Bank arrived in Qina Province, thousands of peasants mortgaged their lands to it, hoping that the new inflow of European capital would ameliorate their deteriorating living conditions.[42] But the great expectations of the province's peasants were soon shattered when they once again lost their lands on a large scale. For example, for many years, farmers in the village of Hasanat suffered from various crises, including the flooding Nile that drowned their houses and harvests in 1887. After the colonial administration had ignored them for so long, the bank seemed to be the last venue of hope. In their urgent petition to Cairo, Hasanat's peasants said, "The bank appeared, with the government partaking in its administration, and we were under the illusion that if we dealt with it, we would ... see good financial results."[43] The Agricultural Bank did grant loans to these peasants, as well as in many other villages in Qina, but within five years the bank was already confiscating peasants' lands and evicting them.

The bank took peasants who defaulted to the mixed court in Cairo, where many European judges heard cases that involved Europeans and Egyptians.[44] The court ruled for the company to seize the land and evict the peasants. In these modern courts, European and modernized Egyptian judges heard the cases of Qina Province's villagers and applied new civil laws and banking regulations. The southern peasants were, without a doubt, unfamiliar with these foreign legal codes and probably had never before been to Cairo—the big capital where their cases were heard without their presence. After seven thousand farmers from Hasanat lost their small plots to the bank, they complained in a petition sent to the government in Cairo:

> The bank's treatment of us was harsh to the worst extent.... We mortgaged our land to the Agricultural Bank at an interest rate of 9 percent.... As for our delay in paying, it is because of the aforementioned reasons [low Nile inundation and bad weather].... When the bank started to dispossess us of our land, it made us pay fees in court that exceeded half of what we originally

owed. It already confiscated the land and took hold of it, and the people are now landless and have nobody to rescue them.... The entirety of the village's fields, 1,300 *faddan*s [acres], are now confiscated by the Agricultural Bank ... and in the meantime God afflicted us with another distress, that is, the existence of the [foreign] water and the sugar companies in Naj' Hammadi.... We suffer from hunger, our children become orphans, we lose our honor, our houses become ruins, and we are forced to migrate.[45]

The farmers of the villages of Armant, Khuzam, Nagada, and Isna had an even worse experience with the bank. While carrying the burden of their bank loans, they faced recurring years of low Nile inundation that left them with poor harvests, as well as high taxes, huge crop shortages, dramatically higher seed prices, and a sugar company that purchased their harvest at unfairly low rates. Furthermore, two foreign water and fertilizer companies had established monopolies in these two commodities in the province. While the water company was intolerably late in installing irrigation machinery, the fertilizer company provided peasants with services at excessively high prices. Qina's peasants lamented that these conditions, coupled with being evicted from their land by the Agricultural Bank, had left their families and children in a state of complete misery.[46]

The Agricultural Bank soon showed signs of failure and collapse, but the colonial administration immediately stepped in to bail it out—unconditionally. The number of peasants borrowing from the bank declined precipitously, likely due to a creeping lack of confidence in the institution. While the bank had 106,373 borrowers in its first few years, this number drastically declined, reaching only 47,081 in 1907. During this crisis, the bank's shareholders in London gratefully asserted that they relied, "not only [on] the financial guarantees of the Egyptian Government, but also on the definite support and encouragement given by that government to the enterprise."[47] In 1906, the Egyptian government guaranteed 3.5 percent of the debentures issued by the bank and allocated 6,570,000 British pounds from the state budget for that purpose. In fact, it was only the large shareholders, holding more than 150,000 British pounds, who would benefit from these advantages.[48]

Meanwhile, the government applied a strict free-market policy of nonintervention when it came to the Egyptian peasantry. Cairo's offices received numerous collective petitions from Qina's farmers protesting their evictions but did nothing to help them.[49] Finally, in 1910, the Parliament suggested that the government initiate negotiations with the Agricultural Bank and other lenders to assist the debtors. The government responded, "The government has made sure that the bank uses its authority moderately against the debtors. The bank is now studying whether there is a way to decrease the debtors' burden relatively. As for the government, it is now working on improving the agricultural conditions in the country, upon which its economic welfare is based, and believes that this is the best cure for the current conditions rather than its interference in the private deals of the banks."[50]

The bank's shareholders in London blocked the only legal exit for the peasants of Qina. In 1912, the government was considering a proposal to modify articles in the civil and commercial code of the mixed courts that would ban the seizure of indebted small properties. From their headquarters at 57½ Old Road Street, London, the committee members of the Agricultural Bank sent an urgent letter to the colonial administration in Egypt with a long memorandum attached opposing the proposal.[51] They argued that they had initially embarked on this enterprise because of the government guarantees and support and declared, "We believe that the proposed legislation would be detrimental, rather than beneficial, to the interests of the Egyptian fellaheen."[52]

The efforts of the shareholders in London met with great success. For several years to follow, hundreds more female and male peasants in the impoverished villages of Qina Province lost their small plots to the almighty bank.[53]

IN THE TIME OF CHOLERA

Years of peripheralization, dispossession, debt, and poverty soon brought about a devastating environmental effect in Qina Province: a cholera epidemic. Cholera had invaded Egypt in its modern history at least twice before, once between 1830 and 1840, during the reign of Muhammad 'Ali Pasha, and another time in the mid-1860s. During the first outbreak, Upper Egypt was spared. Some Cairo residents even fled the capital for the safety of Upper Egypt. The second time cholera hit Egypt, while the informal empire was at work in the north and the marginalization of the south had already begun, the epidemic reached Upper Egypt. Qina Province reportedly lost 250 persons in one day.[54] Under the colonial regime, official reports stated that cholera invaded Egypt in 1895–96, but it had found its way to Qina years before that.

In 1884, Mustapha Agha, the British consular agent at Luxor, attempted to draw attention to several environmental catastrophes he foresaw in Qina. Lord Cromer's administration did not modernize the irrigation system, which affected the subsistence harvest of the peasants and put them into heavy debt. Cholera completed their growing misery:

> The majority of the natives here are suffering a great deal on account of their misery. They continually subsist on bread made of maize and onions.... The causes for all this are numerous: 1. The produce grown by them being barely sufficient for payment of the Government land-taxes and for their maintenance.... 3. The epizooty (cattle disease).... 4. Being dispossessed in former times of cash and cereals.... They borrowed money at high rate of interest for the payment of the monthly installment for taxes and refunded in cereals at low prices.... The feddan [acre] generally yields from 1½ to 2½ ardabes, of which a portion is given to the creditors and the other portion to the Government for land taxes. The produce of the lands irrigated by means of the Shadoof [wooden water lifter] and Sakeyehs [shaykhs] which the natives subsist upon, is not sufficient for the payment of land taxes... the cholera and the epizooty reduced them to the lowest ebb.[55]

The government, nevertheless, did not recognize the disturbing news, and the province went ignored. Cholera lingered in Qina throughout the following years. In 1902, the local administration declared conclusively that "the cholera epidemic is spreading in numerous villages of the province."[56]

One major factor precipitated the appearance of the epidemic in Qina: a lack of clean water for the lower classes. British physicians and sanitary officials of the time had already detected a direct correlation between cholera and the quality of the water supply. One official report stated, "If further evidence were needed to prove that cholera is chiefly a water-borne disease, the late epidemic in Egypt afforded ample." The report continued, in reference to solving the crisis, that "during the period since [the] 1895–1896 epidemic of cholera a certain amount of work has been done in the larger provincial towns to provide the water supply with as much protection as possible from pollution, and some have been supplied from deep tube wells. In none of these towns did the disease assume an epidemic form."[57] Unfortunately, the villages of Qina were not among the lucky areas saved by the colonial regime.

In 1880, the Egyptian government privatized water resources by giving a concession to the Cairo Water Company—a shareholding company managed by a foreign investor.[58] According to the concession, the company was to install free public taps in urban areas in an attempt to provide clean water. The company installed the spigots and the Department of Public Works footed the bill.[59] The company concentrated its work in Cairo, the Delta, and Middle Egypt but neglected Upper Egypt. Thousands of pounds were spent from the country's budget to equip Cairo with free taps and improve the quality of drinking water, which paid off when cholera broke out. A 1902 report asserted that "the steps taken ... to prevent the spread of the disease [cholera] in the town of Cairo, were especially successful."[60] The Delta received similar attention, followed by Middle Egypt, which reduced the severity of the epidemic in the north. For instance, the number of infected cases in Fayoum, south of Cairo, remarkably decreased between 1896 and 1902.[61]

The Cairo Water Company only started to pay attention to Qina Province after the epidemic had already spread. Even once the company did begin projects in Upper Egypt, it provided purified water only for the towns of Qina and Luxor, where state officials and Europeans resided, and ignored tens of surrounding villages. The local committee of the province, consisting of the corrupt landed elite, made most decisions about where to invite the company to undertake public works and install taps. Once the water company installed new systems in Qina, the capital city of the province, water quality finally improved and this successfully halted the disease: "At Keneh [Qina] ... , which formerly drew its water from wells and stagnant backwater of the Nile, an engine, with pump, etc., was erected about eighteen months ago on the Nile. The result of this was very remarkable, only one case of cholera occurring in this town of 27,478 inhabitants whereas during the epidemic of 1896 no less than 422 cases were registered."[62] Elsewhere, the disease severely affected the neglected villages. As a 1902 report attested, "During the cholera epidemic, the inhabitants of Keneh enjoyed immunity from the disease, whilst the surrounding villages were infected."[63]

The committee of Luxor—a town highly frequented by European tourists and residents and with a large population of elite Copts[64]—chose select places along the Nile where they worked on protecting water purity. The committee issued several warnings with preventive procedures to secure clean water, particularly where hotels and houses of wealthy Copts were located. For instance, a 1902 decision prohibited steamships and commercial boats from anchoring in the area between a particular waterwheel and the house of Monsieur Ensenger, as hotels took their water from this area. The decree did not allow common townspeople in Luxor to draw water there, forcing them to use an area south of the waterwheel. It also prohibited them from washing clothes or bathing animals near the designated hotel area, and those inhabitants who did not comply were subject to a fine of between 50 and 100 piasters.[65]

In the time of cholera, the province suffered from severe food shortages, and consequent malnutrition further deteriorated health conditions. The plague broke out as well. Because the Delta and Cairo were busy cultivating cotton, they relied on Upper Egypt for provision of wheat and other staple crops. Thus, the peasants of the south had to pay their tax in grain delivered to the state storehouses in each province. Ironically, when the Parliament was discussing this policy of in-kind tax, it presented it as a relief policy for Upper Egyptians, because Upper Egyptians were unable to submit their dues in cash like the rich Delta.[66] In reality, the peoples of Qina were kept from consuming their wheat in order to sustain the rich north.

Lack of wheat killed many people during these dark times. It was such a rare and expensive commodity that every year during harvest, landless beggars asked charitable farmers for wheat.[67] Sulayman Radwan was part of a gang of thirteen thieves who seasonally robbed peasants of their harvest. One night, his murdered son was found beside the bridge of a village with traces of wheat inside his pockets and shoes. Inspectors found other amounts of wheat buried in fields adjacent to the crime site, and the owners of these fields knew nothing about it—it was probably wheat he had stolen from other fields. More fresh wheat was also found in his house, although he had not grown any that year.[68] Hungry thieves raided peasants' houses during this time, demanding bread. When a gang of fifteen robbers attacked the house of a peasant on his farm to demand bread, the peasant asserted that the bread he had could barely feed him and his son. He brought out all the bread he had, and some of the thieves ate while others did not get a share. Those who remained hungry shot the poor peasant, left him for dead, and fled to the mountains, where they hid.[69]

The plague infected all of Egypt, but British officials affirmed that it was most widespread in the starving south. A 1907 report of the British consul-general stated, "[Of recent years the disease has appeared mostly in Upper Egypt, where it commonly assumes the pneumonic form. This form is especially dangerous on account of the rapidity with which it spreads, its infectious nature, and the high mortality (approximately 100 per cent) attending it.... In 1905 there were reported from Upper Egypt only 3 cases of the plague, occurring in 2 localities; in 1906 there were 412 cases in 26 localities; and in 1907 838 cases in 71 localities."[70] Another report a year later again emphasized that Upper Egypt was a special case. The plague affected the whole country, but "when ... Upper Egypt was invaded, it [the plague] assumed the very infectious and fatal pneumonic form."[71]

Facing peripheralization, misery, and uncured maladies, Qina Province's subalterns had to revolt against the empire and the nation-state. The lower classes of Qina devised their own mode of nonelite, nonnationalist rebellion against the colonial regime and the local ruling class. It was a constant, daily resistance championed by female and male peasants and laborers, and its implacable masterminds were audacious bandits.

At the turn of the twentieth century, the northern elite embarked on a project to forge another "imagined community" in Egypt. The Cairene bourgeoisie were vehemently active in struggling for independence from British occupation, as they advanced a discourse on a national identity and mobilized the masses to serve their goal. They published numerous newspapers and founded political parties, banks, and companies, all under the slogan of national independence from Western economic domination. Cairene bourgeois women joined these political parties, founded charitable associations, and published women's magazines serving the same goal.[72] Despite the absolute marginalization of the south, Cairo's nationalistic discourse insisted on incorporating Qina's peoples into this fabricated nation. The co-opted local elite of the south introduced the northern rhetoric to the province, and many of Qina's corrupt abovementioned parliamentarians acted as the nation's advocates. If education was a main tool deployed in elite invention and diffusion of a national identity, as postcolonial theorists affirm,[73] the local elite of Qina followed the rules. Many boys' schools were founded in the province to help disseminate the Cairene narrative.[74]

Qina's subaltern women and men could not possibly identify with these patriotic discourses or struggles. For them, the hegemonic north and corrupt local elite afflicted them with poverty and killed them with recurring epidemics. Thus, they embarked on their own liberating struggles against the colonizer and the nationalistic elite alike. The living memory, both distant and recent, of the province's massive revolt against former empires invigorated the new wave of resistance. Historical pockets of unrest in places such as Salimiyya, Armant, and Samhud, where numerous widespread and small revolts had erupted in the past, once more became vibrant centers of uprising. New places of relentless unrest joined them, especially in Dishna and Naj' Hammadi, where foreign companies worked.[75]

Everyday resistance in Qina included attacking village shaykhs and mayors, refusing to pay taxes, or sabotaging public works. In 1885, in the village of Busayla, Zaynab Husayn, a widow, and her two younger brothers, Taha and Ali, attacked Shaykh 'Abd al-Jalil, beating him and breaking two of his teeth. When he was in the hospital for treatment for more than ten days, Umm Muhammad, the female maternal cousin of Zaynab, went to his house, attacked his wife, and took a pair of silver bracelets and a golden earring from her. Zaynab and her brothers completely denied the incident, asserting that the shaykh's teeth were already loose from drinking alcohol and this was not the first time he had fabricated a false accusation against innocent people concerning his teeth. Evidently convicted, Zaynab and her brothers were sentenced to thirty days in jail and fined eighty piasters, equal to what the shaykh spent on treatment in the hospital. The shaykh could not prove the charges against Umm Muhammad and had to withdraw his lawsuit against her.[76]

Landless peasants vandalized state projects, probably because they were primarily established for the benefit of the local elite. Some angry peasants cut the irrigation dikes that the Department of Public Works was constructing.[77] Peasants usually kept weapons to use in attacking state symbols, but they hid them from the village authorities, sometimes by burying them underground in their houses.[78] In one incident, angry farmers used those weapons against contractors who used cheap labor from the province in public works. In 1889, the dissatisfied inhabitants of the village of Bayadiyya, whose houses lined the two banks of a canal under construction, collectively took up arms and attacked the contractors and laborers working on the canal. The contractors were attempting to pave a road cutting through the houses of the peasants, in order for their workers to pass and dispose of dirt. The farmers of the village quickly gathered in a crowd with their arms and shot at the workers, who ran away.[79]

In the time of cholera, the *shaqi*s (outlaws) were the group most prolifically rebellious against the empire in Qina. The *shaqi*s inherited the place of the *falatiyya* bandits who had disturbed previous imperial regimes throughout the nineteenth century, and their operations brought back to life the stirring memory of the late legendary bandits of the province. Like the *falatiyya*, the *shaqi*s bandits were also fed by fugitive peasants and workers escaping heavy taxes and corvée labor. They similarly took to the mountains of the province to hide and launch their operations from, and they adopted the same clever tactics and strategies as their forbears.[80]

The new bandits revived one of the traditions of their predecessors: attacking the houses of Parliament members who illegitimately represented them.

Tayʿ Salama—the abovementioned parliamentarian from Qina who kept his seat for more than twenty years against the people's will—was a favorite target of the new bandits. Salama was more than just a corrupt local figure. He was also a voice of northern nationalism and importer of patriotic myths to the south. He was involved in disseminating the nationalist rhetoric through education, as he funded modern boys' schools with religious endowments. The endowment deeds vowed that the goal of these schools was primarily to serve the "nation" and improve the status of "the sons of the fatherland" (*abna' al-watan*).[81] One night, a gang broke into the barn attached to Salama's house and stole four cows and their infant offspring. Barely a year passed before his house was the target of another raid, when four more cows were stolen from the same barn. Gangs and individual bandits who attacked him were mostly from the village of Qammula, whose mayor was Salama himself.[82]

In 1885, on one of the hot August days in the market of the town of Qus, ʿAwwad, a local peasant, sold about two thousand liters of wheat for a decent price. While heading back home with his son Mahmud, twelve armed men robbed them of the money and other possessions and hit ʿAwwad on the head, leaving him seriously injured near a waterwheel. When his son reported the crime, investigations revealed that the attackers were a gang of bandits who had been causing political disturbances for a long time. A few years earlier, this gang had been bigger—consisting of some twenty-five members—and one of its important operations had involved cutting four agricultural bridges in the village of Hajza. They had also stolen tax money, about 33,979 piasters, that had been collected from the same village in 1883. Many of these bandits had already been convicted of other crimes and had served sentences in Qina or Alexandria jails.[83]

The bandits of the province attacked every symbol of the state and the colonial administration. In 1889, they raided a police patrol in the town of Farshut. After exchanging fire, two soldiers were injured and the bandits made off with their weapons. The authorities were never able to apprehend them.[84] In addition to these targets, the bandits also attacked the contractors working for the government and stole from the construction sites of public projects. Also in 1889, a gang of more than fourteen shot at the contractors and workers on the canal project in the village of Bayadiyya, stole a large amount of money, and left.[85] Once, the village guard in Salimiyya caught two bandits on the village's arched bridge, apparently as they were attempting to vandalize it. The captured men tried to bribe the police officer with one pound, to set them free, but it did not work.[86]

Several women in the province joined the world of banditry. Wasfa and Walqan, both from the village of Qammula Middle, formed a gang with a third woman; her husband, Isma'il the bandit; and another man. Interestingly, the three women were more than seventy years old and had never committed a crime before forming the gang. One night in 1883, Wasfa and Walqan took three donkeys and accompanied the two male bandits to a salt source that the state had enclosed in the mountains of a neighboring village. While they were loading the donkeys with the stolen goods, the guard saw them and attempted to arrest them, but one of the male bandits hit him with a gun. The gang managed to escape, leaving the guard injured. Soon after, the police arrested them in possession of about 1,000 liters of salt, along with guns and other weapons. Investigations revealed that one of the donkeys was the property of Wasfa; and the third female bandit, who had accompanied them, had sent another. The three women confessed to the crime. Because of their old age and lack of previous criminal charges, they were sentenced to less than one year in jail.[87]

Deficiencies in the colonial law of the newly instituted modern civil court system in Upper Egypt left the bandits fortunate enough to evade punishment and expand their operations. The new civil codes had no articles for convicting outlaws based only on their infamy (*mashhurin bil-shaqawa*), which the old law had recognized as legal evidence. Thus, many bandits were released after their arrest for lack of hard, documented evidence. Dissatisfied state officials in Upper Egypt, whose efforts to capture the bandits were wasted when the law allowed their release, called for changing the code. For example, Bakhit Hasanayn of Qina raided a place at night before the formation of the first civil court in Upper Egypt. The police arrested and imprisoned Bakhit, but he managed to run away. After many attempts and armed battles between him and the police force, the authorities finally captured him again, this time after the civil court was formed. Bakhit, luckily, stood before a modern judge. No documented evidence supported the charges, so the judge was forced to set him free. On his way back from the court to his home village, he insisted on passing by the district governor, who was sitting in his office. Bakhit taunted the governor: "You had captured me and the government let me go" (Inta masaktini wa al-hukuma sayyabitni).[88]

In the 1890s, the bandit Ziyad al-Shaqi became a national legend, even though the nationalist cause was the furthest thing from his mind. News of his thrilling exploits in Qina Province and throughout Upper Egypt was met with great attention in Cairo. The press played a major role in creating and perpetuating his legend. Cairo newspapers reported so many different—sometimes contradictory—accounts of his story that the truth was almost lost in the telling. Ziyad and his brother apparently led a gang of mountain dwellers that committed "horrifying major sins in Qina that the pen would fail to depict," as one state official put it.[89] The general police inspector himself, Justun Pasha, came from Cairo to execute a plan to capture Ziyad. Information about the operation was leaked to Ziyad, and so he fled with his fellows to the mountains in a neighboring province. The bandits hid in the mountains, but many undercover guards were vigilant day and night, awaiting their appearance. One evening, the gang went to fetch water from a village well and managed to return safely. Furious at their audacity, the next day Justun Pasha led two large forces to launch an assault on the mountains. After a fierce battle in which he was leading the gang from the very front, Ziyad fell to the bullets of the police. Justun Pasha victoriously carried Ziyad back to Qina, where he was interrogated and the gang confessed to all of its crimes.[90]

After the end of World War I, the Egyptian nation's project took a new trajectory. When the famous 1919 uprising took place in Cairo, under the leadership of the bourgeois men and women of the Wafd Party and the mobilized masses of the educated middle class, the British Empire granted the Kingdom of Egypt conditional independence. The Wafd was the delegation of upper-class Egyptians who went to the Versailles conference in Paris at the end of the war to negotiate national liberation. The colonial administration withdrew from many areas yet still maintained military occupation, and the Wafd Party formed a new cabinet and elected Parliament. The nation was officially born then, in the opinion of the northern bourgeoisie and conventional historiography of Egypt.

For the discontented subalterns of Qina Province, the romantic nationalism of the Cairene bourgeoisie was far from reality. The members of the Wafd Party running for parliamentary elections in the province were not received with the expected sentiments of patriotism. In 1949, Makram Pasha 'Ubayd, the leader of the party in Qina, visited the province as part of his election campaign, but his visit ended in a bloody way. When he arrived at the train station, one local clan campaigning for him received him and drove him through town to collect voters' support. A large fight erupted between his entourage and the angry supporters of a rival candidate from a local notable family. The expanding fight reached the town's market, where several of the pasha's opponents were shot dead. The correspondent of the newspaper

Al-Ahram was himself injured in the battle, and the story made it to Cairo's press; this embarrassed the Wafd Party, which claimed to be the only legitimate representative of the "Egyptians."[91]

As their vandalism and assaults on state officials and properties increased, the bandits earned a new name from the national government: *matarid al-jabal*, or the fugitives of the mountains. Between the 1920s and 1940s, the most legendary bandit in Egyptian history appeared in Qina Province to disturb state security in the entirety of the south. Both true and mythical news of al-Khutt's exploits reached the king and the Wafd cabinet in Cairo, and he became the namesake of every other vicious bandit that appeared in Upper Egypt after him, up until today. In a private talk with 'Aziz Abaza Pasha—the chief police commander of Asyut Province in Upper Egypt, a Wafd Party member, and originally a native of the Delta—King Faruq of Egypt alluded to the pasha that he knew of al-Khutt and had ordered his execution. The pasha immediately formed a highly skilled police crew and called it Team Death, ordering its members to get him al-Khutt's head, or he would take theirs.[92]

One day, as the legend goes, 'Aziz Abaza Pasha went to a movie theater after he had become exhausted with looking for al-Khutt. He was trying to light a cigarette when he realized he had no matches, but a man sitting next to him kindly lit it. The next morning, the pasha received a letter, signed by al-Khutt, thanking him for the nice time they had spent together at the movies. Al-Khutt, née Muhammad Muhammad Mansur, was the blond, blue-eyed grandson of a famous shari'a law scholar who memorized the Qur'an in the village of Drunka. His criminal career started early in his teenage years when he shot the son of a village shaykh, after this shaykh prevented him from grazing his sheep in a field and slapped him on the face. After killing nineteen other members of the same shaykh's family, al-Khutt ran away to the mountains with all of his brothers and formed the most fearless gang that the south ever witnessed. The police vigorously searched for him, but his tricks and wit always saved his life. When al-Khutt was finally captured and shot in 1947, a memorial photo was taken of his dead body lying on the ground among the many proud officers who murdered him.[93]

British capitalism had many success stories in different places in the modern world, where it unified local markets and assisted the birth of nation-states. But Upper Egypt has an alternative story to tell. It is a story of incompetent imperial capitalism and a nation that was never truly born. Colonial attempts at collaborating with Cairo's bourgeoisie to create a unified market in Egypt through carrying British capitalism to the south utterly failed and ended with bailout crises. Moreover, as the British generated environmental catastrophes—the most apparent of which was the cholera epidemic—daily-life resistance of the subaltern classes in the south mounted and attempts at forging a nation were consequently aborted. Upper Egypt stands as but one case that testifies to the stumbling existence of world history's imagined empires.

EPILOGUE

America—The Last Imagined Empire?

On the eve of the Egyptian Revolution of 2011, the US administration was acting as another empire, a sole global hegemon, in the south and north of Egypt and most of the world. After the end of the Cold War, many theorists asserted that America functioned as an "informal," "postmodern" empire that penetrated its dependencies with minimal to no military interference and invented nuanced discursive tools of soft hegemony in a globalized realm of action. In Egypt and elsewhere, American imperialism aimed to take place through the neoliberal dictum of the so-called Washington Consensus, or by pressuring satellite regimes to transform their economies from remaining socialisms to free markets. The United States assumed its market model to be like a holy scripture: applicable to all times and places. Once more, the empire's market failed, in the south and north of Egypt alike, and this failure created immense social disparities that are directly responsible for the outbreak of the 2011 revolution that Qina Province joined.

Like the other five world empires of the last five hundred years examined in this book, the United States extended its reach into the farthest places in Upper Egypt—Qina Province—and disturbed the order of things. As with every previous empire, Upper Egypt and Qina Province have a unique story to tell about myths of and rebellion against empire. This is a different narrative about US penetration and hegemony and how the province's youth and subalterns created their own Tahrir Squares and protested in the south.

During the early 1990s, the United States advocated one path toward economic development in former socialist countries: transformation to the market economy. During the 1960s, many postcolonial states in the Third World, including Egypt, opted for socialist systems, and after the fall of the Soviet Union, the triumphant American capitalist model attempted to reshape these states. US neoliberal economic principles were advanced in underdeveloped countries worldwide, through programs of the World Bank and International Monetary Fund (IMF). Transition to the market was supposed to go hand in hand with transition to democracy, or from single-party systems to pluralism. The United States designed a specific checklist for former socialist governments to follow, to withdraw from the economy and consequently achieve economic development. The principle items on this checklist were privatizing the public sector; eliminating farmers' subsidies; reversing populist land-reform laws in order to free rents (i.e., raise the ceiling on rents) and to return agricultural plots that socialist states had seized and distributed to small peasants to old elites; instituting deregulation; and other measures. Experts dispatched from Washington, DC, to former socialist states were very busy during these years, supervising the transition to the market in various places.

In 1992, the United States pressured Hosni Mubarak's regime in Egypt to liberalize the economy in return for debt rescheduling, aid, and strategic alliance. Mubarak ostensibly agreed. In Cairo, the Parliament and the government closely followed the checklist: they changed the socialist constitution and laws inherited from the Nasser period, privatized the public sector or sold the state-owned enterprises to the private sector, and eliminated subsides given to peasants, among other measures. Meanwhile, far away in Upper Egypt, the appointed governors eliminated farmers' subsidies but maintained state enterprises under their control. The ruling echelon also formed clientelist relations with a rising elite of corrupt business tycoons, and they collaborated to exploit the peoples of the south. The World Bank's reports that praised the successful transition barely noticed the state monopolies in Upper Egypt. At the same time, the provincial governors allowed the US Agency for International Development programs in the south to open offices and fund local NGOs that encouraged peasants to engage in insignificant experiments with market-oriented activities. USAID's "market missionaries" proclaimed they were having a significant impact, but as far as Upper Egyptian peasants were concerned their work had a trivial effect.

Such economic ambiguity between state control and the free market added to the impoverishment of Qina Province and pushed its youth to join fellow Facebook activists in Cairo in revolting against both the repressive state and the failed empire on the eve of the 2011 revolution. For example, while USAID was sharing cheerful "success stories" of Upper Egyptian peasants who embraced market ethics, the sugarcane cultivators of Qina Province were protesting against the monopolies of the state-owned sugar factory over their harvest. The US Empire probably suffered another crisis of images similar to what the French Empire experienced in the late 1700s. American financial and business experts thought they could go anywhere on earth, quickly learn its language and understand its conditions, and then competently develop that place to make it better according to a US neoliberal viewpoint. In 1798, Napoléon Bonaparte's campaign arrived in Egypt and assumed it would be able to proficiently exploit local resources and bring about progress. But Napoléon was manipulated and deceived by cunning, dark natives. In the 1990s and first decade after the year 2000, one could detect another crisis of images in how the American administration dealt with the authoritarian regime of Egypt.

In what follows, this epilogue first engages in a discussion with the recent theoretical stances concerning the US Empire and its market. Then it moves to the situation in Qina Province a few years before the 2011 revolution, tracing how the province joined the Tahrir protesters to fight against the consequences of the failures of neoliberalism.

Early in the 1990s, when many viewed the United States as an imperial force on the rise upon the fall of the Soviet Union, Immanuel Wallerstein affirmed instead that it was already declining. Wallerstein, the founder of the world-system theory, explained that this empire had grown due to "God's blessings," and God was apparently was taking his blessings back:

> God, it seems, has distributed his blessings to the United States thrice: in the present, in the past, and in the future.... The problem with God's blessings is that they have a price. And the price we are willing to pay is always a call upon our righteousness. Each blessing has been accompanied by its contradiction. And it is always obvious that those who received the blessing were those who paid the price. As we move from today into tomorrow, it is time once again to count our blessings, assess our sins, and behold our reckoning sheet.[1]

Again, in 2003, after the US invasion of Iraq, Wallerstein noted the US inability to act strongly on the global stage and recommended that the country's power not be overestimated: "We have entered a chaotic world. It has to do with the crisis of capitalism.... The United States government drifted in a situation that it is trying to manage all over the place and that it will be incapable of managing. This is neither good nor bad, but we should not overestimate these people nor the strength on which they rely."[2]

When the US blueprint of transition to the market was not working as hoped in places such as Russia, Joseph Stiglitz, economist and author of *Globalization and Its Discontents,* debunked the myth of the market and pointed out the failure of US neoliberal domination from its onset. In 2002, Stiglitz wrote, "We have focused so hard on our own economic mythology, and on managing globalization to our short-term benefits, that we have been blind to what we are doing to ourselves and the world."[3] Adopting political economy theorist Karl Polanyi's refutation of the self-regulating market and relying on financial evidence, Stiglitz asserted that the collapse of some American big firms was primarily due to excessive deregulation. Therefore, he called on the state to play an essential role in running the economy—or to "bring the state back in," as many other political economists have argued before him.[4] Outside the United States, the Washington Consensus rhetoric promised long-awaited human and economic development—and then imposed unfair free-trade agreements and programs of structural adjustment that benefited Western economic interests. "Liberalization has thus, too often, not been followed by the promised growth, but by increased misery," Stiglitz insists.[5]

From a postcolonial perspective, Timothy Mitchell also refutes US mythology surrounding the greatness of the market economy, and he looks at Upper Egypt in this regard. Mitchell investigates the discipline of economics as a Western discourse in itself, and he traces the genealogy of the making of the field in colonial and postcolonial contexts. Also referencing Polanyi, Mitchell shows how the market economy—the conventional wisdom in liberal and neoliberal theories of economics—was introduced to the colonized as a mythical "universal model" that never functioned in the ideal way that the empire claimed. Mitchell adds that in the past, under the British Empire, European experts, their modern technology, and self-regulating markets resulted in only human and environmental catastrophes. In the present, international institutions of US capitalism, mainly the IMF and the World Bank, still perpetuate this myth and generate more catastrophes in the societies where they insist on applying economic liberalization programs. In Egypt at large and Upper Egypt in particular, Mitchell illustrates that market capitalism has resulted in profound environmental crises and social disparities throughout the last two centuries.[6]

In *Empire,* Michael Hardt and Antonio Negri insist that traditional imperial expansion is dead and there is not a single nation-state today that can play this role alone. "*The United States does not, and indeed no nation-state can today, form the center of an imperialist project.* Imperialism is over. No nation will be world leader in the way modern European nations were."[7] They argue that, in fact, that a transition occurred from imperialism to empire, and they trace the genealogy of this transition from European to Euro-American global control. Whereas imperialism involved territorial expansion, empire has no territorial boundaries or fixed borders. The authors also investigate a transformation in the "paradigm of rule," and they use Michel Foucault's notion of "the biopolitical" to understand this newly formed paradigm. For them, Western capitalism is a key part of the logic of the new empire, just as it had been a pivotal facet of old imperialism. Hardt and Negri argue that the control of production and labor have turned into a biopolitical process in which the body and the entire life of the citizen are disciplined toward economic goals. "Biopower is a form of power that regulates social life from its interior," they write, "following it, interpreting it, absorbing it, and rearticulating it."[8] They predict that the postmodern empire will decline because it carries within itself the seeds of revolution—which will be led by globalized social classes they call the "multitude."[9]

Touching on the same topic, Gayatri Spivak—a founding figure in subaltern studies—recognizes US imperialism and contemplates subaltern resistance against it. Spivak indicates that in its early theoretical connotation, "'subaltern' referred to persons and groups cut off from upward—and, in a sense, 'outward'—social mobility" in colonial societies under European empires.[10] However, Spivak explains that in the new context of imperial America and the invention of new means of soft penetration, such as NGOs and human rights associations, the subaltern today is highly connected and assimilated into the globalized structure of power. She adds that today's US-inspired and largely US-funded international civil society and NGOs act among subaltern individuals for the interest of global capitalism, through means such as women's microenterprise and pharmaceutical dumping. For example, today's subaltern "is no longer cut off from lines of access to the centre, as represented by the Bretton Woods agencies and the World Trade Organizations, is altogether interested in the rural and indigenous subalterns as [a] source of trade-related intellectual property or TRIPs."[11] The new subaltern is no longer isolated and voiceless; rather, s/he is reachable by forces of multinational corporations and affiliated NGOs that exploit her/his indigenous knowledge for global postindustrial capitalism.

All of the above theorization about US imperial domination through the market applies to Upper Egypt. Nevertheless, the empire's market did not meet much success there, and the subalterns of Qina Province did manage to revolt against it.

On eve of the 2011 revolution, Qina Province lived in a mixed and confused situation between transition to the market and conspicuous state intervention. Upon applying an economic reform program in 1992, the authoritarian regime in Cairo allowed USAID officers, or "market missionaries," access to Upper Egypt, including Qina, in order to fund many agricultural programs with local NGOs. These programs targeted both female and male peasants who owned small plots and aimed to convert their mode of production from "traditional" farming techniques addressing local needs to a "modernized" method that conformed to the international market. For example, a program called El-Shams (the Sun), started in 2003 and taught peasants how to cultivate green beans, cantaloupe, and charentais melons for exportation to Europe. The program claimed that it changed the life of thousands of farmers in Upper Egypt and improved the living standards of whole villages.[12] One of the success stories it shared was about another program, AgReform: "Hasan Aly Shehata is a farmer from Dandara village in the governorate of Qena. He is married, with five daughters who are all in school, and a two-year-old son. Hasan is not well-to-do; he cultivates land in a village 40 kilometers away from his house. Hasan's family income and well-being have improved as he started cultivating cantaloupe (not a traditional crop)—a decision based on AgReform's technical support to Al-Waqf Farmer NGO (FNGO), of which he is an active member."[13]

USAID also partnered with a gigantic food corporation, Heinz, in funding a five-year agribusiness project targeting small farmers in Qina and other provinces, beginning in 2008. According to its managers, the project "applies a market-driven value chain approach. It invests in the vast but largely unrealized potential of thousands of Upper Egypt's small farmers to meet modern-day market demands."[14] It was designed to target a large number of peasants—nearly eight thousand—and to foster continuous contact between them and the global market.

Aside from the fact that a large percentage of these programs' budgets were allocated to the high salaries of foreign employees and payments to American experts, local peasants in Qina asserted that the projects had little impact. One could barely notice any change in the mode of production and the lives of the inhabitants of the province's numerous villages. In an interview with an older farmer from Armant in the fall of 2010, he told me that peasants were unable to compete on the international market with their minute plots and without state subsidies. He explained that the European Union granted subsidies to its farmers, who worked with advanced machinery and technology, and gave Qina's farmers limited access to their markets. Economic liberalization eliminated subsidizes for fertilizers, seeds, and machinery. Thus, with ever-increasing rents, small-plot tenant farmers—who were often targeted by USAID-funded NGOs—found it almost impossible to enter the highly competitive global market.

In the meantime, the sugarcane cultivators of Qina Province went on strike. The government purchased their harvest for the province's state-owned sugar factories at unfairly cheap prices, and corrupt officials assisted private businesses in doing the same. In 2008, the farmers of Armant and Ruzayqat refused to deliver their harvest to the state factories unless the government raised prices. One of the province's Parliament members, 'Abd al-Rahim al-Ghul of Qus, who had held his seat for thirty years as a member of the northern ruling party, the National Democratic Party, condemned the strike. He characterized it as an illegal action of public disobedience that the people of the province were not naturally inclined to commit, asserting that it was incited by oppositional groups and human rights organizations.[15]

The same sugarcane farmers were also losing their lands to the old elite families of the colonial era, since the new legal codes of market reform reversed the Arab socialist codes and introduced private property laws anew. Thousands of Qina's peasants had been evicted, or were awaiting eviction, from their plots in order to cede their land back to the large old families. These were the same families that were the co-opted local elite and propertied class during the period of British colonialism, before the 1952 military coup and subsequent socialist reforms. Under Mubarak, these families were co-opted by the northern authoritarian regime through membership in the ruling party and allocation of parliamentary seats.[16] The Washington Consensus preached market reforms as the only way for promised economic and human development. However, in reality these reforms worked for the benefit of the business and rural elite, who controlled the ruling party and the Parliament, at the expense of the peasants and laborers of Qina.

When widespread bread riots swept the province in 2007, there was a huge USAID wheat silo in the fields bordering the city of Qus. The struggle to purchase subsidized bread killed many people in the villages of Qina during the months preceding the outbreak of a national crisis in Cairo. In the long lines in front of state bakeries, Qina's villagers shot each other to get a share of the cheap bread, while preachers in mosques called upon them to consume less and not to waste leftovers.[17] Egypt is "traditionally the largest U.S. wheat consumer," through the USAID aid program.[18] The annual influx of US aid to Egypt mostly takes the form of imported American products, and wheat makes up a considerable portion of these goods. Despite its calls for global free trade, the US government has pressured the Egyptian state to buy the more expensive American wheat instead of the cheaper alternatives from other countries, such as former Soviet states. Concurrently, economic liberalization measures have compelled the Egyptian government to eliminate its subsidies to peasants, including wheat cultivators, while the US government gives generous subsidies to its wheat cultivators.[19]

On the eve of the 2011 revolution in Qina, legendary bandits still hid in the mountains to show their discontent with the confused situation. Building on the traditions of two hundred years of subaltern unrest in Qina, stories of southern bandits took new trajectories. Many such bandits began their careers cooperating with the corrupt regime and its security apparatus, which then disowned them when they became a threat to the central government. Many years ago, there was a legendary bandit known as al-Khutt, whose name has become the title given to every other great bandit appearing in the province after him. Nawfal Sa'd, who finally fell to police bullets in 2007, was another *khutt* who inherited the terrifying persona of his predecessor. Nawfal was an unemployed forty-year-old from the Hawwara clan that independently ruled Upper Egypt for centuries during Ottoman times. He started his criminal career in Qina in the 1990s, when he assisted the regime in crushing Islamic fundamentalists and in violently supporting the candidates of the ruling National Democratic Party during parliamentary elections. He became friends with high-ranking police officers, who protected him in return for a considerable share of his illicit income. In a village in Naj' Hammadi, his house was a huge fort protected from the back by the mountains, hidden in the front behind the high sugarcane fields, and guarded day and night by his heavily armed gang. The security apparatus soon came to view him as a threat, and the time came to terminate him. The police shot Nawfal in a fierce battle on account of many charges against him: aside from drug dealing, robbery, and murder, he was charged several times for resisting the authorities and threatening public security. For many months after he died, his wife attempted to avenge his death by murdering the village traitors who had assisted the police in reaching him.[20]

FIGURE 6. *(top)* Protesting women in Karnak, Luxor, during the 2011 revolution.

FIGURE 7. *(botton)* The McDonald's sign appears next to a revolutionary crowd in Luxor, January 2011.

Finally, on 25 January 2011, the discontented youth of the province created their own Facebook groups to join Cairene compatriots in making the revolution. Youth coalitions quickly took form in every town in Qina, and they led thousands of lower- and middle-class groups to meet in every big and small square in the province to foster the spirit of Tahrir.[21] The Egyptian Revolution in the south and the north rendered America another "imagined empire." Its neoliberal market stumbled just as the British liberal market before it, and the subalterns of the south revived their means to rebel.

NOTES

INTRODUCTION

1. Many world historians use the concept of "informal empire" to refer to indirect forms of imperial hegemony that do not include military occupation. See Niall Ferguson, *Colossus: The Price of America's Empire* (New York: Penguin, 2004), 10. On US aid in general, and USAID's wheat aid in particular and Egyptian dependency, see Galal Amin, *Egypt's Economic Predicament* (Leiden: Brill, 1995).

2. Joseph Stiglitz's *Globalization and Its Discontents* (London: W.W. Norton, 2003) insists that the United States spreads the neoliberal myth of development through market reform in the third world. On the impact of market reform policies on Qina's peasants, see the reports of the Land Center of Human Rights, 2000–2008, Cairo, www.lchr-eg.org (accessed 11 February 2012).

3. See UNDP (UN Development Programme), *Arab Human Development Report* 2004 (New York: UNDP, 2005); World Bank, "Egypt Project and Programs," http://go.worldbank.org/C15AQ9EG50 (accessed 5 October 2008).

4. Facebook group, http://www.facebook.com/group.php?gid=8412576147 (accessed 9 March 2010). The movie's title is *Al-Jazira,* and among the popular TV series on Upper Egyptian mountain-based bandits are *Hada'iq al-Shaytan* and *Dhi'ab al-Jabal.*

5. This book uses the term *microhistory* differently from its original meaning, proposed by historians such as Giovanni Levi, Carlo Ginzburg, and Macro Ferrari, which focuses on the peoples and internal dynamics of small European villages and towns. Rather, this book looks at small places while putting their internal dynamics and transformations into the larger context of the world economy and global imperialism.

6. Qina in this book refers to a province that has consisted of many towns, such as Qina, Qus, Luxor, Isna, and Farshut, and numerous villages, including Salimiyya, Armant, Qammula, Samhud, Maris, and others. During the nineteenth century, the government sometimes split the province into two provinces, *mudiriyya*s of Qina and Isna, for administrative purposes. Today, the province is administratively

split into the two governorates of Qina and Luxor. Regardless of administrative divisions, this book deals with Qina as historically one province at all times.

7. Edouard de Montulé, *Voyage en Amérique, en Italie, en Sicile et en Égypte pendant les années 1816, 1817, 1818 et 1819* (Paris: Delaunay, 1821), 2:271.

8. Ibid.; 'Ali Mubarak, *Al-Khitat al-Tawfiqiyya al-Jadida li-Misr al-Qahira* (Cairo: Matba'at Bulaq, 1887), 14:120.

9. Vivant Denon, *Voyage dans le Basse et la Haute Égypte, pendant les Campagne du Général Bonaparte* (Paris: Imprimerie de P. Didot l'aine, 1802), 235–36.

10. Mubarak, *Al-Khitat al-Tawfiqiyya*, 14:128–29. Also see Taqyy al-Din al-Maqrizi, *Al-Mawa'iz wa-l-I'tibar bi Dhikr al-Khitat wa-l-'Athar* (Cairo: Maktabat al-Thaqafa al-Diniyya, 1987), 1:202–3. And also see Abu al-Fadl al-Idfawi, *Al-Tali' al-Sa'id al-Jami' li Asma' Nujaba' al-Sa'id* (Cairo: al-Dar al-Misriyya lil-Ta'lif wa-al-Tarjama, 1966), 13, 18.

11. W.J. Fischel, "The Spice Trade in Mamluk Egypt," in M.N. Pearson (ed.), *Spices in the Indian Ocean World* (London: Ashgate Variorum, 1996), 56.

12. Mubarak, *Al-Khitat al-Tawfiqiyya*, 14:129, 133–34.

13. See Andre Gunder Frank, *ReOrient: Global Economy in the Asian Age* (Berkeley: University of California Press, 1998); Janet Abu Lughod, *Before European Hegemony: The World System A.D. 1250–1350* (New York: Oxford University Press, 1989); K.N. Chaudhuri, *Trade and Civilization in the Indian Ocean: An Economic History from the Rise of Islam to 1750* (Cambridge: Cambridge University Press, 1985).

14. See Muhammad al-Maraghi al-Jirjawi, *Tarikh Wilayyat al-Sa'id fi al-'Asrayn al-Mamluki wa-l-'Uthmani al-Musamma bi Nur al-'Uyun bi-Dhikr Jirja fi 'Ahd Thalathat Qurun* (Cairo: Maktabat al-Nahda, 1997); Layla 'Abd al-Latif Ahmad, *Al-Sa'id fi 'Ahd Shaykh al-'Arab Hammam* (Cairo: al-Hay'a al-Misriyya al-'Amma lil-Kitab, 1987).

15. On the 1820s revolts, see J.A. St. John, *Egypt and Nubia* (London: Chapman and Hall, 1845), 378–81; and 'Ali Mubarak, *Al-Khitat al-Tawfiqiyya al-Jadida li-Misr al-Qahira* (Cairo: al-Hay'a al-Misriyya al-'Amma lil-Kitab, 1994), 12:116–17.

16. On the 1864 revolt, see Lucie Austin Duff-Gordon, *Letters from Egypt* (London: Macmillan, 1865), 341–71.

17. See, for example, Afaf Lutfi al-Sayyid Marsot, *A History of Egypt: From Arab Conquest to the Present* (Cambridge: Cambridge University Press, 2007); Beth Baron, *Egypt as a Woman: Nationalism, Gender, and Politics* (Berkeley: University of California Press, 2005); and the Arabic books published by Silsilat Tarikh al-Misriyyin during 1980s and 1990s in Cairo by al-Hay'a al-Misriyya al-'Amma lil-Kitab.

18. Peter Gran, "Upper Egypt in Modern History: 'A Southern Question'?," in Nicholas Hopkins and Reem Saad (eds.), *Upper Egypt: Identity and Change* (Cairo: American University in Cairo Press, 2004), 81.

19. See Martina Rieker, "The Sa'id and the City: Subaltern Spaces in the Making of Modern Egypt," PhD dissertation, Temple University, 1997.

20. Michael Hardt and Antonio Negri, *Empire* (Cambridge, MA: Harvard University Press, 2000), xii, xv (emphasis in original).

21. Ibid., xiv.
22. Giovanni Arrighi, "The Three Hegemonies of Historical Capitalism," *Review*, Summer 1990, 366.
23. Ibid., 365–408. Also see Giovanni Arrighi, *The Long Twentieth Century* (London: Verso, 2002).
24. Arrighi, "Three Hegemonies of Historical Capitalism," 399.
25. See Immanuel Wallerstein, *The Modern World-System*, vol. 3 (New York: Academic Press, 1989); Andre Gunder Frank, *Dependent Accumulation and Underdevelopment* (London: Macmillan, 1978); and Samir Amin, *Imperialism and Unequal Development* (New York: Monthly Review Press, 1977).
26. Bill Ashcroft, Gareth Griffiths, and Helen Tiffin (eds.), *The Post-colonial Studies Reader* (London: Routledge, 2006), 1.
27. See Michel Foucault's *History of Sexuality*, vol. 1 (New York: Vintage, 1990); *Discipline and Punish: The Birth of Prison* (New York: Penguin, 1979); and *The Birth of the Clinic* (London: Routledge, 1989). See also, for example, a postcolonial study that applies Foucault's work to the study of the empire: Ann Laura Stoler, *Race and the Education of Desire: Foucault's "History of Sexuality" and the Colonial Order of Things* (Durham, NC: Duke University Press, 1995).
28. Stoler, *Race and the Education of Desire*, 4.
29. See Judith Tucker, *Women in Nineteenth Century Egypt* (Cambridge: Cambridge University Press, 1985), 20.
30. See, for instance, the collection of articles in Huri İslamoğu-İnan, *The Ottoman Empire and the World-Economy* (Cambridge: Cambridge University Press, 2004). See also Joel Benin, *Workers and Peasants in the Middle East* (Cambridge: Cambridge University Press, 2001).
31. For example, see Omnia Shakry, *The Great Social Laboratory: Subjects of Knowledge in Colonial and Postcolonial Egypt* (Stanford, CA: Stanford University Press, 2007); Eugene Rogan (ed.), *Outside In: On the Margins of the Modern Middle East* (London: I.B. Tauris, 2002); and Leila Abu Lughod, *Remaking Women: Feminism and Modernity in the Middle East* (Princeton, NJ: Princeton University Press, 1998).
32. Timothy Mitchell, *Rule of Experts: Egypt, Techno-Politics, Modernity* (Berkeley: University of California Press, 2002), 1–15.
33. See Gayatri Spivak's "Can the Subaltern Speak?" in Ashcroft, Griffiths, and Tiffin, *Post-colonial Studies Reader*, 28–37.
34. Ranajit Guha, "On Some Aspects of the Historiography of Colonial India," in Vinayak Ghaturvedi (ed.), *Mapping Subaltern Studies and the Postcolonial* (London: Verso, 2000), 1.
35. Quoted in David Arnold, "Gramsci and Peasant Subalternity in India," in Ghaturvedi, *Mapping Subaltern Studies and the Postcolonial*, 34–35.
36. Eric Hobsbawm authored an interesting account of social bandits in south Italy, arguing for the progressive nature of their actions. Hobsbawm's approach greatly inspires this book. See Eric Hobsbawm, *Social Bandits and Primitive Rebels: Studies in Archaic Forms of Social Movement in the 19th and 20th Centuries* (New York: Free Press, 1960).

37. The National Archives of Egypt, or Dar al-Watha'iq al-Qawmiyya, are undertaking an extensive project to create digital databases for millions of unknown, uncataloged documents. Researchers in this project informed me about thousands of documents, particularly concerning Qina Province, that were never discovered or touched before, which this book heavily relies on. Great thanks are due Emad Helal, a senior historian and supervisor in this digitization project.

38. For Qina Province in the Ottoman period, the court of Isna is the only court whose records are accessible in the National Archives of Egypt. Despite references to them in Isna Court documents, court records of other towns and villages in the province are not present.

39. This book uses these archival sources with an awareness of their limitations and biases as products of specific political contexts. Many of these documents, such as petitions, rulings of the Supreme Court, or parliamentary minutes, sometimes were recorded in a way that reflected the power structure in state and society. These records must be contextualized and, in some cases, perceived as state discourses rather than simple bearers of facts. Furthermore, this study is selective about the documents it considers as references to actions of political rebellion. While archival records deliver tens of thousands of stories that could fall in a vague area between regular crimes and political resistance, this study includes only highly politicized cases for analysis as subaltern actions of revenge. Specific criteria in making these selections include choosing only crimes targeting state bureaucrats, state buildings, government money, or the propertied politicians. The criteria also include selecting for certain characteristics of the person who committed the action, focusing on peasants, laborers, or women whose lives were hurt in one way or another by the regime.

CHAPTER 1: OTTOMANS, PLAGUE, AND REBELLION

1. Ahmad Pasha Cezzar, *Ottoman Egypt in the Eighteenth Century: The Nizam-name-i Misir* (Cambridge, MA: Harvard University Press, 1962), 44 (Turkish transliteration replaced with Arabic transliteration).

2. See George A. Haddad, "A Project of the Independence of Egypt, 1801," *Journal of the American Oriental Society* 90 (2) (April–June 1970): 174. Prominent Egyptian intellectual Rifa'a al-Tahtawi (d. 1873) referred to the Ottoman-era southern Egyptian state as a *jumhuriyya*. See Layla 'Abd al-Latif Ahmad, *Al-Sa'id fi 'Ahd Shaykh al-'Arab Hammam* (Cairo: al-Hay'a al-Misriyya al-'Amma lil-Kitab, 1987), 21.

3. These events were observed by the contemporary historian and Mamluk officer Ahmad al-Damurdashi (d. ca. 1755) in *Al-Durra al-Musana fi 'Akhbar al-Kinana*, Abd al-Rahim Abd al-Rahman Abd al-Rahim (ed.) (Cairo: Maktabat al-Ma'had al-Faransi, 1989), 40–60 (the quotation is from this source; the plague is discussed on 40–41. Also, late eighteenth-century historian 'Abd al-Rahman al-Jabarti (d. 1822) accounted for these events in *'Aja'ib al-Athar fi-l-Tarajim wa-l-Akhbar* (Cairo: Maktabat Madbuli, 1997), 1:136–39.

4. On these recent theoretical arguments see, Suraiya Faroqhi, *Ottoman Empire and the World Around It* (London: I. B. Tauris, 2006), 14–15; and Karen Barkey, *Empire of Difference: The Ottomans in Comparative Perspective* (Cambridge: Cambridge University Press, 2008), 93–98.

5. On the three-century state see, Salah Ahmad Haridi, *Dawr al-Sa'id fi Misr al-'Uthmaniyy,* 923/1213–1517/1898 (Cairo: Dar al-Ma'arif, 1984). On the Indian Ocean world economy and the place of the Ottoman Empire in it, see Andre Gunder Frank, *ReOrient: Global Economy in the Asian Age* (Berkeley: University of California Press, 1998).

6. Stanford Shaw, *The Financial and Administrative Organization and Development of Ottoman Egypt,* 1517–1798 (Princeton, NJ: Princeton University Press, 1962), 14; Layla 'Abd al-Latif Ahmad, *Al-'Idara fi Misr fi-l-'Asr al-'Uthmani* (Cairo: Matba'at Jami'at 'Ayn Shams, 1978), 39.

7. Ahmad Fou'ad Mitwalli (ed.), "Qanun Misr (Qanun-name Misr)," in al-Jabarti, 'Aja'ib al-Athar, 1:557–59.

8. The *iltizam* system was applied throughout the Arab provinces of the Ottoman Empire after 1617. See Donald Quataert, *The Ottoman Empire, 1700–1922* (Cambridge: Cambridge University Press, 2000), 29–30, 48–50; and Ariel Salzman, "An Ancien Regime Revisited: 'Privatization' and Political Economy in the Eighteenth Century Ottoman Empire," *Politics and Society,* 21 (4) (1993): 393–423.

9. Ahmad, *Al-Sa'id fi 'Ahd Shaykh al-'Arab Hammam,* 102–8; Shaw translation notes in Huseyn Efendi, *Ottoman Egypt in the Age of the French Revolution* (Cambridge, MA: Harvard University Press, 1964), 141,144; Shaw, *Financial and Administrative Organization,* 14, 79.

10. Shaw, *Financial and Administrative Organization,* 14.

11. Vivant Denon, *Voyage dans la Basse et la Haute Égypte* (Paris: Imprimerie de P. Didot l'aine, 1802), 255–56; Ahmad, *Al-Sa'id fi 'Ahd Shaykh al-'Arab Hammam,* 102–8; Shaw translation notes in Huseyn Efendi, *Ottoman Egypt in the Age of the French Revolution,* 141, 144; Shaw, *Financial and Administrative Organization,* 14, 79; James Bruce, *Travels to Discover the Source of the Nile, in the years 1768, 1769, 1770, 1771, 1772, and 1773* (Edinburgh: Printed by J. Ruthven, for G. G. J. and J. Robinson, London, 1790), 1:100.

12. Muhammad Ibn Abd Allah al-Amir al-Maliki, "Risala fi man Tawalla al-Sa'id min al-'Umara al-Jarakisa," 5–7, unpublished manuscript, Manuscript No. 6686, al-Azhar Library, Cairo; Haridi, *Dawr al-Sa'id fi Misr al-'Uthmaniyya,* 168–69.

13. See K. N. Chaudhuri, *Trade and Civilization in the Indian Ocean: An Economic History from the Rise of Islam to 1750* (Cambridge: Cambridge University Press, 1985); R. J. Barendse, *The Arabian Seas: The Indian Ocean World of the Seventeenth Century* (Armonk, NY: M. E. Sharpe, 2002); Janet Abu Lughod, *Before European Hegemony: The World System A.D. 1250–1350* (New York: Oxford University Press, 1989); and Frank, *ReOrient.*

14. About Qina Province's trade in the Mamluk period, see Taqyy al-Din al-Maqrizi, *Al-Mawa'iz wa-l-I'tibar bi Dhikr al-Khitat wa-l-'Athar* (Cairo: Maktabat

al-Thaqafa al-Diniyya, 1987), 1:202–3; Muhammad 'Abdu al-Hajjaji, *Qus fi-l-Tarikh al 'Islami* (Cairo: al-Hay'a al-Misriyya al-'Amma lil-Kitab, 1982); Abu al-Fadl al-'Idfawi, *Al-Tali' al-Sa'id al-Jami' li Asma' Nujaba' al-Sa'id* (Cairo: al-Dar al-Misriyya lil-Ta'lif wa-al-Tarjama, 1966); and Jean-Claude Garcin, *Un centre musulman de la Haute-Égypte médiévale: Qûs* (Cairo: Institut Français d'Archéologie Orientale du Caire, 1976).

15. Fred Lawson, *The Social Origins of Egyptian Expansionism during the Muhammad Ali Period* (New York: Columbia University Press, 1992), 58–61; Fred Lawson, "Rural Revolt and Provincial Society in Egypt, 1820–1824," *International Journal of Middle East Studies* 13 (2) (May 1981): 132–33; Nabil al-Sayyid al-Tukhi, *Sa'id Misr fi 'Ahd al-Hamla al-Faransiyya, 1798–1801* (Cairo: al-Hay'a al-Misriyya al-'Amma lil-Kitab, 1997), 61.

16. Muhammad al-Maraghi al-Jirjawi, *Tarikh Wilayyat al-Sa'id fi al-'Asrayn al-Mamluki wa-l-'Uthmani al-Musamma bi Nur al-'Uyun bi-Dhikr Jirja fi 'Ahd Thalathat Qurun* (Cairo: Maktabat al-Nahda, 1997), 107. Ahmad, *al-Sa'id fi 'Ahd Shaykh al-'Arab Hammam,* 32. About sugar cultivation in Farshut see, Ahmad al-Hitta, *Tarikh Misr al-Iqtisadi* (Alexandria: Matba'at al-Misri, 1967), 8, 16, 111; and Haridi, *Dawr al-Sa'id fi Misr al-'Uthmaniyy,* 263.

17. Abu Lughod, *Before European Hegemony,* 232.

18. Shaw, *Financial and Administrative Organization,* 78.

19. Cezzar, *Ottoman Egypt in the Eighteenth Century,* 41.

20. Haridi, *Dawr al-Sa'id fi Misr al-'Uthmaniyya,* 263; Shaw translation notes in Huseyn Efendi, *Ottoman Egypt in the Age of the French Revolution,* 138–39.

21. Copts are the native Orthodox Christians. The distinction between "Arabs" and "Copts" here applies only to this period, relying on the contemporary literature. Later developments and historical interpretations render the line drawn between the two groups inaccurate.

22. Ahmad, *Al-Sa'id fi 'Ahd Shaykh al-'Arab Hammam,* 55.

23. Shaw, *Financial and Administrative Organization,* 24–25.

24. al-Damurdashi, *Al-Durra al-Musana,* 45–49.

25. Shaw translation notes in Huseyn Efendi, *Ottoman Egypt in the Age of the French Revolution,* 141.

26. Richard Pococke, *A Description of the East, and Some Other Countries* (London: Printed for the author, by W. Bowyer, 1743–45), 1:89; Shari'a Court Records of Isna (hereafter Isna Court), Sijill 1, Case 59, p. 48, 12 Rabi' Akhir 1170, and Isna Court, Sijill 1, Case 66, p. 54, 8 Rabi' Akhir 1170, both in National Archives of Egypt, Cairo (hereafter NAE).

27. Pococke, *Description of the East,* 1:68–69, 77.

28. Haridi, *Dawr al-Sa'id fi Misr al-'Uthmaniyya,* 159–72.

29. Bruce, *Travels to Discover the Source of the Nile,* 1:146–49.

30. For example, Isna Court, Sijill Ishhadat 7, Case 70, 12 Rajab 1173, p. 37; Isna Court, Sijill Ishhadat 14, Part 2, Case 63, p. 42, 1177; Sijill Ishhadat 15, Part 1, Case 129, p. 87, 1178; Isna Court, Sijill Ishhadat 17, Part 1, Case 1, p. 1, 9 Shawwal 1179; and Qina Court, Portfolio No. 1, Dhu al-Hijja 1180, all records found in Haridi, *Dawr*

al-Saʿid fi Misr al-ʿUthmaniyya, appendix 22, 446–47. Some historians mistakenly claim that the land between Asyut and Aswan was communal, or *mashaʿ*, and peasants enjoyed no usufruct rights to it and the Arab shaykhs and large tax farmers distributed different plots each year. This differed from the *'athariyya* land known in Lower and Middle Egypt. The *'athariyya* is enclosed by borders that divided the land of one peasant from that of another. These borders did not change from year to year, as the same peasant kept the same holding each year, unless transactions took place among peasants. Al-Hitta, *Tarikh Misr al-'Iqtisadi,* 5–6. Nonetheless, court records of Isna and Qina show that the same system of landholding was applied in Upper Egypt as in the Delta.

31. Muhammad ʿAfifi, *Al-ʾAqbat fi Misr fi al-ʿAsr al-ʿUthmani* (Cairo: al-Hayʾa al-Misriyya al-ʿAmma lil-Kitab, 1992), 152–53; Isna Court, Sijill Ishhadat 53, Case 317, p. 143, 10 Ramadan 1216; Sijill Ishhadat 52, Case 294, p. 146, 7 Shaʿban 1215, both in NAE.

32. Ahmad, *Al-ʾIdara fi Misr fi-l-ʿAsr al-ʿUthmani,* 273–91.

33. See Isna Court, Sijill Ishhadat, 1172–1215, NAE.

34. Ibid.

35. Isna Court, Portfolio 3, 25 Jumada al-Awwal 1221, records found in Haridi, *Dawr al-Saʿid fi Misr al-ʿUthmaniyya,* appendix 4, 407.

36. See al-Damurdashi, *Al-Durra al-Musana,* 51; and Ahmad, *Al-Saʿid fi ʾAhd Shaykh al-ʾArab Hammam,* 26–29.

37. Haridi, *Dawr al-Saʿid fi Misr al-ʿUthmaniyya,* 193–203.

38. al-Damurdashi, *Al-Durra al-Musana fi ʾAkhbar al-Kinana,* 41. The translation is courtesy of Daniel Crecelius and ʿAbd al-Wahhab Bakr, trans., *Al-Damurdashi's Chronicle of Egypt, 1688–1755* (Leiden, Netherlands: E.J. Brill, 1991), 81.

39. al-Damurdashi, *Al-Durra al-Musana fi ʾAkhbar al-Kinana,* 40–41.

40. al-Jabarti, *ʾAjaʾib al-Athar,* 1:139.

41. Edward Lane, *An Account of the Manners and Customs of Modern Egyptians: Written in Egypt During the Years 1833, 34, and 35* (London: Charles Knight and Co., 1837), 1:3.

42. al-Damurdashi, *Al-Durra al- Musana,* 40–41.

43. al-Damurdashi, *Al-Durra al-Musana,* 41. The translation is courtesy of Crecelius and Bakr, *Al-Damurdashi's Chronicles of Egypt,* 82.

44. Ibid.

45. Ibid.

46. Ibid., 49–60. The translation is courtesy of Crecelius and Bakr, *Al-Damurdashi's Chronicles of Egypt,* 94.

47. Ibid.

48. Ibid.

49. Denon, *Voyage dans la Basse et la Haute Égypte,* 2:255–56; Ahmad, *Al-Saʿid fi ʾAhd Shaykh al-ʾArab Hammam,* 102–8; Shaw translation notes in Huseyn Efendi, *Ottoman Egypt in the Age of the French Revolution,* 141, 144; Bruce, *Travels to Discover the Source of the Nile,* 1:100; Shaw, *Financial and Administrative Organization,* 14, 79.

50. Bruce, *Travels to Discover the Source of the Nile*, 1:117–18.
51. Haddad, "Project of the Independence of Egypt, 1801," 174.
52. Ahmad, *Al-Saʿid fi ʿAhd Shaykh al-ʿArab Hammam*, 21.
53. al-Jabarti, *ʿAjaʾib al-ʿAthar*, 2:349–50.
54. Bruce, *Travels to Discover the Source of the Nile*, 1:117–18 (quotations preserve historical spellings).
55. Pococke, *Description of the East*, 1:84–85.
56. Lawson, *Social Origins of Egyptian Expansionism*, 59.
57. Shaw translation notes in Huseyn Efendi, *Ottoman Egypt in the Age of the French Revolution*, 138–39.
58. A French report observed this in 1753. See also Terence Walz, *Trade between Egypt and Bilad As-Sudan* (Cairo: Institute Français d'Archéologie Orientale du Caire, 1978), 10; and Bruce, *Travels to Discover the Source of the Nile*, 1:151, 195–96, 200. About Hammam's control over Qusayr, see Cezzar, *Ottoman Egypt in the Eighteenth Century*, 44.
59. Walz, *Trade between Egypt and Bilad As-Sudan*, 1–39. A third route passed through the western oasis.
60. Bruce, *Travels to Discover the Source of the Nile*, 1:116–118.
61. Henry Light, *Travels in Egypt, Nubia, Holy Lands, Mount Lebanon and Cyprus in the Year 1814* (London: Rodwell and Martin, 1818), 48. About Farshut's sugar, also see Bruce, *Travels to Discover the Source of the Nile*, 1:116–18.
62. al-Jabarti, *ʿAjaʾib al-ʿAthar*, 2:350.
63. Ibid.; Denon, *Voyage dans la Basse et la Haute Égypte*, 255–56.
64. Qina Court, Portfolio 2, no date, cited in Haridi, *Dawr al-Saʿid fi Misr al-ʿUthmaniyya*, appendix 13, 422.
65. al-Jabarti, *ʿAjaʾib al-ʿAthar*, 2:350.
66. Isna Court, Sijill Ishhadat 15, Part 1, 1178; Isna Court, Sijill 1, Case 59, p. 48, 12 Rabiʿ Akhir 1170; Isna Court, Sijill 1, Case 66, p. 54., 8 Rabiʿ Akhir 1170, all in NAE.
67. Pococke, *Description of the East*, 1:89; Isna Court, Sijill 1, Case 59, p. 48, 12 Rabiʿ Akhir 1170, and Isna Court, Sijill 1, Case 66, p. 54, 8 Rabiʿ Akhir 1170, both in NAE; Ahmad, *Al-Saʿid fi ʿAhad Shaykh al-ʿArab Hammam*, 113.
68. ʿAfifi, *Al-ʿAqbat fi Misr fi al-ʿAsr al-ʿUthmani*, 102.
69. Haddad, "Project of the Independence of Egypt, 1801," 174.
70. Bruce, *Travels to Discover the Source of the Nile*, 1:147 (quotation), 151.
71. For example, Isna Court, Sijill Ishhadat 15, Part 1, 1178; Isna Court, Sijill 1, Case 59, p. 48, 12 Rabiʿ Akhir 1170; Isna Court, Sijill 1, Case 66, p. 54, 8 Rabiʿ Akhir 1170, all in NAE.
72. For example, Isna Court, Sijill Ishhadat 6, Case 224, p. 121, 21 Jumada al-Awwal 1172; from the same sijill and the same year, Case 58, p. 36; Isna Court, Sijill Ishhadat 15, Part 1, Case 94, p. 78, 12 Muharram 1178, all in NAE.
73. Isna Court, Sijills Ishhadat 1–80, 1170–1231, NAE.
74. Isna Court, Sijill Ishhadat 6, Case 224, p. 121, 21 Jumada al-Awwal 1172, NAE.

75. Al-Amir, "Risala fi man Tawalla al-Saʿid min al-'Umara al-Jarakisa," 2–3.
76. Isna Court, Sijill Ishhadat 1, Case 148, p. 107, 17 Rajab 1170, NAE.
77. Isna Court, Sijill Ishhadat 5, Part 1, Case 7, p. 3, 8 Rabiʿ al-Awwal 1173, NAE.
78. Mentions of the Habatirs can be found, for example, in Isna Court, Sijill Ishhadat 53, case 180, p. 67, 11 Jumad Awwal 1216, NAE.
79. al-Jabarti, *ʿAjaʾib al-ʾAthar*, 2:72–73.
80. Ibid., 2:350.
81. Cezzar, *Ottoman Egypt in the Eighteenth Century*, 41; al-Jabarti, *ʿAjaʾib al-ʾAthar*, 2:306; Ahmad, *Al-Saʿid fi ʿAhd Shaykh al-ʾArab Hammam*, 137.
82. Daniel Crecelius, *The Roots of Modern Egypt: A Study of the Regimes of ʿAli Bey al-Kabir and Muhammad Bey Abu al-Dhahab, 1760–1775* (Minneapolis: Bibliotheca Islamica, 1981), 51, 59–61; Ahmad, *Al-Saʿid fi ʿAhd Shaykh al-ʾArab Hammam*, 137–40.
83. Ahmad, *Al-Saʿid fi ʿAhd Shaykh al-ʾArab Hammam*, 146–47; Crecelius, *Roots of Modern Egypt*, 60–62; Denon, *Voyage dans la Basse et la Haute Égypte*, 2:255–56
84. See Ahmad, *Al-Saʿid fi ʿAhd Shaykh al-ʾArab Hammam*.
85. Qina Court, Portfolio 1, 10 Shaʿban 1187 in Haridi, *Dawr al-Saʿid fi Misr al-ʿUthmaniyya*, appendix 14, 423–25.
86. Cezzar, *Ottoman Egypt in the Eighteenth Century*, 27–28.
87. Gabor Agoston and Bruce Masters (eds.), *Encyclopedia of the Ottoman Empire* (New York: Facts on File, 2009), 462–63.
88. Lane, *Account of the Customs and Manners of the Modern Egyptians*, 3.
89. According to a medical report by Colonel Wilson, who came with British troops to Egypt in 1800. The report is quoted a few years later in John Redman Coxe, *The Philadelphia Medical Museum* (Philadelphia: T & G Palmer, 1809), 6:9–10.
90. Ibid., 10.
91. Edward Lane, *Description of Egypt* (Cairo: American University in Cairo Press, 2000), 32–33. Clot Bey mentioned this theory but then refuted it in Clot Bey, "On the Plague of Egypt," in *The Eclectic Journal of Medicine, Vol. IV from November 1839 to October 1840* (Philadelphia: Haswell et al., 1840), 379.
92. Haridi, *Dawr al-Saʿid fi Misr al-ʿUthmaniyya*, 236–37, 244; M. Claude Savary, *Lettres sur l'Égypte*, new ed. (Paris: Chez BLXUET jeune, 1789), 2:16; C. S. Sonnini, *Travels in Upper and Lower Egypt Undertaken by Order of the Old Government of France* (London: T. Gillet, printer, 1799), 1:673. See also al-Jabarti, *ʿAjaʾib al'Athar*, vol. 3. And for full account, see Jane Hathaway, *A Tale of Two Factions* (Binghamton: SUNY Press, 2003).
93. Clot Bey, "On the Plague of Egypt," 378.
94. Olivier, *Travels in the Ottoman Empire, Egypt, and Persia*, 161.
95. Agoston and Masters, *Encyclopedia of the Ottoman Empire*, 462.
96. Bruce McGowan, "The Age of the Ayan, 1699–1812," in Halil Inalcik, Donald Quataert, et al. (eds.), *An Economic and Social History of the Ottoman Empire* (Cambridge: Cambridge University Press, 1994), 651.
97. Haridi, *Dawr al-Saʿid fi Misr al-ʿUthmaniyy*, 236–37. About the deaths of Mamluk knights from the plague, see al-Jabarti, *ʿAjaʾib al-Athar*, vol. 3.

98. John Campbell, *The Travels and Adventures of Edward Brown, Esq.* (London: Printed by J. Applebee, 1739), 335.
99. Ahmad, *Al-'Idara fi Misr fi al-'Asr al-'Uthmani*, 424–25.
100. Cezzar, *Ottoman Egypt in the Eighteenth Century*, 27–28.
101. Ibid., 250–51.
102. Denon, *Voyage dans la Basse et la Haute Égypte*, 2:207–8, 217.
103. Isna Court, Sijill Ishhadat No.53, Case 286, p. 123, Jumada al-Akhir 1216, NAE.
104. Ibid.
105. Isna Court, Sijill Ishhadat 53, Case 269, p. 113, Rabi 'Awwal 1216, NAE.

CHAPTER 2: THE FRENCH, PLAGUE ENCORE, AND JIHAD

1. Vivant Denon, *Voyage dans le Basse et la Haute Égypte, pendant les Campagne du Général Bonaparte* (Paris: Imprimerie de P. Didot l'aine, 1802), 2:120. The translation is from Vivant Denon, *Travels in Upper and Lower Egypt* (New York: Arno Press, 1973), 2:199.
2. About Copts, see Nasir Ahmad Ibrahim, *Al-Faransiyyun fi Sa'id Misr: Al-Muwajaha al-Maliyya*, 1798–1801 (Cairo: Darl-Kutub wal-Watha'iq al-Qawmiyya, 2005), 135–73. About the Arab tribes, see Denon, *Voyage dans le Basse et la Haute Égypte*, 2:139–40.
3. Bill Ashcroft, Gareth Griffiths, and Helen Tiffin (eds.), *The Post-colonial Studies Reader* (London: Routledge, 2006), 93–116.
4. Edward Said, *Orientalism* (New York: Vintage, 1979), 66.
5. Ibid., 7 (emphasis in original).
6. See 'Ilham Muhamamd Dhuhni, *Misr fi Kitabat al-Rahhala wal-Qanasil al-Faransiyyin fil-Qarn al-Thamin 'Ashr* (Cairo: al-Hay'a al-Misriyya al-'Amma lil-Kitab, 1992); and Ilham Muhamamd Dhuhni, *Misr fi Kitabat al-Rahhala wal-Qanasil al-Faransiyyin fil-Qarn al-Tsi' 'Ashr* (Cairo: al-Hay'a al-Misriyya al-'Amma lil-Kitab, 1995).
7. *Monthly Review or Literary Journal* 76 (January–June 1787): 567.
8. M. Claude Savary, *Lettres sur l'Égypte*, new ed. (Paris: Chez BLXUET jeune, 1789), 2:109–10.
9. Ibid., 2:115–16. The translation is from M. Claude Savary, *Letters on Egypt*, 3rd ed. (London: G. G. and J. Robison, 1799), 2:28–29.
10. Savary, *Lettres sur l'Égypte*, 2:279–182.
11. Ibid., 3:19–22, 184.
12. C. S. Sonnini, *Travels in Upper and Lower Egypt Undertaken by Order of the Old Government of France* (London: T. Gillet, printer, 1799), 1:287.
13. Ibid., 1:192–94. Also see 264–65.
14. Ibid., 1:196–97.
15. Ibid., 1:312.

16. Ibid., 1:186.
17. Ibid., 1:188 (emphasis in original).
18. Ibid., 1:239. Quote is on 244.
19. Ibid., 1:203.
20. Ibid., 1:311.
21. Ibid., 1:214.
22. Ibid., 1:230–31. Also see 232–33.
23. Ibid., 1:204, 215.
24. Juan Cole, *Napoleon's Egypt: Invading the Middle East* (New York: Palgrave Macmillan, 2008), 12–20.
25. Ibid., 16.
26. Jennifer Pitts, *A Turn to Empire: The Rise of Imperial Liberalism in Britain and France* (Princeton, NJ: Princeton University Press, 2005), 168–73.
27. Michael Doyle, *Empires* (Ithaca: Cornell University Press, 1986), 307.
28. Cole, *Napoleon's Egypt*, 15.
29. Ibid., 5–6.
30. Ibid., 11–12.
31. 'Abd al-Rahman al-Jabarti, *Al-Jabarti's Chronicle of the French Occupation*, Shamuel Moreh (trans.) (Princeton, NJ: Markus Wiener, 1975), 26–27.
32. 'Abd Al-'Aziz Jamal al-Din, "Al-'Amaliyyat al-'Askariyya fi Sa'id Misr bayn 'Aamayy 1798/1799," appendix 1 in 'Abd al-Rahman al-Jabarti, *'Aja'ib al-Athar fil-Tarajim wal-Akhbar* (Cairo: Lajnat al-Bayan al-'Arabi, 1958–), 4:382–85.
33. Isna Court, Sijill Ishhadat 50, pp. 111–14, 21 Rabi' al-Awwal 1213, Archival Code 1169–000050; Isna Court, Sijill Ishhadat 50, pp. 116–118, 3 Jumada al-Awwal 1213, Archival Code 1169–000050, both in NAE.
34. Isna Court, Sijill Ishhadat 51, p. 284, 35 Dhu al-Qi'da 1214, Archival Code 1169–000051, NAE.
35. 'Izzat Hasan Effendi al-Darandali, *Al-Hamla al-Faransiyya 'ala Misr fi Daw' Makhtut 'Uthmani, Makhtutat Dianama*, Jamal Sa'id 'Abd al-Ghani (trans. and ed.) (Cairo: al-Hay'a al-Misriyya al-'Amma lil-Kitab, 1999), 367; Husam Muhammad 'Abd al-Mu'ti, *Al-'Ilaqat al-Misriyya al-Hijaziyya fi al-Qarn al-Thamin 'Ashr* (Cairo: al-Hay'a al-'Amma lil-Kitab, 1999), 63–70; Jamal al-Din, "al-'Amaliyyat al-'Askariyya fi Sa'id Misr," 382–85.
36. Jamal al-Din, "al-'Amaliyyat al-'Askariyya fi Sa'id Misr," 410–27; E. L. F Haut, *Mémoires d'un officier de l'armée française* (Cairo: Bibliothèque et Archives Nationales d'Egypte, 2005), 252–70; D. J. Larrey, *Memoirs of Military Surgery and Campaigns of the French Army*, Richard Willmott Hall (trans.) (Baltimore: Joseph Cushing, 1914), 1:128; Nabil al-Sayyid al-Tukhi, *Sa'id Misr fi 'Ahd al-Hamla al-Faransiyya, 1798–1801* (Cairo: al-Hay'a al-Misriyya al-'Amma lil-Kitab, 1997).
37. *Mémoires sur l'Égypte, publiés pendant les campagnes du Général Bonaparte* (Paris: Imprimerie de P. Didot l'aine, 1800), 146–55.
38. Vivant Denon, "Discourse du citoyen Denon," in *Mémoires sur l'Égypte*, 410.
39. Ibid.

40. Denon, *Voyage dans le Basse et la Haute Égypte*, 2:120–21. The translation is from Denon, *Travels in Upper and Lower Egypt*, 2:199–200.
41. See, for example, Denon, *Voyage dans le Basse et la Haute Égypte*, 2:131–32.
42. Ibid., 149.
43. Ibid., 230–31, 235–36.
44. Ibid., 191. The translation is from Denon, *Travels in Upper and Lower Egypt*, 2:295.
45. Ibid., 197–99.
46. Napoleon secretly fled Egypt because of many military defeats in September 1799. After Napoleon, General Kléber was appointed as the commander in chief for less than a year before he was assassinated in June 1800. Kléber was succeeded by the General Menou, who was the third and last commander in chief of the campaign, as the French were finally defeated and forced to depart by joint British-Ottoman troops in 1801.
47. Madiha Dus (ed.), *Mukhtarat min Watha'iq al-Hamla al-Faransiyya, 1798–1801* (Cairo: Dar al-Kutub wal-Watha'iq al-Qawmiyya, 2006), 78–82, 87–91, 108–9.
48. Ibid., 86–91.
49. Ibrahim, *Al-Faransiyyun fi Sa'id Misr*, 136–37.
50. Ibid., 135–73.
51. Ibid. About Menou and the Copts, also see Dus, *Mukhtarat min Watha'iq al-Hamla al-Faransiyya*, 114–15, 116–17.
52. Denon, *Voyage dans le Basse et la Haute Égypte*, 3:139–40.
53. Isna Court, Sijill Ishhadat 50, p. 286, 5 Shawwal 1214, Archival Code 1169-000051, NAE.
54. Dus, *Mukhtarat min Watha'iq al-Hamla al-Faransiyya*, 118.
55. Ibid., 109–33; Khalid Abu al-Rus, "Madinat Isna fil-Qarn al-Thamin 'Ashr," PhD dissertation, Cairo University, 2008, 56.
56. Ibid.
57. Denon, *Voyage dans le Basse et la Haute Égypte*, 2:195–97. The translation is from Denon, *Travels in Upper and Lower Egypt*, 2:300–301.
58. Denon, *Voyage dans le Basse et la Haute Égypte*, 2:233–34.
59. Dus, *Mukhtarat Min Watha'iq al-Hamla al-Faransiyya*, 112–13, 136, 144; Jamal al-Din, appendix 10, in al-Jabarti, *'Aja'ib al-'Athar fil-Tarajim wal-'Akhbar*, 4:433–35.
60. Jamal al-Din, appendix 15, in al-Jabarti, *'Aja'ib al-'Athar fil-Tarajim wal-'Akhbar*, 4:439.
61. Denon, *Voyage dans la Basse et la Haute Égypte*, 2:151–52. The translation is from Denon, *Travels in Upper and Lower Egypt*, 2:243–44.
62. al-Jabarti, *'Aja'ib al-'Athar fil-Tarajim wal-'Akhbar*, 4:592–601.
63. Jamal al-Din, "Mu'ahadat al-sulh bayna Kilibar wa-Murad Bey," in al-Jabarti, *'Aja'ib al-'Athar fil-Tarajim wal-'Akhbar*, 4:301–3; *The Annual Register; or, a View of the History of Politics and Literature for the Year 1801* (London: Printed by T. Burton, 1802), 212–17, 225; Louis Adolphe Thires, *History of the Consulate and the*

Empire of France under Napoleon, D. Forbes Campbelle and John Stebbing (trans.) (London: Chatto and Windus, 1893), 1:304–5; Dus, *Mukhtarat min Watha'iq al-Hamla al-Faransiyya,* 109–10.

64. Jamal al-Din, "al-Amir Murad Bey," in al-Jabarti, *'Aja'ib al-athar fil-tarajim wal-akhbar,* 4:592.

65. Edward Lane, *An Account of the Manners and Customs of Modern Egyptians: Written in Egypt During the Years 1833, 34, and 35* (London: Charles Knight and Co., 1837), 1:3.

66. Gabor Agoston and Bruce Masters (eds.), *Encyclopedia of the Ottoman Empire* (New York: Facts on File, 2009), 462–63.

67. T. C. Hansard (ed.), *The Parliamentary Debate, Forming a Continuation of the Work Entitled "The Parliamentary History of England from the Earliest Period to 1803"* (London, 1825), 12:1323–24.

68. *Mémoires sur l'Égypte,* 155.

69. Larrey, *Memoirs of Military Surgery and Campaigns of the French Army,* 1:370.

70. 'Abd al-Rahman al-Jabarti, *Muzhir al-Taqdis bi Zawal Dawlat al-Faransis* (Cairo: Dar al-Kutub wal-Watha'iq al-Misriyya, 1998), 250. The translation is from LaVerne Kuhnke, *Lives at Risk: Public Health in Nineteenth-Century Egypt* (Berkeley: University of California Press, 1990), 76.

71. Hansard, *Parliamentary Debate,* 12:1325–26.

72. "The Diseases of Egypt, from Observations Made during the British Expedition in That Country under Sir R. Abercromble, K.C.B., in 1801," *Medical Press and Circular, a Weekly Journal of Medicine and Medical Affairs,* July–December 1882, 152–53.

CHAPTER 3: THE PASHA'S SETTLERS, BULLS, AND BANDITS

1. J. A. St. John, *Egypt and Nubia* (London: Chapman and Hall, 1845), 378–81.

2. 'Ali Mubarak, *Al-Khitat al-Tawfiqiyya al-Jadida li-Misr al-Qahira* (Cairo: al-Hay'a al-Misriyya al-'Amma lil-Kitab, 1994), 12:116–17; Afaf Lutfi al-Sayyid Marsot, *Egypt in the Reign of Muhammad Ali* (Cambridge: Cambridge University Press, 1984), 133.

3. See, for example, 'Abd al-Rahman al-Rafi'i, *'Asr Muhammad 'Ali* (Cairo: Dar al-Ma'arif, 1930); and Marsot, *Egypt in the Reign of Muhammad Ali.*

4. Khaled Fahmy, *All the Pasha's Men: Mehmed Ali: His Army and the Making of Modern Egypt* (Cambridge: Cambridge University Press, 1997). Fahmy also argues against Muhammad 'Ali intending to build an empire and claims instead that he maintained his position as a loyal viceroy of the Ottoman sultan.

5. Michael Hechter, *Internal Colonialism: The Celtic Fringe in British National Development,* 2nd ed. (New Brunswick, NJ: Transaction, 1998).

6. Marsot, *Egypt in the Reign of Muhammad Ali,* 66; 'Abd al-Rahman al-Jabarti, *'Aja'ib al-'Athar fi-l-Tarajim wa-l-'Akhbar* (Cairo: Lajnat al-Bayan al-'Arabi, 1958–), 7:155–57, 162.

7. al-Jabarti, *'Aja'ib al-'Athar,* 7:167. Ibrahim held the position of *al-daftardar.* Ra'uf 'Abbas et al. (eds.), *Al-'Awamir wa-l-Mukatabat al-Sadira min 'Aziz Misr Muhammad 'Ali* (Cairo: Dar al-Kutub wa-al-Watha'iq al-Qawmiyya, 2005–6), 1:1, 23.

8. al-Jabarti, *'Aja'ib al-'Athar,* 7:234–35.

9. Ibid.

10. Amin Sami, *Taqwim al-Nil* (Cairo: Matba'at Dar al-Kutub al-Misriyya, 1936), introduction, p. 128; 2:290.

11. al-Jabarti, *'Aja'ib al-'Athar,* 7:175–76.

12. Ibid., 7:367.

13. Helen Anne Rivlin, *The Agricultural Policy of Muhammad 'Ali in Egypt* (Cambridge, MA: Harvard University Press, 1961), 171–74.

14. Ibid, 171–72; Muhamad Fu'ad Shukri et al., *Bina' Dawlat Misr Muhammad 'Ali: Al-Siyasa al-Dakhiliyya* (Cairo: Dar al-Fikr al-'Arabi, 1948), 54.

15. Fred Lawson, *The Social Origins of Egyptian Expansionism during the Muhammad Ali Period* (New York: Columbia University Press, 1992), 69.

16. John Bowring, *Report on Egypt and Candia, 1840, Addressed to the Right Hon. Lord Viscount Palmerston* (London: W. Clowes and Sons, 1840), 67.

17. 'Abbas et al., *Al-'Awamir wa-l-Mukatabat,* 1:435, 439; 2:286–87.

18. al-Jabarti, *'Aja'ib al-'Athar,* 7:185, 269; Marsot, *Egypt in the Reign of Muhammad Ali,* 153; Rivlin, *Agricultural Policy,* 146; 'Abbas et al., *Al-'Awamir wa-l-Mukatabat,* 1:240.

19. Marsot, *Egypt in the Reign of Muhammad Ali,* 149.

20. See Marsot, *Egypt in the Reign of Muhammad Ali,* 127–28, 145–53; Rivlin, *Agricultural Policy,* chapter 8; and Shukri et al., *Bina' Dawlat Misr,* 130–51.

21. 'Abbas et al., *Al-'Awamir wa-l-Mukatabat,* 1:75. For the campaigns, see al-Jabarti, *'Aja'ib al-'Athar,* vol. 7.

22. See 'Abd al-Rahim 'Abd al-Rahman 'Abd al-Rahim, *Muhammad 'Ali wa Shibh al-Jazira al-'Arabiyya, 1819–1840* (Cairo: Dar al-Kitab al-Jami'i, 1981), 55–56, 508; and Shukri et al., *Bina' Dawlat Misr,* 55, 130–51.

23. See Salah Ahmad Haridi, *Dawr al-Sa'id fi Misr al-'Uthmaniyy, 923/1213–1517/1898.* (Cairo: Dar al-Ma'arif, 1984); and Terence Walz, *Trade between Egypt and Bilad As-Sudan* (Cairo: Institut Français d'Archéologie Orientale du Caire, 1978).

24. Arthur T. Holroyd, *Egypt and Mahomed Ali Pacha in 1837: A Letter, Containing Remarks upon "Egypt as It Is in 1837"; Addressed to the Right Hon. Viscount Palmerston.* London: James Ridgeway and Sons, 1838., 18.

25. Quoting Colonel Campbell, the British consul general, in Bowring, *Report on Egypt and Candia,* 37.

26. Ibrahim later traveled to the Delta and applied his southern system there. al-Jabarti, *'Aja'ib al-'Athar,* 7:178, 233.

27. Isna Court, Sijill Ishhadat 80, Case 41, p. 16, 4 Dhu al-Hijja 1231, NAE.

28. Isna Court, Sijill Ishhadat 94, Part 1, Case 66, p. 23, end of Dhu al-Qi'da 1229, NAE.

29. Isna Court, Sijill Ishhadat 94, Part 1, Case 75, p. 27, 6 Dhu al-Hijja 1229, NAE.
30. See Marsot, *Egypt in the Reign of Muhammad Ali*, 133–35.
31. al-Jabarti, *'Aja'ib al-'Athar*, 7:481.
32. Gabriel Baer, "Submissiveness and Revolt of the Fallah," in *Studies in the Social History of Modern Egypt* (Chicago: University of Chicago Press 1969); Fred Lawson, "Rural Revolt and Provincial Society in Egypt, 1820–1824," *International Journal of Middle East Studies* 13 (2) (May 1981): 131–53; Marsot, *Egypt in the Reign of Muhammad Ali*, 133–35.
33. Marsot, *Egypt in the Reign of Muhammad Ali*, 133–34.
34. 'Ali Mubarak, *Al-Khitat al-Tawfiqiyya*, 12:116–17; St. John, *Egypt and Nubia*, 381; Marsot, *Egypt in the Reign of Muhammad Ali*, 133.
35. St. John, *Egypt and Nubia*, 378–81.
36. Ibid., 380–81.
37. Ibid., 379–81.
38. Ibid., 382.
39. Khaled Fahmy, "Mutiny in Mehmed Ali's New *Nizami* Army, April–May 1824," *International Journal of Turkish Studies* 8 (1–2) (2002): 129–38.
40. St. John, *Egypt and Nubia*, 382–84.
41. Ibid.; 'Ali Mubarak, *Al-Khitat al-Tawfiqiyya*, 12:116–17; Marsot, *Egypt in the Reign of Muhammad Ali*, 133.
42. 'Abbas et al., *Al-'Awamir wa-l-Mukatabat*, 1:130–31, 13 Dhu al-Hijja 1239.
43. See, for example, Isna Court, Sijill Ishhadat, 1254–56; and Sadir Mudiriyyat, Isna, 1260–1261, both in NAE.
44. Filib Jallad, *Qamus al-'Idara wal-Qada'* (Al-Iskandariyyu: al-Matba'a al-Bukhariyyah, 1891–), 1:12–15, 1255–56; Zayn al-'Abidin Shams al-Din Najm, *Mu'jam al-'Alfaz wa-l-Mustalahat al-Tarikhiyya* (Cairo: Dar al-Fikr al-'Arabi, 2006), 29–30 (on *ab'adiyya*), 35 (on *'uhda*), 183–84 (on *çiftlik*).
45. See, for example, Sadir Mudiriyyat, Isna, 18 Shawwal 1260; and p. 129, 15 Jumada al-Awwal 1260, both in NAE.
46. Isna Court, Sijill Ishhadat 96, Part 1, Case 102, p. 48, 30 Shawwal 1253, NAE.
47. Isna Court, Sijill Ishhadat 96, Part 1, Case 237, p. 121, 22 Jumada al-Awwal 1254; Sijill 97, Part 1, Case 12, p. 3, 2 Safar 1255, both in NAE.
48. Mudiriyyat Qina Court, Sijill Murafa'at 1, Case 11, p. 12, 25 Jumada al-Awwal 1262, NAE.
49. For examples of cases of elite intermarriages, see Isna Court, Sijill Ishhadat 94, Part 1, Case 275, p. 281, 12 Ramadan 1252; Sijill 96, Part 1, Case 38, p. 18, 22 Muharram 1254; Sijill 96, Case 73, p. 35, 9 Safar 1254; Sijill 96, Case 323, pp. 168–69, 17 Sha'ban 1254; Sijill Ishhadat 94, Part 1, Case 63, p. 192, 7 Rabi' al-Awwal 1252; Sijill Ishhadat 94, Case 155, p. 230, 12 Jumada al-Awwal 1252; Sijill 96, Part 1, Case 104, p. 51, 24 Safar 1254; and Sijill 96, Case 109, p. 53, 1 Rabi' al-Awwal 1254, all in NAE.
50. Isna Court, Sijill Ishhadat 94, Part 1, Case 247, p. 270, 14 Sha'ban 1252. For more examples, see Sijillat Sadir and Warid Mudiriyyat, Qina and Isna, 1260–64;

Isna Court, Sijills Ishhadat 94–97, 1252–56; Isna Court, Sijill 94, Part 1, Case 121, pp. 213–15, 9 Rabiʿ al-Thani 1252; Isna Court, Sijill 95, Part 1, Case 38, p. 21, 5 Dhu al-Hijja 1253; Isna Court, Sijill 95, Case 43, p. 23, 4 Dhu al-Hijja 1253; Isna Court, Sijill 96, Part 1, Case 102, p. 48, end of Shawwal 1253; Isna Court, Sijill 95, Part 1, Case 2, pp. 1–2, 22 Ramadan 1253; Qina Court, Sijill Murafaʿat, Cases 384–92, p. 88, 1 Rabiʿ al-Awwal 1262; Qina Court, Sijill Murafaʿat, Case 91, p. 23, 15 Shaʿban 1262, all in NAE.

51. See Sadir Mudiriyyat, Qina and Isna, 1261–63; Isna Court, Sijill Ishhadat 94, Part 1, Case 247, p. 270, 14 Shaʿban 1252, both in NAE.

52. For example, see Isna Court, Sijill Ishhadat 95, Part 1, Case 2, pp. 1–2, 22 Ramadan 1253, NAE.

53. File "Sadir ʿArdhalat Mufattish ʿUmum Qibli," p. 385, 16 Rabiʿ al-Thani 1263, NAE. Bureaucrats did not enjoy property rights to these lands, which were still state property. This would change when the regime introduced private property laws.

54. Sadir Mudiriyyat, Isna, p. 7, 1 and 3 Ramadan 1260; p. 12, 23 Ramadan 1260; and p. 389, 2 Jumada al-Thani 1260, all in NAE.

55. Sadir Mudiriyyat, Isna, p. 129, 15 Jumada al-Awwal 1260; Sadir Mudiriyyat, Isna, p. 15, 6 Jumada al-Awwal 1260, both in NAE.

56. See, for example, Sadir Mudiriyyat, Isna, p. 13, 15 Jumada al-Awwal 260, NAE.

57. Maʿiyya Saniyya, Turkish, Microfilm 24, p. 45, 17 Jumada al-Akhir 1251, NAE.

58. See Sadir and Warid Mudiriyyat, Qina and Isna, Sijills, 1260–64, NAE.

59. See Maʿiyya Saniyya, Turkish, Daftars 80–85; and Sadir Mudiriyyat, Isna, Ramadan 1260, both in NAE.

60. Sadir Mudiriyyat, Isna, p. 367, 23 Jumada al-Awwal 1261, NAE. See also Sadir Mudiriyyat, Isna, p. 168, 19 Safar 1260, NAE.

61. Sadir Mudiriyyat, Isna, Part 2, p. 387, 1261, NAE.

62. Sadir Mudiriyyat, Isna, p. 322, 10 Rabiʿ al-Awwal 1261, NAE. Also see Sadir Mudiriyyat, Isna, p. 149, 9 Safar 1260, NAE.

63. For example, the pasha adopted the term *al-ahali* in his then newly published official gazette, *Al-Waqaʾiʿ al-Misriyya* (49) (8 Rabiʿ al-Awwal 1245).

64. Antonio Gramsci's concept of hegemony refers to the modern state use of certain institutions in subjugating the ruled classes to the ruling elite, who promote their interests as the interests of all, or as the greater good, by subtle and inclusive control over the economy rather than by force. Gramsci considered the legislature, judiciary, and executive institutions "naturally . . . organs of political hegemony, but in different degrees." Antonio Gramsci, *Selections from the Prison Notebooks* (New York: International Publishers, 1971), 246.

65. Muhammad Khalil Subhi, *Tarikh al-Haya al-Niyabiyya fi Misr* (Cairo: Matbaʿat Dar al-Kutub al-Misriyya, 1947), 4:9–11; Sami, *Taqwim al-Nil*, 2:598. See also the minutes of the council's sessions in *Al-Waqaʾiʿ al-Misriyya*, issues of years 1245–49.

66. Sami, *Taqwim al-Nil*, 2:351–52.

67. For example, see *Al-Waqa'i' al-Misriyya,* 8 Ramadan 1247, 15 Shawwal 1247, 8 Dhu al-Qi'ada 1247, 22 Shawwal 1247, and 19 Rajab 1247.; Najm, Zayn al-'Abidin Shams al-Din (ed.), *Daftar Majmu' 'Idara wa-'Ijra'at,* 1240–1280/1825–1863 *(Watha'iq Tarikh Misr wa-l-'Arab al-Hadith)* (Cairo: Dar al-Fikr al-'Arabi, 2003), 21 Rabi' al-Awwal 1245, pp. 402–3. See also Sami, *Taqwim al-Nil,* 377–79; and *La'ihat Zira'at al-Fallah wa-Tadbir 'Ahkam al-Siyasa bi-Qasd al-Falah* (Cairo: Matba'at Sahib al-Sa'ada, 1829), 20.

68. *Qanun al- Siyasatnama,* in Subhi, *Tarikh al-Hayah al-Niyabiyya,* 5:40–75. See also F. Robert Hunter, *Egypt under the Khedives, 1805–1879: From Household Government to Modern Bureaucracy* (Pittsburgh: University of Pittsburgh Press, 1984), 17–32.

69. Ma'iyya Saniyya, Arabic, Microfilm 24, 17 Safar 1245, 7 Shawwal 1251, end of Muharram 1252, and 5 Safar 1252, NAE. During this period, Upper Egypt was divided into two provinces, and the southern one, Nisf Thani Qibli, included Qina and Isna and their rural vicinities.

70. See Zayn al-'Abidin Shams al-Din Najm, *'Idarat al-'Aqalim fi Misr, 1805–1882* (Cairo: Dar al-Kitab al-Jami'i, 1988), 128–32.

71. For example, see Isna Court, Sijill Ishhadat 94, Part 1, Case 199, p. 250, 5 Rajab 1252; Sijill 95, Part 1, Case 98, p. 62, 28 Dhu al-Qi'da 1253; and Sijill 96, Part 1, Case 2, p. 4, 25 Safar 1254, and Case 3, p. 4, 25 Safar 1254, and Case 102, p. 48, end of Shawwal 1253, and Case 143, p. 71, 18 Rabi' al-Awwal 1254, all in NAE.

72. Isna Court, Sijill Ishhadat 94, Part 1, Case 100, p. 204, 3 Rabi' al-Thani 1252, and Case 176, p. 75, 5 Jumada al-Awwal 1252; Isna Court, Sijill Ishhadat 97, Part 1, Case 139, pp. 82–83, Rabi' al-Akhir 1255, all in NAE.

73. 'Abbas et al., *al-'Awamir wa-l-Mukatabat,* 2:114, 24 Rajab 1253.

74. Ibid., 2:30, 14 Rajab 1251.

75. Ibid., 2:99, end of Muharram 1252.

76. Sadir Mudiriyyat, Isna, 18 Shawwal 1260, NAE.

77. Warid Mudiriyyat, Isna, p. 30, 25 Shawwal 1263, NAE.

78. Sadir 'Ardhalat Mufattish 'Umum Qibli, p. 385, 16 Rabi' al-Thani 1263, NAE; 'Ali Mubarak, *Al-Khitat al-Tawfiqiyya,* 9:217.

79. 'Abbas et al., *Al-'Awamir wa-l-Mukatabat,* 2:308.

80. Isna Court, Sijill Ishhadat 94, Part 1, Case 356, p. 320, 22 Dhu al-Qi'da 1252, NAE.

81. Sadir 'Ardhalat Mufattish 'Umum Qibli, p. 347, 9 Rabi' Thani 1263, NAE. Records do not show how the case was concluded and whether the state punished the transgressing shaykhs and bureaucrat.

82. Qina Court, Sijill Murafa'at, Case 249, p. 57, 29 Rabi' al-Awwal 1263, NAE.

83. See Sadir Mudiriyyat, Isna, years 1260–63, NAE. For example, see Sadir Mudiriyyat, Isna, p. 7, 1 and 3 Ramadan 1260; p. 12, 23 Ramadan 1260; p .389, 2 Jumada al-Thani 1260; and p. 368, 23 Jumada al-Awwal 1261, all in NAE.

84. Sadir Mudiriyyat, Isna, p. 7, 3 Ramadan 1260; p. 19, 5 Ramadan 1260; p. 29, 6 Ramadan 1260; p. 19, 23 Ramadan and 12 Shawwal 1260, all in NAE.

85. Sadir Mudiriyyat, Isna, p. 399, 4 Rajab 1261, NAE.

86. Sadir Mudiriyyat, Qina, p. 214, 17 Rabiʿ al-Awwal 1262, NAE; ʿAli Mubarak, *Al-Khitat al-Tawfiqiyya,* 12:135.
87. Sadir Mudiriyyat, Qina, p. 301, 4 Shaʿban 1262, NAE.
88. Sadir Mudiriyyat, Qina, p. 271, 24 Jumada al-Thani 1262, NAE.
89. Qina Court, Sijill Murafaʿat, Case 100, p. 26, 7 Muharram 1263, NAE.
90. Sadir Mudiriyyat, Qina, p. 209, 11 Rabiʿ al-Awwal 1262, NAE.
91. Sadir Mudiriyyat, Qina, p. 256, 1 Jumada al-Thani 1262; p. 296, 25 Rajab 1262; and p. 323, 15 Ramadan 1262, all in NAE. See also ʿAli Mubarak, *Al-Khitat al-Tawfiqiyya,* 11:32–33.

CHAPTER 4: "COMMUNIST" REBELLION

1. Lucie Austin Duff-Gordon, *Letters from Egypt* (London: Macmillan, 1865), 341–42.
2. Ibid., 345–69.
3. See, for example, from liberal historiography, Niall Ferguson, *Empire: The Rise and Demise of the British World Order and the Lessons for Global Power* (New York: Basic Books, 2003); and David Landes, *The Wealth and Poverty of Nations: Why Some Are So Rich and Some So Poor* (New York: W. W. Norton, 1999). And from Marxist historiography, see Immanuel Wallerstein, *The Modern World-System* (New York: Academic Press, 1974–).
4. Niall Ferguson, *Colossus: The Price of America's Empire* (New York: Penguin, 2004), 10.
5. Ibid., 25–26.
6. See Giovanni Arrighi, *The Long Twentieth Century* (London: Verso, 2002); and Giovanni Arrighi, "The Three Hegemonies of Historical Capitalism," *Review,* Summer 1990, 365–408.
7. For dependency theory, see Andre Gunder Frank, *Dependent Accumulation and Underdevelopment* (London: Macmillan, 1978); and Samir Amin, *Imperialism and Unequal Development* (New York: Monthly Review Press, 1977). For world-system theory, see Wallerstein, *Modern World-System,* vol. 3.
8. See, for example, Roger Owen, *The Middle East in the World Economy, 1800–1914* (London: I. B. Tauris, 1993), chapter 5; Charles Issawi, *An Economic History of the Middle East and North Africa* (New York: Columbia University Press, 1982); and Amin, *Imperialism and Unequal Development.*
9. See Owen, *Middle East in World Economy,* 122–26.
10. Amin Sami, *Taqwim al-Nil,* vol. 1 (Cairo: Matbaʿat Dar al-Kutub al-Misriyya, 1936), part 3, 80.
11. Duff-Gordon, *Letters from Egypt,* 332. Also see Sadir Mudiriyyat Qina, year 1275, NAE.
12. Sadir Mudiriyyat Qina, Part 10, p. 9, 29 Safar 1279; Part 1, p. 34, 4 Safar 1275; Part 2, Safar 1275; Part 7, p. 88, 15 al-Hijja 1278; and Madabit Majlis al-Ahkam, Sadir al-Aqalim al-Qibliyya, Microfilm 367, p. 6, 19 Muharram 1276, all in NAE.

13. For example, Sadir Mudiriyyat Qina, p. 118, 13 Shaʿban 1270, NAE.
14. Sadir Mudiriyyat Qina, Part 7, p. 88, 15 Dhu al-Hijja 1278; Part 2, Safar 1275; Part 7, p. 90, 19 Dhu al-Hijja 1278, all in NAE.
15. See, for example, Sadir Mudiriyyat Qina, Part 2, p. 12, Safar 1275; and Sadir Mudiriyyat Qina, 1272, both in NAE.
16. Zayn al-ʿAbidin Sham al-Din Najm (ed.), *Daftar Majmuʿ 'Idara wa-'Ijraʾat, 1240–1280/1825–1863 (Wathaʾiq Tarikh Misr wa-l-ʿArab al-Hadith)* (Cairo: Dar al-Fikr al-ʿArabi, 2003), 401.
17. See Sadir Mudiriyyat Qina, year 1270, NAE.
18. For example, see Farshut Court, Sijill Ishhadat 1, p. 3, Jumada al-Thani 1273; and Farshut and Najʿ Hammadi Courts, Sijill Ishhadat 1, Case 516, p. 56, 14 Muharram 1274, both in NAE. *Salam* is a type of credit contract accepted by shariʿa law and was a common practice in rural areas in the Muslim world.
19. Duff-Gordon, *Letters from Egypt*, 45; ʿAli Mubarak, *Al-Khitat al-Tawfiqiyya al-Jadida li-Misr al-Qahira* (Cairo: al-Hayʾa al-Misriyya al-ʿAmma lil-Kitab, 1994), 8:175. An example of wives suing their husbands for failure to support the household with enough food is Farshut and Najʿ Hammadi Courts, Sijill 2, Case 3, p. 1, 12 Jumada al-Awwal 1273, NAE.
20. Madabit Majlis al-Ahkam, Sadir al-Aqalim al-Qibliyya, Microfilm 367, p. 6, 19 Muharram 1276, NAE.
21. Madabit Majlis al-Ahkam, Microfilm 434, Sijill 666, Case 690, 16 Rajab 1275, NAE.
22. Madabit Majlis al-Ahkam, Microfilm 434, Sijill 663, Case 115, pp. 52, 20 Safar 1274, NAE.
23. Sami, *Taqwim al-Nil*, vol. 1, part 3, 298.
24. Archival records of Qina Province reflect the idleness and decentralization of the state during the reign of ʿAbbas Pasha. As opposed to Muhammad ʿAli's state, the administrative and central planning activities in Qina during ʿAbbas Pasha's rule were drastically reduced and matters were left to provincial bureaucrats. See Sadir and Warid Mudiriyyat Qina and Isna, Sijills, years 1265, 1269, and 1270, NAE. Ehud Toledano attempted to present a positive vision on that viceroy in *State and Society in Mid-Nineteenth-Century Egypt* (Cambridge: Cambridge University Press, 1990). About land seizures, see, for example, Sami, *Taqwim al-Nil*, vol. 1, part 3, 19, 33; and Sadir Mudiriyyat Qina and Isna, part 2, Jumada al-Awwal 1270, NAE.
25. About the development of the code and the role of internal forces or landed elite in the promulgation of the 1858 code, see Denis Jorgens, "A Comparative Examination of the Provisions of the Ottoman Land Code and Khedive Saʿid's Law of 1858," in Roger Owen (ed.), *New Perspectives on Property and Land in the Middle East* (Cambridge, MA: Harvard University Press, 2000), 93–119; and Kenneth Cuno, *The Pasha's Peasants: Land, Society, and Economy in Lower Egypt, 1740–1858* (Cambridge: Cambridge University Press, 1992), chapter 10. Both Cuno and Jorgens emphasize that Saʿid's code in fact presented a continuity of old Ottoman codes rather than a modern rupture.
26. See Sadir Mudiriyyat Qina and Isna, 1269–1270; pp. 130–31, 22 Shaʿban 1270, all in NAE. Village shaykhs also rented medium-sized *abʿadiyya*s while

peasants rented small *ab'adiyya*s of a few acres. Peasants bid to buy small *ab'adiyya*s of less than five acres, or a group of them shared small farms. For examples, see Farshut and Naj' Hammadi Court, Sijills Ishhadat 1 and 2, 1273, NAE.

27. Filib Jallad, *Qamus al-'Idara wa-l-Qada'* (Al-Iskandariyya: al-Matba'a al-Bukhariyya, 1891–), 1:182–90; Zayn al-'Abidin Shams al-Din Najm, *Mu'jam al-Alfaz wa-l-Mustalahat al-Tarikhiyya* (Cairo: Dar al-Fikr al-'Arabi, 2006), 30.

28. Madabit Majlis al-Ahkam, Microfilm 434, Case 842, pp. 77, 18 Shawwal 1275, NAE.

29. Sadir Mudiriyyat, Qina, p. 237, 21 Safar 1272; 2 and 9 Safar 1275; p. 245, 23 Safar 1272; p. 257, 28 Safar 1272; p. 1, 1 Rabi' al-Awwal 1275; p. 257, 28 Safar 1272, all in NAE.

30. Sadir Mudiriyyat, Qina, Part 10, pp. 4–5, 25 Safar 1279; p. 75, Rabi' al-Thani 1275; p. 34, 27 Rabi' al-Awwal 1279; p. 83, 15 Rabi' al-Akhir 1275; Part 2, Safar 1275; Part 7, pp. 72–73, 76, 6 Dhu al-Hijja 1278; and Part 7, 19 Dhu al-Hijja 1278, all in NAE.

31. 'Awamir Karima, No. 1898, 23 Jumada al-Akhir 1278; No. 1905, 24 Rabi' al-Thani 1279, both in NAE.

32. Sadir Mudiriyyat Qina, Part 1, p. 98, 21 Safar 1275; Part 2, p. 72, 25 Safar 1275; Part 13, 17 Ramadan 1275, all in NAE.

33. For example, see Sadir 'Ardhalat Taftish 'Umum Qibli, p. 32, 3 Safar 1273; and Farshut and Naj' Hammadi Courts, Sijill Ishhadat 43, 1277–78, both in NAE.

34. Sadir 'Ardhalat Taftish 'Umum Qibli, p. 5, 15 Muharram 1273, NAE.

35. See, for example, the Hanafi state mufti Muhammad Al-'Abbasi al-Mahdi's *Al-Fatawa al-Mahdiyya fil-Waqa'i' al-Misriyya*, 7 vols. (Cairo: al-Matba'a al-Azhariyya, 1301/1883); and the Maliki scholar Hasan al-'Adawi al-Hamzawi's *Tabsirat al-Qudah wa-l-Ikhwan fi Wad' al-Yadd* (Cairo: al-Matba'a al-Amiriyya, 1276/1859).

36. 'Awamir Karima, No. 1891, 18 Jumada al-Thani 1275; Sadir Mudiriyyat Qina, Part 1, p. 67, 23 Rabi' al-Akhir 1279, both in NAE.

37. For a case of corruption of shari'a judges in land matters, see Madabit Majlis al-Ahkam, Sadir al-Aqalim al-Qibliyya, Microfilm 367, 1276, NAE.

38. See Mudiriyyat Qina Shari'a Court, Sijill Tarikat 10, years 1277–78, NAE.

39. See Sadir Mudiriyyat Qina, Part 1, 1279, NAE.

40. Farshut and Naj' Hammadi Courts, Sijill 45, Case 1, p. 1, 28 Safar 1277; Case 4, p. 1, 28 Safar 1277; Case 5, p. 1, 29 Safar 1277; Case 9, p. 2, 29 Safar 1277; Case 21, p. 3, 2 Rabi' al-Awwal 1277; Sadir Mudiriyyat Qina, part 2, p. 73, 26 Safar 1275, all in NAE.

41. See, for example, Landes, *Wealth and Poverty of Nations*.

42. On modernity and trust of European experts, see Anthony Giddens, *The Consequences of Modernity* (Stanford, CA: Stanford University Press, 1990), chapter 3. Giddens discuses how "traditional" societies' trust of modernity as an abstract system comes with blind trust of European professional expertise. Timothy Mitchell's *Rule of Experts* uses these theoretical insights to illustrate how trustworthy Western experts and their technology most of the time only brought about human

and environmental catastrophes. On imperialism and international labor migration, especially in the field of mining, see J. R. McNeill and William McNeill, *The Human Web* (New York: W. W. Norton, 2003), 262–63. On British imperialism and coal, see J. R. McNeill et al. (ed.), *Encyclopedia of World Environmental History* (New York: Routledge, 2004), 1:169–70.

43. Ma'iyya Saniyya, Turkish, No. 3, 4 Dhu al-Qi'da 1234; 18 Dhu al-Hijja 1241; No. 67, 28 Rajab 1251; Diwan Khidiwi, Turkish, No. 729, 28 Dhu Qi'da 1241; No. 779, 5 Rabi' al-Awwal 1248; Ma'iyya Saniyya, Arabic, No. 63, 28 Sha'ban 1267, all in NAE.

44. Sa'id generally invited extensive European expertise and embarked on many large European-Egyptian ventures that involved state funds and European experts. The Suez Canal was one of those ventures initiated by French experts that ended up with heavy indebtedness on the part of Sa'id and his successors. See Owen, *Middle East in the World Economy*.

45. Sadir Mudiriyyat, Qina and Isna, Part 1, pp. 8 and 26, 3 Safar 1275; p. 14, 7 Safar 1275; 'Awamir Karima, Sijill 1889, 10 Dhu al-Qi'da 1274; 24 Shawwal 1274, all in NAE.

46. Sadir Mudiriyyat, Qina and Isna, Part 1, p. 86, 27 Safar 1275, NAE.

47. Sadir Mudiriyyat, Qina and Isna, Part 1, p. 26, 3 Safar 1275, NAE.

48. Sadir Mudiriyyat, Qina and Isna, Part 1, pp. 1, 10, 13, 38, and 42, 1275, NAE.

49. Sadir Mudiriyyat, Qina and Isna, Part 1, pp. 10 and 14, Safar 1275; p. 21, 20 Safar 1275; p. 42, 21 Safar 1275; Part 4, p. 6, 27 Rabi' al-Awwal 1275, all in NAE.

50. Sadir Mudiriyyat, Qina and Isna, Part 4, p. 6, 17 Rabi' al-Awwal 1275, NAE.

51. Sadir Mudiriyyat, Qina and Isna, Part 2, p. 14, 7 Safar 1275, NAE.

52. Sadir Mudiriyyat, Qina and Isna, Part 2, p. 21, 19 Safar 1275; p. 42, 23 Safar 1275, both in NAE.

53. 'Awamir Karima, No. 1891, 8 Sha'ban 1275, NAE.

54. See Ma'iyya Saniyya, Turkish (Arabic summaries), Sijill 45, 7 and 19 Rabi' al-Awwal 1286; Sijill 3, 7 Dhu al-Qi'da 1270; Sadir al-Ma'iyya, Arabic, Sijill 135, Part 8, 24 Rajab 1270; Majlis al-Ahkam, Sijills 1880–81, 3 Sha'ban 1271; 16 Jumada al-Awwal 1271; Sadir Mudiriyyat Qina, p. 29, 4 Rabi' al- Awwal 1274; Madabit Majlis al-Ahkam, Microfilm 434, Case 842, p. 77, 18 Shawwal 1275; Sadir Mudiriyyat Qina, Part 2, p. 33, 2 Rabi' al-Awwal 1275; Sadir Mudiriyyat Qina, p. 290, 11 Rabi' al-Awwal 1272; Sadir Mudiriyyat Qina, pp. 215 and 241, 22–23 Safar 1272, all in NAE.

55. Issawi, *Economic History of the Middle East*, 30–31; 'Ali Mubarak, *Nukhbat al-Fikr fi Tadbir Nil Misr* (Cairo: Matba'at Wadi al-Nil, 1297/1879), 166–69.

56. Karl Polanyi, *The Great Transformation: the Political and Economic Origin of Our Time* (Boston: Beacon, 2001), 191–92.

57. About the Corn Laws, see Cheryl Schonhardt-Bailey, *The Rise of Free Trade*, vol. 4 (London: Routledge, 1997), chapters 2 and 3. About the wheat of Upper Egypt, see Mubarak, *Nukhbat al-Fikr fi Tadbir Nil Misr*, 169.

58. Mubarak, *Nukhbat al-Fikr fi Tadbir Nil Misr*, 169.

59. Sadir Madabit Majlis al-Ahkam, Microfilm 367, p. 125, 23 Rabi' al-Awwal 1280, NAE.
60. For example, see Sadir Mudiriyyat Qina, Part 10, p. 56, 14 Rabi' al-Awwal 1279, NAE.
61. For example, see Sadir Mudiriyyat Qina, Part 1, p. 53, 4 Rabi' al-Akhir 1279, NAE.
62. Sadir Mudiriyyat Qina, Part 1, pp. 32–33, 25 Rabi' al-Awwal 1279, NAE.
63. For example, see Madabit Majlis al-Ahkam, Microfilm 434, Sijill 666, Case 682, p. 123, Rajab 1275, NAE.
64. Sadir Mudiriyyat Qina, p. 239, 23 Safar 1272; Part 1, p. 13, 19 Rabi' al-Awwal 1279, both in NAE.
65. Sadir Mudiriyyat Qina, Part 13, p. 67, 8 Shawwal 1275, NAE.
66. Sadir Madabit Majlis al-Ahkam, Microfilm 367, p. 166, 29 Dhu al-Hijja 1280, NAE.
67. Madabit Majlis al-Ahkam, Microfilm 434, Case 842, pp. 77–82, 18 Shawwal 1275, NAE.
68. For example, see Madabit Majlis al-Ahkam, Microfilm 434, Sijill 668, Case 1217, 23 Jumada al-Awwal 1275, NAE.
69. Madabit Majlis al-Ahkam, Microfilm 421, 12 Dhu al-Qi'da 1288, NAE.
70. Mubarak, *Al-Khitat al-Tawfiqiyya*, 14:95. Mubarak misspells the name of the village as Qaw; the actual name of the village that existed in Qina is Faw.
71. Duff-Gordon, *Letters from Egypt*, 364. It seems that Duff-Gordon had received confusing accounts, because a Copt was not allowed to buy a Muslim female slave according to shari'a law.
72. Ibid., 345–46.
73. Ibid., 346–47.
74. Ibid., 347–48.
75. Ibid., 362–63.
76. Ibid., 341–71. Quote is on 369.
77. For example, Delta families that gained politically were the Abazas and the Shawarbis. For details about officials and parliamentarians and their elite families, see Sami, *Taqwim al-Nil*, vol. 2, part 3; and Muhammad Khalil Subhi, *Tarikh al-Haya al-Niyabiyya fi Misr*, vol. 6 (Cairo: Matba'at Dar al-Kutub al-Misriyya, 1939–47).
78. See G. R. Rubin and David Sugarman, *Law, Economy and Society, 1750–1914: Essays in the History of English Law* (Abingdon, UK: Professional Books, 1984).
79. Sadir 'Ardhalat Taftish 'Umum Qibli, p. 103, 19 Safar 1271; p. 110, 25 Safar 1271, both in NAE.
80. Farshut and Naj' Hammadi Courts, Sijill Ishhadat 13, Case 13, p. 3, 22 Shawwal 1274, NAE.
81. See Sami, *Taqwim al-Nil*, vol. 1, part 3; Madabit Majlis al-Ahkam microfilms, NAE; and Mubarak, *Al-Khitat al-Tawfiqiyya*, 8:85.
82. Jallad, *Qamus al-'Idara wa-l-Qada'*, 1:183.
83. Mubarak, *Al-Khitat al-Tawfiqiyya*, 11:39, 14:69; Sa'ida Muhammad Husni (ed.), *Mahadir Majlis Shura al-Nuwwab: Al-Hay'a al-Niyabiyya al-'Ula, 1866–1869*

(Cairo: Dar al-Kutub wa-l-Watha'iq al-Misriyya, 2001), 49–53; Madabit Majlis al-Ahkam, Microfilm 434, Sijill 961, Case 274, 2 Dhu al-Qi'da 1306, NAE.

84. Husni, *Mahadir Majlis Shura al-Nuwwab: al-Hay'a al-Niyabiyya al 'Ula, 1866–1869*, 156–61; Ma'iyya Saniyya, Arabic, No. 23, Part 1, 24 Dhu al-Hijja 1285, NAE.

85. Madabit Majlis al-Ahkam, Microfilm 429, Sijill 889, Case 14, 11 Rabi' al-Akhir 1302, NAE.

86. See Sadir Mudiriyyat, Qina and Isna, Parts 1–2, 1287, NAE.

87. The 1869 law was abolished in 1881, and the women of Qina Province then hurried to shari'a courts and the Supreme Court in Cairo to redeem their long-lost properties. See Jallad, *Qamus al-'Idara wa-l-Qada'*, 1:190. Also see Madabit Majlis al-Ahkam, Microfilm 428, Sijill 876, Case 15, 23 Rajab 1301, NAE.

88. Mubarak, *Nukhbat al-Fikr fi Tadbir Nil Misr*, 166–69.

89. Sami, *Taqwim al-Nil*, vol. 3, part 3, p. 1307; Sadir Mudiriyyat, Qina and Isna, Part 1, p. 55, 4 Rajab 1287, NAE; Mubarak, *Al-Khitat al-Tawfiqiyya*, 9:263.

90. Sadir Mudiriyyat, Qina and Isna, Part 1, p. 95, 15 Rajab 1287, NAE.

91. Majlis Khususi (summaries), No. 71, 20 Jumada al-Thani 1282; Madabit Majlis al-Ahkam, Microfilm 429, Sijill 885, Case 454, 2 Muharram 1301, NAE.

92. Sadir Mudiriyyat, Qina and Isna, Part 1, p. 80, 11 Rajab 1287, NAE.

93. See Sadir Mudiriyyat, Qina and Isna, Part 1, 1287; Part 2, p. 35, 9 Sha'ban 1287; and Part 1, p. 27, 28 Rajab 1287, all in NAE. See also Mubarak, *Al-Khitat al-Tawfiqiyya*, 13:78.

94. For example, see Sadir Mudiriyyat Qina and Isna, Part 3, p. 91, 27 Ramadan 1287, NAE. Court records of this period show the decline of the native traditional sugar businesses.

95. Sadir Mudiriyyat Qina and Isna, Part 3, p. 57, 26 Shawwal 1287, NAE.

96. See, for example, Sadir Mudiriyyat Qina and Isna, Part 1, p. 73, 12 Ramadan 1287, NAE.

97. Sadir Mudiriyyat Qina and Isna, Part 1, pp. 25 and 30, 21 and 24 Jumada al-Thani 1287; Part 2, p. 24, 24 Rajab 1287, both in NAE.

98. Sadir Mudiriyyat Qina and Isna, Part 2, p. 30, 25 Jumada al-Thani 1285; Part 1, p. 44, p. 49, 3 Rajab 1287, both in NAE.

99. Madabit Majlis al-Ahkam, Microfilm 422, 5 Rabi' Akhir 1299, NAE.

100. Madabit Majlis al-Ahkam, Microfilm 421, Case 141, end of Dhu al-Hijja 1289, NAE.

101. See Owen, *Middle East in the World Economy*, 145, and chapter 5.

CHAPTER 5: A REBELLION IN THE TIME OF CHOLERA

1. Madabit Majlis al-Ahkam, Microfilm 43, Sijill 897, 20 Muharram 1303, NAE; *Further Correspondence Respecting the Affairs of Egypt*, 1884 (London: Harrison and Sons, 1884), 48–49, British National Archives, Kew (hereafter BNA).

2. See Benedict Anderson, *Imagined Communities: Reflections on the Origin and Spread of Nationalism* (London: Verso, 1983).

3. Niall Ferguson, *Empire: The Rise and Demise of the British World Order and the Lessons for Global Power* (New York: Basic Books, 2003), xxv and xx.

4. Anderson, *Imagined Communities*, 63; see also 37 and 46. Anderson's theoretical analysis influences postcolonial historiography on the formation of nation-states. For example, on India, see Partha Chatergie, *The Nation and Its Fragments: Colonial and Post-colonial Histories* (Princeton, NJ: Princeton University Press, 1993); on Syria see, James Gelvin, *Divided Loyalties: Nationalism and Mass Politics in Syria at the Close of Empire* (Berkeley: University of California Press, 1999).

5. See, for example, Muhammad Farid Hashish, *Hizb al-Wafd, 1936–1952* (Cairo: al-Hay'a al-Misriyya al-'Amma lil-Kitab,1999); and Eric M. Davis, *Challenging Colonialism: Bank Misr and the Political Economy of Industrialization in Egypt, 1920–1941* (Princeton, NJ: Princeton University Press, 1983).

6. Evelyn Baring Cromer, *Modern Egypt* (London: Macmillan, 1908), 1:532. Cromer used the word *remote* to refer to the south more than once (2:326) (emphasis added).

7. For example, see ibid., 1:30, 57.

8. The concept of "free-trade imperialism" is borrowed from the classical article John Gallagher and Ronald Robinson, "The Imperialism of Free Trade," *Economic History Review*, second series, vol. 6 (1) (1953): 1–15. The rulers of Egypt, officially viceroys of the Ottoman sultan, had to abide by an Anglo-Turkish free-trade agreement from 1838.

9. For more details on the economic policies of Sa'id and Isma'il, see Roger Owen, *The Middle East in the World Economy 1800–1914* (London: I. B. Tauris, 1993), chapter 5.

10. Following the names of big families in 'Ali Mubarak's books and biographical collections of notables of this period, one finds that only few Upper Egyptian families made it to high positions in the government and joined the notable class. See Ahmad Taymur, *Tarajim 'A'yan al-Qarn al-Thalith 'Ashr wa-Awa'il al-Rabi' 'Ashr* (Cairo: Multazim al-Tab' 'Abd al-Hamid Ahmad Hanafi, 1940).

11. Sa'ida Muhammad Husni, *Al-Majalis al-Niyabiyya fi Misr fi 'Ahd al-Ihtilal al-Biritani, 1882–1914* (Cairo: al-Hay'a al-Misriyya al-'Amma lil-Kitab, 1990), 14–18.

12. For details about council members, parliamentary minutes, and discussions on matters related to cotton, see Sa'ida Muhammad Husni (ed.), *Mahadir Majlis Shura al-Nuwwab: al-Hay'a al-Niyabiyya al-'Ula, 1866–1869* (Cairo: Dar al-Kutub wa-l-Watha'iq al-Misriyya, 2001); Sa'ida Muhammad Husni (ed.), *Mahadir Majlis Shura al-Nuwwab: Al-Hay'a al-Niyabiyya al-Thaniya, 1870–1873* (Cairo: Dar al-Kutub wa-l-Watha'iq al-Misriyya, 2006); Amin Sami, *Taqwim al-Nil* (Cairo: Matba'at Dar al-Kutub al-Misriyya, 1936), vol. 2, part 3; Muhammad Khalil Subhi, *Tarikh al-Haya al-Niyabiyya fi Misr*, vol. 6 (Cairo: Matba'at Dar al-Kutub al-Misriyya, 1939–47).

13. Husni, *Mahadir Majlis Shura al-Nuwwab: Al-Hay'a al-Niyabiyya al-'Ula, 1866–1869*, 13–15, 55–57; Sami, *Taqwim al-Nil*, vol. 3, part 2, 671. On Muslim identity, see, for example, Sami, *Taqwim al-Nil*, vol. 3, part 2, 784.

14. Husni, *Mahadir Majlis Shura al-Nuwwab: Al-Hay'a al-Niyabiyya al-'Ula, 1870–1873*, 212. The writings of 'Ali Pasha Mubarak—a high state official and land-

owner educated in Europe—is an example of this intellectual discourse. See 'Ali Mubarak, *Nukhbat al-Fikr fi Tadbir Nil Misr* (Cairo: Matba'at Wadi al-Nil, 1297/1879), 4.

15. See Roger Owen, *Lord Cromer: Victorian Imperialist, Edwardian Proconsul* (Oxford: Oxford University Press, 2005), chapters 8 and 9, and p. 178.

16. Cromer, *Modern Egypt*, 2:271.

17. "Memorandum on Egyptian Affairs: Course of Events and Progress of Reforms in Egypt since the Conclusion of Lord Dufferin's Special Mission," February 1, 1884, pp. 3–4, FO 881/4906, BNA; Husni, *Al-Majalis al-Niyabiyya fi Misr fi 'Ahd al-'Ihtilal al-Biritani, 1882–1914*, 14–18.

18. Subhi, *Tarikh al-Haya al-Niyabiyya fi Misr*, 6:37–58.

19. Ibid., 6:29–58.

20. al-Hukuma al-Misriyya, *Mahadir Jalasat Majlis Shura al-Qawanin* (Cairo: Matba'at Fath Allah Ilyas Nuri, 1883–), session no. 24, January 1884.

21. 'Ali Mubarak, *Al-Khitat al-Tawfiqiyya al-Jadida li-Misr al-Qahira* (Cairo: al-Hay'a al-Misriyya al-'Amma lil-Kitab, 1994), 8:85–86.

22. Dishna Court, Sijill Ishhadat, Murafa'at, Mubaya'at, and Tarikat 143, Case 155, pp. 39–40, 20 September 1900, NAE; Majlis al-Wuzara', Iltimasat, Portfolio 8/A, 29 November 1909, NAE.

23. See, for example, "Memorandum on Egyptian Affairs," 1884, p. 8, FO 881/4906, BNA.

24. al-Hukuma al-Misriyya, *Mahadir Jalasat Majlis Shura al-Qawanin*, 29 Rajab 1310 16 February 1893, pp. 23–24.

25. "Villiers to Cromer," 1895, FO 78/4668, BNA, quoted in Martina Rieker, "The Sa'id and the City: Subaltern Spaces in the Making of Modern Egyptian History" (PhD dissertation, Temple University, 1997), 153.

26. 'Abdin Iltimasat, Arabic, Microfilm 476, Sijill 4, p. 133, 20 December 1904, NAE.

27. Majlis al-Wuzara', Majlis Shura al-Qawanin, Portfolio 3/2/B, 22 October 1890, NAE.

28. Majlis al-Wuzara', Jalasat Majlis al-Nuzzar, Portfolio 5/L, 5 June 1890; Portfolio 5/M, 9 July 1890 and 24 July 1890, all in NAE.

29. Majlis al-Wuzara', Jalasat Majlis al-Nuzzar, Portfolio 5/Sin, 20 August 1896, and Portfolio 5/'Ayn, 51 January 1897, both in NAE; *Reports by His Majesty's High Commissioner on the Finance, Administration, and Condition of Egypt and the Soudan in 1898* (London: Harrison and Sons, 1899), 19, BNA.

30. al-Hukuma al-Misriyya, *Mahadir Jalasat Majlis Shura al-Qawanin*, 13 Jumada al-Awwal 1303/17 February 1886, p. 19.

31. Ibid., 13 Jumada al-Awwal 1303/17 February 1886, p. 19, and 17 Dhu al-Qi'da 1303/17 August 1886, p. 61; al-Hukuma al-Misriyya, *Mahadir Jalasat Majlis Shura al-Qawanin*, 29 Jumada al-Akhir 1305/22 February 1888, pp. 2–3.

32. See, for example, Majlis al-Wuzara', Nizarat al-Maliyya, al-Muwazana, I'tirad Lajna min Majlis Shura al-Qawanin 'ala al-Muwazana, Portfolio 9/1/K, 22 December 1896, NAE; and Cromer, *Modern Egypt*, 1:103.

33. Cromer, *Modern Egypt*, 2:569.

34. Majlis al-Wuzara', Majlis Shura al-Qawanin, Portfolio 3/2/Jim, 9 May 1898, NAE.

35. Majlis al-Wuzara', Jalasat Majlis al-Nuzzar, Portfolio 5/'Ayn, 25 January 1897. NAE.

36. Majlis al-Wuzara', Jalasat Majlis al-Nuzzar, Portfolio 5/Nun, 30 July 1896, NAE.

37. *Reports by His Majesty's Agent and Consul-General on the Finance, Administration and Condition of Egypt and the Soudan in 1906* (London: Harrison and Sons, 1907), 49, BNA.

38. 'Abdin Iltimasat, Portfolio 495, 8 May 1917, 20 May 1917, November 1921, NAE.

39. Ibid.

40. *Reports by His Majesty's Agent and Consul-General on the Finance, Administration and Condition of Egypt and the Soudan in 1898*, 16–17, BNA.

41. Owen, *Lord Cromer*, 304–5.

42. See, for example, 'Abdin Iltimasat, Portfolio 496, 30 February 1908, NAE.

43. Petition from the peasants to Cairo, 'Abdin Iltimasat, Portfolio 494, Case 4, 30 January 1911, NAE.

44. The colonial administration developed this reformed legal system in 1883 to allow Europeans to litigate outside the native system of shari'a courts and other modern legal councils.

45. 'Abdin Iltimasat, Portfolio 494, Case 4, 30 January 1911, NAE.

46. For example, see 'Abdin, Arabic, Microfilm 476, Sijill 4, 20 December 1904; 'Abdin Iltimasat, Portfolio 473, 14 March 1915; 'Abdin Iltimasat, Portfolio 469, 2 May 1911; 'Abdin Iltimasat, Portfolio 495, 8 May 1917; and 'Abdin Iltimasat, Portfolio 496, Case 105, 20 April 1915, all in NAE.

47. "Confidential: British Agency in Cairo, Agricultural Bank of Egypt," FO 141/531/2, BNA.

48. *Reports by His Majesty's Agent and Consul-General on the Finance, Administration and Condition of Egypt and the Soudan in 1906*, 14, 52, BNA.

49. See, for example, 'Abdin Iltimasat, Portfolio 473, Case No. 2, 20 January 1917; and Portfolio 496, No. 108, 25 May 1915, both in NAE.

50. *Majmu'at Mahadir Dawr In'iqad al-Jam'iyya al-'Umumiyya, 1910* (Cairo: al-Matba'a al-Amiriyya, 1910–), 69–70.

51. "Confidential: British Agency in Cairo Agricultural Bank of Egypt," 9, FO 141/531/2, BNA.

52. Ibid., 8.

53. For example, see 'Abdin Iltimasat, Portfolio 496, No. 108, 25 May 1915; and Portfolio 496, 7 January 1915, both in NAE.

54. LaVerne Kuhnke, *Lives at Risk: Public Health in Nineteenth-Century Egypt* (Berkeley: University of California Press, 1990), 63, 66.

55. *Further Correspondence Respecting the Affairs of Egypt*, 1884, 48–49, BNA.

56. *Al-Qararat wa-l-Manshurat al-Sadira fi* 1902 (Cairo: al-Matbaʻa al-Amiriyya, 1903), 423.

57. *Reports by His Majesty's Agent and Consul-General on the Finance, Administration and Condition of Egypt and the Soudan in* 1902 (London: Harrison and Sons, 1903), 71, BNA.

58. Egypt was not yet colonized, but after the foreign debt crisis its finances were partially under British-French control.

59. Majlis al-Wuzara', Sharikat wa-Jamʻiyyat, Portfolio 1/B, 16 May 1880, NAE.

60. *Reports by His Majesty's Agent and Consul-General on the Finance, Administration and Condition of Egypt and the Soudan in* 1902, 51, BNA.

61. *Reports by His Majesty's Agent and Consul-General on the Finance, Administration and Condition of Egypt and the Soudan in* 1898, 30, 72, BNA.

62. *Reports by His Majesty's Agent and Consul-General on the Finance, Administration and Condition of Egypt and the Soudan in* 1902, 49, BNA.

63. Ibid.

64. *Al-Qararat wa-l-Manshurat al-Sadira fi* 1901 (Cairo: al-Matbaʻa al-Amiriyya, 1902), 57..

65. *Al-Qararat wa-l-Manshurat al-Sadira fi* 1902, 30, 77.

66. al-Hukuma al-Misriyya, *Mahadir Jalasat Majlis Shura al-Qawanin,* 8 Rajab 1301/May 1884.

67. Madabit Majlis al-Ahkam, Microfilm 428, Sijill 881, Case 288, 6 Shawwal 1301, NAE.

68. Madabit Majlis al-Ahkam, Microfilm 422, 6 Jumada al-Awwal 1299, NAE.

69. Madabit Majlis al-Ahkam, Microfilm 426, Sijill 861, Case 998, 10 Dhu al-Hijja 1300, NAE. This incident happened in 1878, two years after the dual British-French control over Egyptian finances started, upon the debt crisis.

70. *Reports by His Majesty's Agent and Consul-General on the Finance, Administration and Condition of Egypt and the Soudan in* 1907 (London: Harrison and Sons, 1908), 28, BNA.

71. *Reports by His Majesty's Agent and Consul-General on the Finance, Administration and Condition of Egypt and the Soudan in* 1908 (London: Harrison and Sons, 1909), 32, BNA.

72. See, for example, Muhammad Farid Hashish, *Hizb al-Wafd, 1936–1952* (Cairo: al-Hay'a al-Misriyya al-ʻAmma lil-Kitab, 1999); Davis, *Bank Misr and the Political Economy of Industrialization in Egypt, 1920–1941*; and Beth Baron, *Egypt as a Woman: Nationalism, Gender, and Politics* (Berkeley: University of California Press, 2005).

73. See Anderson, *Imagined Communities;* and Bill Ashcroft, Gareth Griffiths, and Helen Griffiths (ed.), *The Post-colonial Studies Reader* (London: Routledge, 2006), part 8.

74. Education was the main means of disseminating nationalist discourse. Tayʻ Salama, an infamous parliamentarian, was involved in founding boys' schools toward this goal. See, for example, Qina Court, Sijill Ishhadat 125, Case 92, pp. 61–62, 4 November 1899; Dishna Court, Sijill Ishhadat, Murafaʻat, Mubayaʻat,

and Tarikat 141, Case 100, pp. 86–87, 22 July 1900; and Dishna Court, Sijill Ishhadat, Murafaʿat, Mubayaʿat, and Tarikat 141, Case 39, pp. 36–38, 24 March 1900, all in NAE.

75. This section of the chapter is theoretically informed by the insights of subaltern studies into writing non-bourgeois-nationalist histories of colonized societies, particularly in India. It attempts to break away from elitist historiography of Egypt that focuses on bourgeois nationalism as the only form of resisting colonialism, opting instead to present a nonelitist narrative showing other modes of resistance of the lower classes in Upper Egypt. See Ranajit Guha, "On Some Aspects of the Historiography of Colonial India," in Vinayak Ghaturvedi (ed.), *Mapping the Subaltern Studies and the Postcolonial* (London: Verso, 2000), 1–7.

76. Madabit Majlis al-Ahkam, Microfilm 43, Sijill 892, Case 187, 15 Rajab 1302, NAE.

77. *Al-Qararat wa-l-Manshurat al-Sadira fi* 1902, 504.

78. Madabit Majlis al-Ahkam, microfilm 422, 6 Jumada al-Awwal 1299.

79. *Al-Qararat wa-l-Manshurat al-Sadira fi* 1889 (Cairo: al-Matbaʿa al-Amiriyya, 1890), 378.

80. The annual report of 1901 recorded a 3 percent increase in "felonies" in Qina Province, parallel to the increase in Grand Cairo. This probably suggests that resistance against the empire was as great in Qina as in Cairo. *Reports by His Majesty's Agent and Consul-General on the Finance, Administration and Condition of Egypt and the Soudan in* 1901 (London: Harrison and Sons, 1902), 29, BNA.

81. These were *waqf* charitable endowments. See, for example, Qina Court, Sijill Ishhadat 125, Case 92, pp. 61–62, 4 November 1899; Dishna Court, Sijill Ishhadat, Murafaʿat, Mubayaʿat, and Tarikat 141, Case 100, pp. 86–87, 22 July 1900; and Dishna Court, Sijill Ishhadat, Murafaʿat, Mubayaʿat, and Tarikat 141, Case 39, pp. 36–38, 24 March 1900, all in NAE.

82. Madabit Majlis al-Ahkam, Microfilm 422, 5 Jumada al-Thani 1299; Microfilm 430, Sijill 893, Case 214, 13 Shawwal 1302, both in NAE.

83. Madabit Majlis al-Ahkam, Microfilm 43, Sijill 893, Case 244, 17 Shawwal 1302, NAE.

84. *Al-Qararat wa-l-Manshurat al-Sadira fi* 1889, 813.

85. Ibid., 501.

86. Ibid., 813.

87. Madabit Majlis al-Ahkam, Microfilm 426, Sijill 859, Case 875, 17 Shawwal 1300, NAE.

88. *Majmuʿat al-Taqarir al-Marfuʿa min al-Mudiriyyat wa-l-Muhafazat li Dawlatu Afandim Nazir al-Dakhiliyya wa-l-Maliyya ʿan ʾAʿmal* 1889 (Misr: al-Matbaʿa al-Amiriyya, 1890), 198–99.

89. *Al-Qararat wa-l-Manshurat al-Sadira fi* 1890 (Cairo: al-Matbaʿa al-Amiriyya, 1891), 157–61.

90. Ibid.

91. "Hawadith Muʾsifa fi al-Mahalla al-Kubra wa Qina," *Al-Balagh*, 16 December 1949.

92. "Khutt al-Saʿid," *Al-Ahram*, 31 October 2010. http://gate.ahram.org.eg/Malafat/74/678/%D8%AE%D8%B7-%D8%A7%D9%84%D8%B5%D8%B9%D9%8A%D8%AF-.aspx (accessed 10 January 2011).

93. There are many versions of al-Khutt's story, and facts are mixed with mythical public narratives about him. Personal communication with inhabitants of the village of Drunka, Qina, June 2009.

EPILOGUE

1. Immanuel Wallerstein, *After Liberalism* (New York: New Press, 1995), 177.
2. Immanuel Wallerstein, "U.S. Weakness and the Struggle for Hegemony," *Monthly Review* 55 (2003): 7.
3. Joseph Stiglitz, "The Roaring Nineties," *Atlantic Monthly*, October 2002, 98. See also, Joseph Stiglitz, *Globalization and Its Discontents* (New York: W.W. Norton, 2003); and Joseph Stiglitz and Gerald Meier, *Frontiers of Development Economics* (Oxford: Oxford University Press, 2001).
4. See Peter Evans, Theda Skocpol, and Dietrich Rueschemeyer (eds.), *Bring the State Back In* (Cambridge: Cambridge University Press, 1985).
5. Stiglitz, *Globalization and Its Discontents*, 17.
6. Ibid., 1–15; Mitchell, *Rule of Experts: Egypt, Techno-Politics, Modernity* (Berkeley: University of California Press, 2002), 272–303.
7. Michael Hardt and Antonio Negri, *Empire* (Cambridge, MA: Harvard University Press, 2000), xiv (emphasis in original).
8. Ibid., 23–24.
9. Ibid., 393.
10. Gayatri Chakravorty Spivak, "The New Subaltern: A Silent Interview," in Vinayak Ghaturvedi (ed.), *Mapping Subaltern Studies and the Postcolonial* (London: Verso, 2000), 325.
11. Ibid., 326.
12. USAID, "Success Stories," www.usaideconomic.org.eg/SuccessStories.asp (accessed 12 January 2012).
13. Ibid.
14. ACDI-VOCA, "Egypt—Agribusiness Linkages Global Development Alliance," www.acdivoca.org/site/ID/egyptHeinzGDA (accessed 10 January 2012).
15. See the Cairo-based newspaper, *Al-Masry al-Youm*, 9 and 30 March 2008.
16. See Land Center for Human Rights, *Reports* (Cairo: Land Center for Human Rights, 2005–8); Ray Bush (ed.), *Counter Revolution in Egypt's Countryside: Land and Farmers in an Era of Economic Reform* (London: Zed Books, 2002).
17. *Al-Masry al-Youm*, 22 March 2007.
18. See Lisa Kallal and OsterDowJones Commodity News, "Commodities Report: Wheat Prices Post Big Declines on Selling by Speculative Funds," *Wall Street Journal*, 23 December 2003.

19. See "U.S. Wheat Aid Is Sold to Egyptian Company," *Wall Street Journal*, 30 November 1998; Dyanna DeCola, "Wheat Prices Rise on Egypt's Return as a Buyer," *Wall Street Journal*, 12 April 2001; USAID, "Economic Growth in Egypt," www.usaideconomic.org.eg (accessed 10 January 2012).

20. *Al-Wafd*, 4 August 2007. The story of Nawfal is similar to that of 'Izzat Ali Hanafi, the bandit mentioned in this book's introduction, with regard to allying with the regime in crushing Islamic fundamentalists and forging election results in the interest of the National Democratic Party, the former ruling party.

21. See coverage of the revolution in Qina Province on this Qina-based website: www.qenaonline.com (accessed 15 January 2012). For example, www.qenaonline.com/portal/news-action-show-id-1175.htm (accessed 15 January 2012); www.qenaonline.com/portal/albums-action-show-id-25.htm (accessed 15 January 2012); www.qenaonline.com/portal/news-action-show-id-1211.htm (accessed 15 January 2012); and www.qenaonline.com/portal/news-action-show-id-1189.htm (accessed 15 January 2012).

BIBLIOGRAPHY

ARCHIVAL SOURCES

National Archives of Egypt, Cairo

'Abdin Iltimasat (petitions to the royal palace), portfolios (1890–1920).
'Awamir Karima (royal orders and decrees).
Diwan Khidiwi, Turkish (Arabic summaries).
Madabit Majlis al-Ahkam (minutes of the Supreme Court; cases and *ardhala*s, or petitions), microfilms (1265/1848–1306/1889).
Majlis al-Wuzara' (Cabinet of Ministers), portfolios (1882–1920).
Ma'iyya Saniyya, Arabic and Turkish (Arabic summaries).
Sadir and Warid 'Ardhalat Taftish 'Umum Qibli (petitions sent to the general inspector of Upper Egypt) (1263/1846–1879/1296).
Sadir and Warid Mudiriyyat, Qina and Isna (central government correspondence with Qina Province) (1260/1844–1296/1879).
Shari'a Court Records of Isna (1170/1756–1338/1920).
Shari'a Court Records of Qina, Farshut, Naj' Hammadi, and Dishna (1262/1845–1338/1920).

British National Archives, Kew

"Confidential: British Agency in Cairo, Agricultural Bank of Egypt." FO 141/531/2.
Correspondence Respecting the Finances of Egypt, 1884. London: Harrison and Sons, 1884.
"Egyptian Expeditionary Force, the Cultivation of Cereals in Upper Egypt." FO 141/669/4.
Further Correspondence Respecting the Affairs of Egypt, 1884. London: Harrison and Sons, 1884.
Further Correspondence Respecting the Finances of Egypt [a series of reports]. London: His Majesty's Stationary Office, 1884, 1887, 1888.

"Memorandum on Egyptian Affairs: Course of Events and Progress of Reforms in Egypt since the Conclusion of Lord Dufferin's Special Mission." 1884. FO 881/4906.

Reports by His Majesty's Agent and Consul-General on the Finance, Administration, and Condition of Egypt and the Soudan [a series of annual reports]. London: Harrison and Sons, 1899–1903, 1906–9.

Reports by His Majesty's High Commissioner on the Finance, Administration, and Condition of Egypt and the Soudan. London: His Majesty's Stationary Office, 1914–19.

Report by Sir Evelyn Baring . . . on the Financial Situation of Egypt Dated June 28, 1884. London: Harrison and Sons, 1884.

"Villiers to Cromer." 1895. FO 78/4668.

ARABIC PRIMARY SOURCES AND UNPUBLISHED MANUSCRIPTS

'Abbas, Ra'uf, et al. (eds.). *Al-'Awamir wa-l-Mukatabat al-Sadira min 'Aziz Misr Muhammad 'Ali*. 2 vols. Cairo: Dar al-Kutub wa-al-Watha'iq al-Qawmiyya, 2005–6.

'Abd al-Mu'ti, Husam Muhammad. *Al-'Ilaqat al-Misriyya al-Hijaziyya fi al-Qarn al-Thamin 'Ashr*. Cairo: al-Hay'a al-'Amma lil-Kitab, 1999.

al-'Abbasi al-Mahdi, Muhammad. *Al-Fatawa al-Mahdiyya fil-Waqa'i' al-Misriyya*. 7 vols. Cairo: al-Matba'a al-Azhariyya, 1301/1883.

al-'Adawi al-Hamzawi, Hasan. *Tabsirat al-Qudah wa-l-Ikhwan fi Wad' al-Yadd*. Cairo: al-Matba'a al-Amiriyya, 1276/1859.

al-Amir, Muhammad Ibn Abd Allah al-Maliki. "Risala fi man Tawalla al-Sa'id min al-'Umara al-Jarakisa." Unpublished manuscript. Manuscript No. 6686, al-Azhar Library, Cairo.

al-Damurdashi, Ahmad. *Al-Durra al-Musana fi 'Akhbar al-Kinana*. 'Abd al-Rahim 'Abd al-Rahman 'Abd al-Rahim (ed.). Cairo: Maktabat al-Ma'had al-Faransi, 1989.

al-Darandali, 'Izzat Hasan Effendi. *Al-Hamla al-Faransiyya 'ala Misr fi daw' makhtut 'Uthmani, Makhtutat Dianama*. Jamal Sa'id 'Abd al-Ghani (trans. and ed.). Cairo: al-Hay'a al-Misriyya al-'Amma lil-Kitab, 1999.

al-Hukuma al-Misriyya. *Mahadir Jalasat Majlis Shura al-Qawanin* [a series of annual publications]. Cairo: Matba'at Fath Allah Ilyas Nuri, 1883–.

al-Idfawi, Abu al-Fadl. *Al-Tali' al-Sa'id al-Jami' li Asma' Nujaba' al-Sa'id*. Cairo: al-Dar al-Misriyya lil-Ta'lif wa-al-Tarjama, 1966.

al-Jabarti, 'Abd al-Rahman. *'Aja'ib al-'Athar fi-l-Tarajim wa-l-'Akhbar*. 7 vols. Cairo: Lajnat al-Bayan al-'Arabi, 1958–.

———. *Al-Jabarti's Chronicle of the French Occupation*. Shamuel Moreh (trans.) Princeton, NJ: Markus Wiener, 1975.

———. *Muzhir al-Taqdis bi-Zawal Dawlat al-Faransis*. Cairo: Dar al-Kutub wal-Watha'iq al-Misriyya, 1998.

al-Maqrizi, Taqyy al-Din. *Al-Mawaʻiz wa-l-Iʻtibar bi-Dhikr al-Khitat wa-l-ʾAthar.* 2 vols. Cairo: Maktabat al-Thaqafa al-Diniyya, 1987.

———. *'Ighathat al-'Umma bi-Kashf al-Ghumma.* Cairo: Dar al-Hilal, 1990.

al-Maraghi, Muhammad al-Jirjawi. *Tarikh Wilayyat al-Saʻid fi al-ʻAsrayn al-Mamluki wa-l-ʻUthmani al-Musamma bi-Nur al-ʻUyun bi-Dhikr Jirja fi ʻAhd Thalathat Qurun.* Cairo: Maktabat al-Nahda, 1997.

———. "Taʻtir al-Nawahi wa-l-Arjaʾ bi-Dhikr man Ishtahar min ʻUlamaʾ wa-Aʻyan Madinat al-Saʻid Jirja." 3 vols. Unpublished manuscript. Manuscript No. 2487, Dar Al-Kutub al-Misriyya, Cairo.

Al-Qararat wa-l-Manshurat. Cairo: al-Matbaʻa al-Amiriyya, 1889–1920.

al-Rafiʻi, ʻAbd al-Rahman. *ʻAsr Muhammad ʻAli.* Cairo: Dar al-Maʻarif, 1930.

Al-Waqaʾiʻ al-Misriyya [the Egyptian Official Gazette], 1245–1338/1829–1920.

Crecelius, Daniel, and ʻAbd al-Wahhab Bakr (trans.). *Al-Damurdashi's Chronicle of Egypt, 1688–1755.* Leiden, Netherlands: E. J. Brill, 1991.

Husni, Saʻida Muhammad (ed.). *Mahadir Majlis Shura al-Nuwwab: Al-Hayʾa al-Niyabiyya al-ʾUla, 1866–1869.* Cairo: Dar al-Kutub wa-l-Wathaʾiq al-Misriyya, 2001.

———. *Mahadir Majlis Shura al-Nuwwab: Al-Hayʾa al-Niyabiyya al-Thaniya, 1870–1873.* Cairo: Dar al-Kutub wa-l-Wathaʾiq al-Misriyya, 2006.

Jallad, Filib. *Qamus al-ʾIdara wa-l-Qadaʾ.* 7 vols. Al-Iskandariyyah: al-Matbaʻa al-Bukhariyya, 1891–.

Laʾihat Ziraʻat al-Fallah wa-Tadbir Ahkam al-Siyasa bi-Qasd al-Falah. Cairo: Matbaʻat Sahib al-Saʻada, 1829.

Majmuʻat al-Taqarir al-Marfuʻa min al-Mudiriyyat wl-Muhafazat li-Dawlatu Afandim Nazir al-Dakhiliyya wa-l-Maliyya ʻan Aʻmal 1889. Misr: al-Matbaʻa al-Amiriyya, 1890.

Majmuʻat Mahadir Dawr Inʻiqad al-Jamʻiyya al-ʻUmumiyya, 1910. Cairo: al-Matbaʻa al-Amiriyya, 1910–.

Mubarak, ʻAli. *Al-Khitat al-Tawfiqiyya al-Jadida li-Misr al-Qahira.* Vols. 1–13. Cairo: al-Hayʾa al-Misriyya al-ʻAmma lil-Kitab, 1994.

———. *Al-Khitat al-Tawfiqiyya al-Jadida li-Misr al-Qahira.* Vols. 14–19. Cairo: Matbaʻat Bulaq, 1887.

———. *Nukhbat al-Fikr fi Tadbir Nil Misr.* Cairo: Matbaʻat Wadi al-Nil, 1297/1879.

Najm, Zayn al-ʻAbidin Shams al-Din (ed.). *Daftar Majmuʻ ʾIdara wa-ʾIjraʾat, 1240–1280/1825–1863 (Wathaʾiq Tarikh Misr wa-l-ʾArab al-Hadith).* Cairo: Dar al-Fikr al-ʻArbi, 2003.

Sami, Amin. *Taqwim al-Nil.* 4 vols. Cairo: Matbaʻat Dar al-Kutub al-Misriyya, 1936.

Subhi, Muhammad Khalil. *Tarikh al-Haya al-Niyabiyya fi Misr.* 6 vols. Cairo: Matbaʻat Dar al-Kutub al-Misriyya, 1939–47.

Taymur, Ahmad. *Tarajim ʾAʻyan al-Qarn al-Thalith ʻAshr wa-ʾAwaʾil al-Rabiʻ ʻAshr.* Cairo: Multazim al-Tabʻ ʻAbd al-Hamid Ahmad Hanafi, 1940.

SECONDARY SOURCES

'Abd al-Muttalib, 'Asim Mahrus. *Al-Qutn fi-l-'Alaqat al-Misriyya al-Biritaniyya.* Cairo: al-Hay'a al-Misriyya al-'Amma lil-Kitab, 1993.

'Abd al-Rahim, 'Abd al-Rahim 'Abd al-Rahman. *Muhammad 'Ali wa Shibh al-Jazira al-'Arabiyya,* 1819–1840. Cairo: Dar al-Kitab al-Jami'i, 1981.

Abdel Aal, Mohamed. "Tenants, Owners, and Sugar Cane: Law 96/1992 in Qena and Aswan." In Nicholas Hopkins and Reem Saad (eds.), *Upper Egypt: Identity and Change.* Cairo; New York: American University in Cairo Press, 2004.

Abdel-Malek, Anouar. *Idéologie et renaissance nationale, l'Égypte moderne.* Paris: Éditions Anthropos, 1969.

Abernethy, David. *Dynamics of Global Dominance.* New Haven, CT: Yale University Press, 2001.

Abir, Mordechai. *Ethiopia and the Red Sea: The Rise and Decline of the Solomonic Dynasty and Muslim-European Rivalry in the Region.* London: F. Cass, 1980.

———. *Ethiopia: The Era of The Princes* (New York: Fredrick A. Praeger, 1968).

Abu al-Rus, Khalid. "Madinat Isna fil-Qarn al-Thamin 'Ashr." PhD dissertation, Cairo University, 2008.

Abu Lughod, Janet. *Before European Hegemony: The World System A.D.* 1250–1350. New York: Oxford University Press, 1989.

Abu Lughod, Leila. *Remaking Women: Feminism and Modernity in the Middle East.* Princeton, NJ: Princeton University Press, 1998.

'Afifi, Muhammad. *Al-'Aqbat fi Misr fi al-'Asr al-'Uthmani.* Cairo: al-Hay'a al-Misriyya al-'Amma lil-Kitab, 1992.

Agoston, Gabor, and Bruce Masters (eds.). *Encyclopedia of the Ottoman Empire.* New York: Facts on File, 2009.

Ahmad, Layla 'Abd al-Latif. *Al-'Idara fi Misr fi-l-'Asr al-'Uthmani.* Cairo: Matba'at Jami'at 'Ayn Shams, 1978.

———. *Al-Sa'id fi 'Ahd Shaykh al-'Arab Hammam.* Cairo: al-Hay'a al-Misriyya al-'Amma lil-Kitab, 1987.

al-Hajjaji, Muhammad 'Abdu. *Qus fi-l-Tarikh al-'Islami.* Cairo: al-Hay'a al-Misriyya al-'Amma lil-Kitab, 1982.

al-Hitta, Ahmad. *Tarikh Misr al-'Iqtisadi.* Alexandria: Matba'at al-Misri, 1967.

al-Tukhi, Nabil al-Sayyid. *Sa'id Misr fi 'Ahd al-Hamla al-Faransiyya,* 1798–1801. Cairo: al-Hay'a al-Misriyya al-'Amma lil-Kitab, 1997.

Amin, Galal. *Egypt's Economic Predicament.* Leiden: Brill, 1995.

Amin, Samir. *Imperialism and Unequal Development.* New York: Monthly Review Press, 1977.

Anderson, Benedict. *Imagined Communities: Reflections on the Origin and Spread of Nationalism.* London: Verso, 1991.

Anderson, Perry. *Lineages of the Absolutist State.* London: Verso, 1974.

The Annual Register; or, a View of the History of Politics and Literature for the Year 1801. London: Printed by T. Burton, 1802.

Arnold, David. "Gramsci and Peasant Subalternity in India." In Vinayak Ghaturvedi (ed.), *Mapping Subaltern Studies and the Postcolonial*. London: Verso, 2000).
Arrighi, Giovanni. *The Long Twentieth Century*. London: Verso, 2002.
———. "The Three Hegemonies of Historical Capitalism," *Review,* Summer 1990, 365–408.
Ashcroft, Bill, Gareth Griffiths, and Helen Tiffin. *The Post-colonial Studies Reader*. London: Routledge, 2006.
———. *Post-colonial Studies: The Key Concepts*. London: Routledge, 2000.
Ashtor, Eliyahu. *A Social and Economic History of the Near East in the Middle Ages*. Berkeley: University of California Press, 1976.
Baer, Gabriel. *Studies in the Social History of Modern Egypt*. Chicago: University of Chicago Press, 1969.
Barendse, R. J. *The Arabian Seas: the Indian Ocean World of the Seventeenth Century*. Armonk, NY: M. E. Sharpe, 2002.
Barkey, Karen. *Empire of Difference: The Ottomans in Comparative Perspective*. Cambridge: Cambridge University Press, 2008.
Baron, Beth. *Egypt as a Woman: Nationalism, Gender, and Politics*. Berkeley: University of California Press, 2005.
Benin, Joel. *Workers and Peasants in the Middle East*. Cambridge: Cambridge University Press, 2001.
Bjørkelo, Anders. "Turco-*Jallaba* Relations 1821–1885." In Leif O. Manger (ed.), *Trade and Traders in the Sudan*. Bergen: Department of Social Anthropology, University of Bergen, 1984.
Bowring, John. *Report on Egypt and Candia, 1840, Addressed to the Right Hon. Lord Viscount Palmerston*. London: W. Clowes and Sons, 1840.
Brown, Nathan. "Who Abolished Corvée Labour in Egypt and Why?" *Past and Present,* August 1994, 116–37.
Bruce, James. *Travels to Discover the Source of the Nile, in the Years* 1768, 1769, 1770, 1771, 1772, *and* 1773. 5 vols. Edinburgh: Printed by J. Ruthven, for G. G. J. and J. Robinson, London, 1790.
Bush, Ray (ed.). *Counter Revolution in Egypt's Countryside: Land and Farmers in an Era of Economic Reform*. London: Zed Books, 2002.
Campbell, John. *The Travels and Adventures of Edward Brown, Esq*. London: Printed by J. Applebee, 1739.
Capper, James. *Observations on the Passage to India through Egypt*. London: Printed for W. Faden, J. Robson, and R. Sewell, 1785.
Cargill, William, Esq. *Mehemet Ali, Lord Palmerston, Russia and France: Position of England, Turkey, and Russia, Egypt and Turkey, Negotiations at Alexandria, Objects of Russia, Treaty of July* 15, 1840. London: John Reid and Co., 1840.
Cezzar, Ahmad Pasha. *Ottoman Egypt in the Eighteenth Century: The Nizamname-i Misir*. Cambridge, MA: Harvard University Press, 1962.
Chatergie, Partha. *The Nation and Its Fragments: Colonial and Post-colonial Histories*. Princeton, NJ: Princeton University Press, 1993.

Chaudhuri, K. N., *Trade and Civilization in the Indian Ocean: An Economic History from the Rise of Islam to 1750.* Cambridge: Cambridge University Press, 1985.

Clot Bey. "On the Plague of Egypt." In *The Eclectic Journal of Medicine, Vol. IV from November 1839 to October 1840.* Philadelphia: Haswell et al., 1840.

Cole, Juan. *Napoleon's Egypt: Invading the Middle East.* New York: Palgrave Macmillan, 2008.

Coxe, John Redman. *The Philadelphia Medical Museum.* Philadelphia: T & G Palmer, 1809.

Crecelius, Daniel. "The Importance of Qusayr in the Late Eighteenth Century." *Journal of the American Research Center in Egypt* 24 (1987): 53–60.

———. *The Roots of Modern Egypt: A Study of the Regimes of ʿAli Bey al-Kabir and Muhammad Bey Abu al-Dhahab, 1760–1775.* Minneapolis: Bibliotheca Islamica, 1981.

Cromer, Evelyn Baring. *Modern Egypt.* 2 vols. London: Macmillan, 1908.

Cuno, Kenneth. *The Pasha's Peasants: Land, Society, and Economy in Lower Egypt, 1740–1858.* Cambridge: Cambridge University Press, 1992.

Davis, Eric M. *Challenging Colonialism: Bank Misr and the Political Economy of Industrialization in Egypt, 1920–1941.* Princeton, NJ: Princeton University Press, 1983.

de Montulé, Edouard. *Voyage en Amérique, en Italie, en Sicile et en Égypte pendant les années 1816, 1817, 1818 et 1819.* 2 vols. Paris: Delaunay, 1821.

Denon, Vivant. *Travels in Upper and Lower Egypt.* New York: Arno Press, 1973.

———. *Voyage dans la Basse et la Haute Égypte pendant les Campagne du Général Bonaparte.* Paris: Imprimerie de P. Didot l'aine, 1802.

Dhuhni, Ilham Muhamamd. *Misr fi kitabat al-rahhala wal-qanasil al-Faransiyyin fil-qarn al-thamin ʿashr.* Cairo: al-Hayʾa al-Misriyya al-ʿAmma lil-Kitab, 1992.

———. *Misr fi kitabat al-rahhala wal-qanasil al-Faransiyyin fil-qarn al-tsiʿ ʿashr.* Cairo: al-Hayʾa al-Misriyya al-ʿAmma lil-Kitab, 1995.

"The Diseases of Egypt, from Observations Made during the British Expedition in That Country under Sir R. Abercromble, K.C.B., in 1801." *Medical Press and Circular, a Weekly Journal of Medicine and Medical Affairs,* July–December 1882, 152–53.

Doyle, Michael. *Empires.* Ithaca: Cornell University Press, 1986.

Duff-Gordon, Lucie Austin. *Letters from Egypt.* London: Macmillan, 1865.

Dus, Madiha (ed.). *Mukhtarat min Wathaʾiq al-Hamla al-Faransiyya, 1798–1801.* Cairo: Dar al-Kutub wal-Wathaʾiq al-Qawmiyya, 2006.

Evans, Peter, Theda Skocpol, and Dietrich Rueschemeyer (eds.). *Bring the State Back In.* Cambridge: Cambridge University Press, 1985.

Fahmy, Khaled. *All the Pasha's Men: Mehmed Ali, His Army, and the Making of Modern Egypt.* Cambridge: Cambridge University Press, 1997.

———. "Mutiny in Mehmed Ali's New *Nizami* Army, April–May 1824." *International Journal of Turkish Studies* 8 (1–2) (2002): 129–38.

Faroqhi, Suraiya. *Ottoman Empire and the World Around It.* London: I. B. Tauris, 2006.

Ferguson, Niall. *Colossus: The Price of America's Empire*. New York: Penguin, 2004.
———. *Empire: The Rise and Demise of the British World Order and the Lessons for Global Power*. New York: Basic Books, 2003.
Fischel, W.J. "The Spice Trade in Mamluk Egypt." In M.N. Pearson (ed.), *Spices in the Indian Ocean World*. London: Ashgate Variorum, 1996.
Foucault, Michel. *The Birth of the Clinic*. London: Routledge, 1989.
———. *Discipline and Punish: The Birth of Prison*. New York: Penguin, 1979.
———. *History of Sexuality*. New York: Vintage, 1990.
Frank, Andre Gunder. *Dependent Accumulation and Underdevelopment*. London: Macmillan, 1978.
———. *ReOrient: Global Economy in the Asian Age*. Berkeley: University of California Press, 1998.
Franklin, J., Esq. *The History of Ancient and Modern Egypt* 3 vols. London, 1800–1802.
Gallagher, John, and Ronald Robinson. "The Imperialism of Free Trade." *Economic History Review*, second series, vol. 6 (1) (1953): 1–15.
Garcin, Jean-Claude. *Un centre musulman de la Haute-Égypte médiévale: Qûs*. Cairo: Institut Français d'Archéologie Orientale du Caire, 1976.
Gelvin, James. *Divided Loyalties: Nationalism and Mass Politics in Syria at the Close of Empire*. Berkeley: University of California Press, 1999.
Giddens, Anthony. *The Consequences of Modernity*. Stanford, CA: Stanford University Press, 1990.
Graham, Gerald. *Great Britain in the Indian Ocean: A Study of Maritime Enterprise, 1810–1850*. Oxford: Clarendon Press, 1967.
Gramsci, Antonio. *Selections from the Prison Notebooks*. New York: International Publishers, 2003.
Gran, Peter. "Upper Egypt in Modern History: 'A Southern Question'?" In Nicholas Hopkins and Reem Saad (eds.), *Upper Egypt: Identity and Change*. Cairo: American University in Cairo Press, 2004.
Guha, Ranaja. "On Some Aspects of the Historiography of Colonial India." In Vinayak Ghaturvedi (ed.), *Mapping Subaltern Studies and the Postcolonial*. London: Verso, 2000.
Guo, Li. *Commerce, Culture and Community in a Red Sea Port in the Thirteenth Century*. Leiden: Brill, 2004.
Haddad, George A. "A Project of the Independence of Egypt, 1801." *Journal of the American Oriental Society* 90 (2) (April–June 1970): 169–83.
Hanna, Nelly. *Making Big Money in 1600: The Life and Times of Isma'il Abu Taqiyya, Egyptian Merchant*. New York: Syracuse University Press, 1998.
Hansard, T.C. (ed.). *The Parliamentary Debate, Forming a Continuation of the Work Entitled "The Parliamentary History of England from the Earliest Period to 1803."* London, 1825.
Hardt, Michael, and Antonio Negri. *Empire*. Cambridge, MA: Harvard University Press, 2000.

Haridi, Salah Ahmad. *Dawr al-Sa'id fi Misr al-'Uthmaniyy,* 923/1213–1517/1898. Cairo: Dar al-Ma'arif, 1984.

Hashish, Muhammad Farid. *Hizb al-Wafd,* 1936–1952. Cairo: al-Hay'a al-Misriyya al-'Amma lil-Kitab, 1999.

Haut, E. L. F. *Mémoires d'un officer de l'armée française.* Cairo: Bibliothèque et Archives Nationales d'Egypte, 2005.

Hechter, Michael. *Internal Colonialism: The Celtic Fringe in British National Development.* 2nd ed. New Brunswick, NJ: Transaction, 1998.

Hobsbawm, Eric. *Social Bandits and Primitive Rebels: Studies in Archaic Forms of Social Movement in the 19th and 20th Centuries.* New York: Free Press, 1960.

Holroyd, Arthur T., *Egypt and Mahomed Ali Pacha in 1837: A Letter, Containing Remarks upon "Egypt as It Is in 1837"; Addressed to the Right Hon. Viscount Palmerston.* London: James Ridgeway and Sons, 1838.

Hunter, F. Robert. *Egypt under the Khedives, 1805–1879: From Household Government to Modern Bureaucracy.* Pittsburgh: University of Pittsburgh Press, 1984.

Huseyn Efendi. *Ottoman Egypt in the Age of the French Revolution.* Stanford Shaw (ed.). Cambridge, MA: Harvard University Press, 1964.

Husni, Sa'ida Muhammad. *Al-Majalis al-Niyabiyya fi Misr fi 'Ahd al-'Ihtilal al-Biritani,* 1882–1914. Cairo: al-Hay'a al-Misriyya al-'Amma lil-Kitab, 1990.

Ibrahim, Nasir Ahmad. *Al-Faransiyyun fi Sa'id Misr: Al-Muwajaha al-Maliyya,* 1798–1801. Cairo: Darl-Kutub wal-Watha'iq al-Qawmiyya, 2005.

Inalcik, Halil, Donald Quataert, et al. (eds.). *An Economic and Social History of the Ottoman Empire.* 2 vols. Cambridge: Cambridge University Press, 1994.

The Institute of Egypt. *Memoirs Relative to Egypt, Written in that Country during the Campaigns of General Bonaparte, in the Years 1798 and 1799, by the Learned and Scientific Men Who Accompanied the French expedition.* London: Printed by T. Gillet, for R. Phillips, 1800.

İslamoğu-İnan, Huri. *The Ottoman Empire and the World-Economy.* Cambridge: Cambridge University Press, 2004.

Issawi, Charles. *An Economic History of the Middle East and North Africa.* New York: Columbia University Press, 1982.

Jorgens, Denis. "A Comparative Examination of the Provisions of the Ottoman Land Code and Khedive Sa'id's Law of 1858." In Roger Owen (ed.), *New Perspectives on Property and Land in the Middle East.* Cambridge, MA: Harvard University Press, 2000.

Kennedy, Paul. *The Rise and Fall of the Great Powers.* New York: Vintage, 1989.

Kincaid, Jamaica. *A Small Place.* New York: Farrar, Straus and Giroux, 2000.

Kuhnke, LaVerne. *Lives at Risk: Public Health in Nineteenth-Century Egypt.* Berkeley: University of California Press, 1990.

Land Center for Human Rights. *Reports.* Cairo: Land Center for Human Rights, 2005–8. www.lchr-eg.org.

Lane, Edward. *An Account of the Manners and Customs of Modern Egyptians: Written in Egypt During the Years* 1833, 34, *and* 35. London: Charles Knight and Co., 1837.

———. *Description of Egypt.* Cairo: American University in Cairo Press, 2000.

Landes, David. *The Wealth and Poverty of Nations: Why Some Are So Rich and Some So Poor.* New York: W. W. Norton, 1998.

Lapidus, Ira. "The Grain Economy of Mamluk Egypt." Journal of the Economic and Social History of the Orient 12 (1) (January 1969): 1–15.

———. Review of "*Un centre musulman de la Haute-Égypte médiévale: Qús.*" Journal of the Economic and Social History of the Orient 21 (3) (October 1978): 331–34.

Larrey, D. J. *Memoirs of Military Surgery and Campaigns of the French Army.* Richard Willmott Hall (trans.). Baltimore: Joseph Cushing, 1914.

Lawson, Fred. "Rural Revolt and Provincial Society in Egypt, 1820–1824." International Journal of Middle Eastern Studies 13 (2) (May 1981): 131–53.

———. *The Social Origins of Egyptian Expansionism during the Muhammad Ali Period.* New York: Columbia University Press, 1992.

Light, Henry. *Travels in Egypt, Nubia, Holy Lands, Mount Lebanon and Cyprus in the Year 1814.* London: Rodwell and Martin, 1818.

Marsot, Afaf Lutfi al-Sayyid. *Egypt in the Reign of Muhammad Ali.* Cambridge: Cambridge University Press, 1984.

———. *A History of Egypt: From Arab Conquest to the Present.* Cambridge: Cambridge University Press, 2007.

McGowan, Bruce. "The Age of the Ayans, 1699–1812." In Halil Inalcik, Donald Quataert, et al. (eds.), *An Economic and Social History of the Ottoman Empire, 1600–1914.* Cambridge: Cambridge University Press, 1994.

McNeill, J. R., et al. (eds.). *Encyclopedia of World Environmental History.* New York; London: Routledge, 2004.

McNeill, J. R., and William McNeill. *The Human Web.* New York: W. W. Norton, 2003.

Mémoires sur l'Égypte, publiés pendant les campagnes du Général Bonaparte. Paris: Imprimerie de P. Didot l'aine, 1800.

Mitchell, Timothy. *Rule of Experts: Egypt, Techno-Politics, Modernity.* Berkeley: University of California Press, 2002.

Monthly Review or Literary Journal 76 (January–June 1787).

Motyl, Alexander. *Imperial Ends: The Decay, Collapse, and Revival of Empires.* New York: Columbia University Press, 2001.

Najm, Zayn al-'Abidin Shams al-Din. *'Idarat al-'Aqalim fi Misr, 1805–1882.* Cairo: Dar al-Kitab al-Jami'i, 1988.

———. *Mu'jam al-Alfaz wa-l-Mustalahat al-Tarikhiyya.* Cairo: Dar al-Fikr al-'Arabi, 2006.

O'Brien, Patrick. "Imperialism and the Rise and Decline of the British Economy, 1688–1989." New Left Review 1 (238) (November–December 1999): 49–80.

O'Fahey, R. S., and J. L. Spaulding. *Kingdoms of the Sudan.* London: Methuen, 1974.

Owen, Roger. *Cotton and the Egyptian Economy, 1820–1914.* Oxford: Clarendon Press, 1969.

———. *Lord Cromer: Victorian Imperialist, Edwardian Proconsul.* Oxford: Oxford University Press, 2005.

———. *The Middle East in the World Economy, 1800–1914*. London: I. B. Tauris, 1993.

Pearson, Michael. *The Indian Ocean*. London: Routledge, 2003.

Peirce, Leslie. *Morality Tales: Law and Gender in the Ottoman Court of Aintab*. Berkeley: University of California Press, 2003.

Pitts, Jennifer. *A Turn to Empire: The Rise of Imperial Liberalism in Britain and France*. Princeton, NJ: Princeton University Press, 2005.

Pococke, Richard. *A Description of the East, and Some Other Countries*. 2 vols. London: Printed for the author, by W. Bowyer, 1743–45.

Polanyi, Karl. *The Great Transformation: The Political and Economic Origin of Our Time*. Boston: Beacon, 2001.

Quataert, Donald. *The Ottoman Empire, 1700–1922*. Cambridge: Cambridge University Press, 2005.

Raymond, André. *Arab Cities in the Ottoman Period: Cairo, Syria, and the Maghreb*. Burlington, VT.: Ashgate, 2002.

———. *Cairo*. London: Harvard University Press, 2000.

Rieker, Martina. "The Sa'id and the City: Subaltern Spaces in the Making of Modern Egypt." PhD dissertation, Temple University, 1997.

Rivlin, Helen Anne. *The Agricultural Policy of Muhammad 'Ali in Egypt* (Cambridge, MA: Harvard University Press, 1961).

Rogan, Eugene (ed.). *Outside In: On the Margins of the Modern Middle East*. London: I. B. Tauris, 2002.

Rubin, G. R., and David Sugarman. *Law, Economy and Society, 1750–1914: Essays in the History of English Law*. Abingdon, UK: Professional Books, 1984.

Said, Edward. *Orientalism*. New York: Vintage, 1979.

Salzman, Ariel. "An Ancien Regime Revisited: 'Privatization' and Political Economy in the Eighteenth Century Ottoman Empire." *Politics and Society* 21 (4) (1993): 393–423.

Savary, M. Claude. *Lettres sur l'Égypte*. New ed. Paris: Chez BLXUET jeune, 1789.

———. *Letters on Egypt*. 3rd ed. London: G. G. and J. Robison, 1799.

Schonhardt-Bailey, Cheryl. *The Rise of Free Trade*. London: Routledge, 1997.

Shakry, Omnia. *The Great Social Laboratory: Subjects of Knowledge in Colonial and Postcolonial Egypt*. Stanford, CA: Stanford University Press, 2007.

Shaw, Stanford. *The Financial and Administrative Organization and Development of Ottoman Egypt, 1517–1798*. Princeton, NJ: Princeton University Press, 1962.

Shukri, Muhamad Fu'ad, et al. *Bina' Dawlat Misr Muhammad 'Ali: Al-Siyasa al-Dakhiliyya*. Cairo: Dar al-Fikr al-'Arabi, 1948.

Sonnini, C. S. *Travels to Upper and Lower Egypt Undertaken by the Order of the Old Government of France*. 3 vols. London: T. Gillet, printer, 1799.

Spivak, Gayatri. "Can the Subaltern Speak?" In Bill Ashcroft, Gareth Griffiths, and Helen Griffiths (ed.), *The Post-colonial Studies Reader*, 324–40. London: Routledge, 2006.

———. "The New Subaltern: A Silent Interview." In Vinayak Ghaturvedi (ed.), *Mapping Subaltern Studies and the Postcolonial*. London: Verso, 2000.

Stiglitz, Joseph. *Globalization and Its Discontents.* London: W. W. Norton, 2003.
———. "The Roaring Nineties." *Atlantic Monthly,* October 2002.
Stiglitz, Joseph, and Gerald Meier. *Frontiers of Development Economics.* Oxford: Oxford University Press, 2001.
St. John, J. A. *Egypt and Nubia.* London: Chapman and Hall, 1845.
Stoler, Ann Laura. *Race and the Education of Desire: Foucault's "History of Sexuality" and the Colonial Order of Things.* Durham, NC: Duke University Press, 1995.
Thires, Louis Adolphe. *History of the Consulate and the Empire of France under Napoleon.* D. Forbes Campbelle and John Stebbing (trans.). London: Chatto and Windus, 1893.
Toledano, Ehud. *State and Society in Mid-Nineteenth-Century Egypt.* Cambridge: Cambridge University Press, 1990.
Tucker, Judith. *In the House of the Law: Gender and Islamic Law in Ottoman Syria and Palestine.* Berkeley: University of California Press, 1998.
———. *Women in Nineteenth-Century Egypt* (Cambridge: Cambridge University Press, 1985).
UNDP (UN Development Programme). *Arab Human Development Report* 2004. New York: UNDP, 2005.
Wallerstein, Immanuel. *After Liberalism.* New York: New Press, 1995.
———. *The Modern World-System.* 3 vols. New York: Academic Press, 1974–.
———. "U.S. Weakness and the Struggle for Hegemony." *Monthly Review* 55 (2003).
Walz, Terence. *Trade between Egypt and Bilad As-Sudan, 1700–1820.* Cairo: Institute Français d'Archéologie Orientale du Caire, 1978.
Wilkinson, Sir John Gardner. *Three Letters on the Policy of England towards the Porte and Muhammad Ali.* London: John Murray, 1840.
Wright, Donald R. *The World and a Very Small Place in Africa: A History of Globalization in Niumi, the Gambia.* Armonk, NY: M. E. Sharpe, 2004.

ART CREDITS

Figure 1. Sir Gardner Wilkinson, *Hand-book for Travellers in Egypt* (London: John Murray, 1847), 449. Book is courtesy of Oberlin College's Mudd Library.

Figure 2. R. J. C. Broadhurst (trans.), *The Travels of Ibn Jubayr* (London: Jonathan Cape, 1951), 30–31. Book is courtesy of Ohio University Library.

Figure 3. Sir Gardner Wilkinson, *Hand-book for Travellers in Egypt* (London: John Murray, 1847), 441. Book is courtesy of Oberlin College's Mudd Library.

Figure 4. Winifred S. Blackman, *The Fellahin of Upper Egypt* (London: George G. Harrap and Company, 1927), 127. Book is courtesy of Oberlin College's Mudd Library.

Figure 5. Winifred S. Blackman, *The Fellahin of Upper Egypt* (London: George G. Harrap and Company, 1927), 29. Book is courtesy of Oberlin College's Mudd Library.

Figures 6 and 7. Courtesy of Nasr Wahbi al-Qusi, journalist and political activist from Luxor.

INDEX

'Ababida, 24, 33, 37–38, 40–41, 59, 107
'Abbas, Khedive, 101, 190
'Abd al- Rahim al-Ghul, 153
'Ali Bey al-Kabir, 36–37
*'ardhala*s, 14, 72, 90
'Urf, 25

Abnud, 58
Agricultural Bank of Egypt, 133–6
Ahmad al-Salah, 70, 78–80
Ahmad al-Tayyib, 95, 112–4
al-Khutt, 145, 154
al-La'iha al-Sa'idiyya, 101–2
American Civil War, 109, 118
Andre Gunder Frank, 9, 22
Antonio Gramsci, 7, 12
Armant, 79, 84, 86, 119–20, 122, 131, 133, 135, 140, 152, 153
Asyut, 21, 30, 68, 79–80, 87, 92, 94, 128, 145

bandits, 2–3, 13, 15, 71, 73, 89–94, 100, 120–3, 140, 141–5, 154
Benedict Anderson, 122–123, 199
British Foreign Office, 15
British liberalism, 15, 96, 125

Cabinet of Ministers, 15, 128–9, 130
cholera, 3, 7, 122–124, 136–9, 141, 146
coal mines, 97, 105–9
commercial agriculture, 4, 22, 31, 118, 123, 125
Copts, 5, 14, 23–25, 32–35, 40–45, 47–53, 55–63, 66, 76–77, 79, 81, 83, 88, 90, 95, 98, 99, 101–2, 113, 138

corvée labor, 78, 82–85, 89–91, 93, 98, 102, 120, 141
Cromer, Lord, 125–8, 130–6

Daira Saniyya, 118–21, 128, 131
darb al-jallaba, 32
Department of Public Works, 128–129, 137, 141
Department of Railways, 129. *See also* railways
Dependency Theory, 1, 8–9, 11, 31, 96–97
Dufferin, Lord, 127

East Africa, 4, 22, 65, 72, 76–77
Edward Said, 10, 45
Egyptian Revolution of 2011, 1, 3, 147, 154–6
environmental, 1, 3, 12, 18, 26, 29, 44, 64, 68, 123, 136, 146, 150
Eurocentric, 10

Facebook, 2, 148, 156
falatiyya, 89, 92–95, 100, 110–3, 120, 141. *See also* bandits
Farshut, 22–23, 28, 30–32, 37, 76–77, 83, 89, 98, 102, 104, 116, 118, 142
Foucauldian, 10–11. *See also* Michel Foucault.

Gayatri Spivak, 10, 151
Girga, 21, 26–29, 128
gunpowder factories, 85, 109, 111

Hammam Ibn Yusuf, Shaykh al-'Arab, 14, 17, 29–37, 41, 63, 80

Hanafi, School of Islamic law, 25, 88–89, 104
Hawwara Tribe, 5, 17–40, 77, 154
Hijaz, 5, 21, 26, 31, 57, 65, 70, 72, 75–76, 80, 99

Ibrahim Pasha, 73–78
iltizam, 19, 24, 27–30, 37, 50. *See also* tax farms
Immanuel Wallerstein, 9, 149
Indian Ocean world economy, 4–6, 18, 22, 31, 46, 49, 72, 76
internal colonialism, 15, 71–73, 81
International Monetary Fund (IMF), 8, 148
Isma'il, Khedive 109, 112–6, 118, 121, 125–6
Isna, 13–14, 22, 25, 35, 41, 57–58, 63, 76–77, 83, 86, 88, 91, 93–94, 100, 102, 110, 128–9, 135
Istanbul, 6, 14, 18–19, 21–23, 25, 28, 30–32, 36–37, 39, 42, 57, 73–75

Jeddah, 23, 34, 57, 76

Karl Polanyi, 12, 150
Karnak, 92, 102, 111, 155
khawaja, 100, 103, 105–8

law, 15, 19, 24–27, 30, 41,54, 77, 82, 84–85, 87–89, 93, 97, 99, 101–4, 107, 112–9, 125–9, 132, 134, 143, 145, 148, 153; 1858 land law, 101, 115–6; 1869 land law, 114, 117
liberalism, 15, 53
Lucie Duff-Gordon, Lady, 15, 95, 112–4
Luxor, 46, 50–52, 92, 98, 103, 110, 112, 129, 136, 138, 155

Majlis al-Ahkam, 15, 116, 189–90, 192, 194, 196–9, 206, 208, 213
Majlis Shura al-Nuwwab, 15, 16, 116, 125, 197–8, 200–201, 217
Makram 'Ubayd Pasha, 144
Maliki, School of Islamic Law, 25, 88–9
Mamluks, 5–6, 19–29, 35–42, 47–48, 50, 54, 56, 58–61, 64–67, 72–73
market economy, 3, 12, 15, 96, 99, 133, 147, 150. *See also* market reforms

market reforms, 2, 153, 157. *See also* market economy
Marxist Theory, 8–9, 12, 96
Mecca, 4, 21, 23, 26, 57, 65–66, 78
Michel Foucault, 10, 45, 151. *See also* Foucauldian
Mocha, 23, 49, 73, 76
Modern World-System, 9, 11, 161
modernity, 3–4, 12, 15, 96–97, 101, 105, 114–115, 118, 120–121
Morocco, 5
Mubarak, Muhammad Husni 1, 2, 112, 148, 153
Muhammad 'Ali Pasha, 6, 14, 42, 70–94, 105, 123, 136
Murad Bey, 39, 50, 56–57, 60, 63, 66–67

Nagada, 31, 41, 91–92, 120, 135
Naj' Hammadi, 118, 132, 135, 140, 154
Napoléon Bonaparte, 4, 43, 54, 149
National Democratic Party (NDP), 153–4
neoliberalism, 1, 12, 147–50, 156. *See also* Washington Consensus

Parliament, 15, 46, 115–117, 122, 125–32, 135, 139, 141, 144, 148, 153
paternalistic, 115
patriarchal, 114, 118
peripheralization, 7, 11, 89, 125, 136, 140
plague, 3, 6, 17–19, 26–27, 36–40, 63–68, 79, 139
plantation, 73, 75, 81–85, 90–92, 95, 102–4, 111–2, 115–6, 122, 125, 127, 129
poll-tax, 57
Postcolonial theory, 8, 10–12, 44–45, 122–123, 140, 147, 150

Qus, 4–5, 22, 31, 49, 52, 59, 78, 86, 91, 98, 102–104, 111, 127, 142, 153
Qusayr, 22–24, 31–32, 34, 41, 47–49, 52, 57, 59, 65–67, 75–76, 78, 80, 105, 109, 129

railways, 119, 129, 132
Revolt of Qina, in 1820–1824, 6, 70, 78–80; in 1864, 6, 95, 109–114

Sa'id, Khedive, 97, 100–101, 104–5, 108–9, 115, 125

Salimiyya, 70, 78, 95, 97–98, 101–3, 111–3, 116, 140, 142
Samir Amin, 9
Savary, M., 47–49, 54–55, 58, 65
shari'a court, 13–15, 25, 33–35, 40, 42, 72, 83, 87–88, 91, 93, 100, 115
shari'a judges, 104, 192
Sharif Hasan of Mecca, 58
Société Générale des Sucreries, 131–3
Sonnini, C. S., 48, 49, 50, 51, 52, 53, 54, 55, 58, 61, 63, 64, 65, 172, 174, 229
steamships, 97–101
subaltern, 3–4, 7–8, 12–15, 18, 23, 26, 28–29, 32, 37, 40, 72–73, 94–97, 109, 114, 118, 120–4, 140, 144, 146–7, 151–6
Sudan, 5, 23, 31–32, 71–73, 76, 84–86, 98, 105
sugarcane plantations, 22, 118–21
sulfur mine, 103, 109, 111
Sultan: Mustafa Khan, 27;
  Selim I, 19;
  Selim III, 41–42;
  Suleiman the Magnificent, 19
Syasatname, 15, 88

Tahrir Square, 147, 149, 156
tax farms, 19, 24, 27–30, 37, 50. *See also itlizam*
textile factories, 77, 86, 91

United States, 8–9, 147–50, 157
USAID, 1, 148, 152–4

Vivant Denon, 4, 41, 43, 58

Wafd Party, 144–5
Washington Consensus, 1, 147, 150, 153. *See also* neoliberalism
World Bank, 2, 148, 150
World War I, 132, 144
World-System theory 8–10, 96, 149

Yemen, 5, 22–23, 48–49, 65, 71, 73, 76